Fraud Watch

Bottom-Line Business Guides

Titles in this series currently include:

Fraud Watch
Second edition
David Davies

Practical Management Consultancy
Third edition
Calvert Markham

Going for Excellence: Achieving Results through Efficiency
Bengt Karlöf

Business Grow-How: The Stepping Stones to Successful Growth
Alan Baines and Raj Sinhal

Directors: Your Responsibilities and Liabilities
Fourth edition
Peter Souster

No Customer–No Business: The True Value of Activity-Based Cost Management
Robin Bellis-Jones and Nick Develin

Fraud Watch

Second edition

David Davies

KPMG

ABG Professional Information
40 Bernard Street
London
WC1N 1LD
Tel: 020 7920 8991
Fax: 020 7920 8992
Website: www.abgweb.com

British Library Cataloguing-in-Publication Data

A catalogue record for this book is available from the British Library.

Typeset by RefineCatch Limited, Bungay, Suffolk
Printed by Bell & Bain, Glasgow

Contents

Preface vii

1 Introduction 1
Creating and keeping value 1
What is fraud? 1
Learning from yesterday's financial disasters 2
Looking at fraud risk in a new way 4
How to look at the causes of fraud 5
Fraud Watch in outline 6

2 Understanding fraud 9
Introduction 9
Fraud case studies 9
Why people commit fraud 18
Behavioural characteristics 22
Common indicators and risk factors 23
Conclusion 33

3 Causes of fraud 35
Introduction 35
Today's fraud arena 35
Business strategy 42
People 45
Culture and ethics 53
Management structures 58
Reward structures 70
Communications 75
Fraud risk management 77
Conclusion 95

Contents

4 Computer fraud and abuse 97

Introduction 97

How computer fraud occurs 101

Fraud on the Internet 109

Hacking 114

Viruses, worms and hoaxes 118

Other computer abuse issues 119

IT security 124

Conclusion 127

5 Accounts manipulation 129

Introduction 129

Sales 131

Purchases 139

Stock 145

Cash 149

Other areas of manipulation 152

Conclusion 155

6 Fraud in manufacturing and services 159

Introduction 159

Purchasing 159

Sales 176

Stock 185

Cash and payments 188

Other areas 193

Conclusion 199

7 Fraud in the financial sector 201

Introduction 201

Banking 201

Investment business 241

Insurance 247

Conclusion 251

8 Managing fraud in the future 253

Introduction 253

Linking risk to value 253

Fraud fundamentals 256

Fraud risk profiling 269

Conclusion 274

Index 277

Preface

The fraudster is like an unwelcome magician conjuring clever tricks. There is a certain mystery about fraud. Yet most fraudsters are not clever at all. Rather the companies they defraud unwittingly play the part of magician's assistant. This book reveals the fraudster's tricks, how companies help frauds to be committed, what motivates fraudsters and what to look out for.

Since the first edition of *Fraud Watch* was published five years ago, business has moved on and fraud has moved on. Computer fraud and abuse has developed dramatically with increased use of the Internet and e-commerce. The chapter on computer fraud and abuse has therefore been considerably expanded to deal with these new issues. Accounts manipulation is much more prevalent than it was, driven in part by overwhelming pressure on management to deliver results, so there is an entirely new chapter on that subject.

Available guidance on risk management and internal control looks at symptoms rather than causes of risk, at risk management frameworks rather than fraudsters. Books by leading management gurus deal with issues that have a fundamental impact on fraud risk but the impact is rarely discussed. A new chapter analyses the causes of fraud in depth. There is also an entirely new chapter on managing fraud risk.

Many frauds occur again and again, so I repeat the core material from the first edition, introducing many new examples.

Corporate fraud is the main focus. My aim is to provide a clear briefing on the common types of fraud facing companies today so that effective measures to combat them can be developed. I do not deal with very specialised frauds affecting particular industry sectors. Money laundering, insider dealing, credit card fraud and commercial crime (i.e., frauds committed by companies) are also excluded as several books and publications on those topics have appeared in recent years.

Today we read much about corporate governance, risk management and internal control. The words occur again and again in guidance, long since detached from the financial disasters that originally gave rise to the corporate governance debate. This book brings the words to life and puts the reader back in touch with the reality of fraud.

I must thank the following people:

Lesley Roberts, formerly KPMG's Director of Information Security Management, now with CGU, and Malcolm Marshall, partner in KPMG's Information Risk Management practice, who wrote Chapter 6;

Alex Plavsic, partner in KPMG Forensic Accounting, for parts of Chapter 8 on fraud risk profiling which were written for *Risk Management and Internal Control*, to be published by GEE Publishing in 2000;

other partners and managers in KPMG, in particular David Eastwood for his input to the common indicators of fraud section in Chapter 2, Gus MacKenzie for material on advance fee fraud in the purchasing section of Chapter 6, Ian Dewar for his contribution on dealing frauds in Chapter 7 and Danny McLaughlin for elements of Chapter 8;

other colleagues and former colleagues in KPMG Forensic Accounting, London for their helpful input and comments to both the current and previous editions of the book;

the secretaries of KPMG Forensic Accounting, London.

David Davies
January 2000

1

Introduction

Creating and keeping value

It's 2005. Your share price has collapsed from £5 to 50 pence. A £100 million 'black hole' has opened up in your group's results due to accounts manipulation and fraud. As chief executive, the City is baying for your blood and that of your fellow directors. Predators loom on the horizon hoping to buy the group at a fraction of its true worth.

A nightmare scenario, maybe. And surely after Barings, BCCI, Maxwell, Polly Peck, Daiwa and Sumitomo, to name but a few, there will not be any more financial disasters. Corporate governance is tighter. All the lessons have been learned.

But how many of those companies thought that it could happen to them? How many of you think that it could happen to your company? Most companies think 'it can't happen here'. History shows that every-one cannot be right.

Are the seeds of disaster already present in your company? Is fraud draining value from your business? Are you unwittingly creating the conditions in which fraud will thrive? *Fraud Watch* enables you to answer those questions. It helps you to create, and keep, value in your company.

What is 'fraud'?

There is no legal or commonly accepted definition of 'fraud' so for the purposes of this book I adopt the following straightforward and wide-ranging one:

1

> All those activities involving dishonesty and deception that can drain value from a business, directly or indirectly, whether or not there is personal benefit to the fraudster.

In other words, the whole range of activity from gross mismanagement involving an element of deception, unauthorised risk taking, irregularities, manipulation and theft through to the major international frauds.

There are of course legal provisions under which fraud is prosecuted but this book is not about the legalities of fraud. Whether or not an incident is capable of prosecution is not the main focus. The key question is: does an incident impact value? If it does, then it concerns the board of a company and its shareholders.

Some companies actively suppress the word 'fraud'. Some companies say that it does not fit with their policy of 'trusting employees' or of 'empowerment'. Management gurus rarely mention the word. The latest management books I looked at recently in a London business bookshop did not index the word once. Perhaps, a fundamental, but unspoken, assumption is being made: that everyone is always honest. You may question that assumption after reading this book.

Learning from yesterday's financial disasters

Many lessons can be drawn from yesterday's financial disasters. I would highlight three in particular.

Pressure

Many cases are driven by overwhelming pressure: business pressure and personal pressure. Pressure is often the root cause of fraud: to reach targets, to meet bonus thresholds, to keep one's job, to maintain a promotion path, to prop up an ailing part of the business. There are also personal pressures: financial problems, serious gambling habits, expensive divorce settlements and extravagant lifestyles.

Of course, some pressures are unavoidable. The key is to recognise and manage them. What pressures are people under in your company? Where are the pressure points? Are you unwittingly creating pressures that will result in fraudulent manipulation? How do you manage the pressures?

Escalation

The majority of frauds are some sort of 'spiral'. Most do not start from an intent to commit fraud. They start with a small error concealed, some minor form of unauthorised risk taking or bad business practice. Lie builds on lie, deception on deception. It is difficult for the rogue trader to say to his boss three months later, 'Sorry, what I told you three months ago was a lie. Can we start again?' The escalation may take place over a few weeks, but more usually over a period of years.

This trend of escalation has fundamental implications for fraud risk management. The challenge is to stop things in the early stages, ideally before the fraudster even joins your company. Rigorous recruitment screening is therefore essential. So too is fraud awareness, at all levels so that the early warning signs of fraud are identified. It is important that there are clear reporting channels and protections for those who have fraud suspicions. In a significant number of cases, someone knew, or suspected, what was going on but did not know who to talk to and/or did not feel that there were adequate protections for them as a whistle blower.

These people skills and issues are just as important as the more traditional forms of control, such as budgets and authority limits, but they are rarely found.

Disasters waiting to happen

Frauds are often 'disasters waiting to happen'. A 'cocktail' of factors creates abnormal risk. It is only a matter of time before a disaster occurs. Some of the factors are to do with risk management and internal control. Others relate to the wider business environment: the people, culture, ethics, management structures, reward structures and communications in a company.

For example, in one company staff said:

> It is a blame culture. If someone makes a mistake it affects their career. Dubious practices occur such as padding estimates. The culture drives

people to make the best profit possible. Certain things force individuals not to act with integrity.

This sub-culture has serious implications, not just for fraud. Projects may appear to be on track and then are suddenly in crisis as the manipulation becomes too big to contain. Delivery deadlines may be missed. Repeat customer business may be lost. Identifying and dealing with the root cause of the sub-culture may eliminate a hundred risks.

Looking at fraud risk in a new way

Business risk management models often omit fraud or include it as a minor sub-category of operational risk. A few visible fraud types such as payments and stock frauds may be covered but more insidious and pervasive frauds such as accounts manipulation and purchasing fraud are ignored. The focus is on employee rather than management fraud.

A more helpful approach is to see fraud risk as a 'shadow profile' of the business risk profile. For each category of business risk there is an equivalent fraud risk. The business risk profile makes the unspoken assumption that everyone is honest. The shadow profile makes the opposite assumption: that from time to time people, including management, will be dishonest.

To illustrate the point, some of the risk categories identified by a major engineering company in its purchasing for major projects are set out in Figure 1.1 below.

The company identified 'quality' as a risk issue: quality of components and equipment supplied and the quality of the production process. It employed a number of quality inspectors and had quality procedures. It ignored the 'shadow profile' which includes bribery of quality inspectors, forged product certifications and other substandard product frauds.

Similarly, the company was concerned to achieve best price in its purchasing. It did not recognise frauds in the shadow profile such as bid rigging and bid fixing, whereby companies pay much more than they need to due to kickbacks and corruption in the cost base.

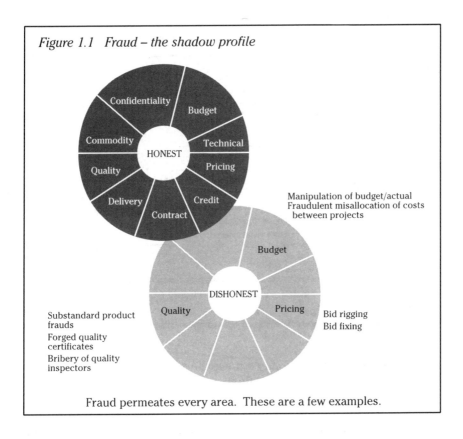

Figure 1.1   Fraud – the shadow profile

Confidentiality
Budget
Commodity
Technical
HONEST
Quality
Pricing
Delivery
Credit
Contract

Manipulation of budget/actual
Fraudulent misallocation of costs
between projects

Budget

DISHONEST

Substandard product
frauds
Forged quality
certificates
Bribery of quality
inspectors

Quality
Pricing

Bid rigging
Bid fixing

Fraud permeates every area. These are a few examples.

Budgets are important in the management of resources in order to complete a project at a profit. The potential for manipulation of budgets, fraudulent misallocation of costs between projects and padding of estimates and contingencies was not considered.

These are dangerous but nevertheless common failings in risk management. Plotting the shadow profile helps management to see the fraud risks more clearly.

How to look at the causes of fraud

I commented above that many frauds are a 'disaster waiting to happen'. Factors come together to create abnormal and unrecognised risk. One way of looking at these factors is set out below.

5

Figure 1.2   *Model for analysing the causes of fraud*

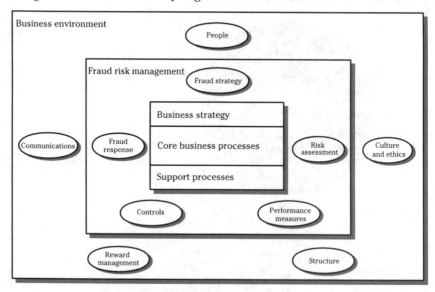

At the centre are the company's business strategy, its core processes and support processes, such as finance, IT and HR.

Fraud risk management covers a range of measures to control fraud risks inherent in business strategy and processes, including the company's fraud strategy, fraud risk assessment, performance measures, detailed controls and fraud response mechanisms.

All these measures sit in the context of the wider business environment: the people, culture, ethics, management structures, reward structures and communications of a company. Factors in the business environment can have a major impact on the implementation of the company's strategy, its business processes and fraud risk management.

Fraud Watch in outline

Fraud Watch is in three parts. In summary, Chapters 2 to 4 open up the subject of fraud and examine the main causes, including computer aspects. Chapters 5 to 7 discuss the main types of corporate fraud and what to look out for. The concluding chapter looks at practical ways to identify and manage fraud risk.

Chapter 2 begins by analysing three fraud cases, using the model in Figure 1.2, highlighting what happened and why. I then discuss why people commit fraud, the behavioural characteristics of fraudsters and other common indicators and risk factors.

Chapter 3 looks at the causes of fraud in greater depth. I highlight the wider issues that define today's fraud arena and the impact of business strategy on fraud risk management. Then I look at the detailed aspects of the internal business environment. Finally, I cover specific problems relating to fraud risk management itself, for example lack of anti-fraud strategy and weaknesses in risk assessment.

Chapter 4 examines computer fraud and abuse. The first part explains the typical frauds at each stage of computer processing: input-related, program-related and output-related fraud. Other problems are then discussed relating to the Internet, hacking, viruses, worms, hoaxes, active content and other aspects of computer abuse.

Chapter 5 covers accounts manipulation. No fewer than 68 common forms of manipulation are discussed. Chapter 6 looks at fraud in manufacturing and services while Chapter 7 discusses the more specialised frauds in the financial sector.

Chapter 8 explores how companies should manage fraud risk in the future. It looks at the fundamentals of effective fraud risk management and practical ways to profile the fraud risks in your company.

2

Understanding fraud

Introduction

Let us now look at how fraud occurs in practice. In three actual cases I explain what happened, what enabled the frauds to occur and how the frauds could have been prevented or picked up earlier. The discussion is then widened to look at what motivates fraudsters, typical behavioural characteristics and common fraud indicators and risk factors.

Fraud case studies

Case study 1: electronic banking fraud

WHO WANTS TO BE A MILLIONAIRE?

An accounts supervisor in a leading chemicals company got £1 million out of a division with £1.5 million profit before tax. He started by stealing £20,000 per month increasing gradually to £80,000 per month. He gained access to the authentication devices for making payments and the related passwords. He hid the fraud by manipulating bank reconciliations which he prepared and by concealing the amounts in poorly controlled areas of the profit and loss account and balance sheet. The fraud would probably never have been picked up if he had kept payments below the £50,000 level. It was eventually picked up in reviewing cash flows at group level.

The key elements highlighted in the previous chapter are present:

(a) **pressure** – the accounts supervisor was under acute personal pressure to commit the fraud. He had mounting gambling debts;

(b) **escalation** – the fraud started with payments of £20,000 per month gradually increasing to payments of £80,000 per month;

(c) a **disaster waiting to happen** – certain aspects within the company made it easy for the fraudster to carry out and conceal the fraud. The company was, unwittingly, the fraudster's assistant.

What enabled the fraud to occur?

The problem areas are illustrated in the following chart.

Figure 2.1   Problem areas in case study 1

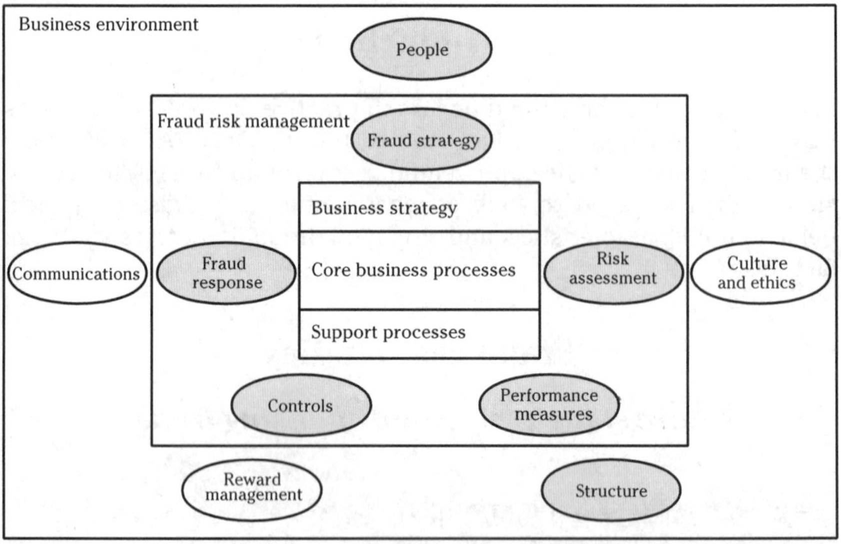

Some of the problems are to do with fraud risk management, others relate to the wider business environment. The interplay between the two elements is crucial.

As regards fraud risk management:

(a) **control** weaknesses were at the heart of the problem. Despite the appearance of controls such as authorisation codes and bank reconciliations, these were more apparent than real. The electronic authentication devices for making payments were kept in a desk drawer. The password for one was written on the guidance booklet attached to the device and the other was probably found out by 'shoulder surfing'. Legitimate payments had been going through for some time without one or both of the authorised personnel being involved. The supervisor did the bank reconciliation and concealed the fraudulent payments by changing the totals formulae on the computer spreadsheet so that the bank reconciliations appeared to add up. Bank reconciliations were reviewed but the review was cursory;

(b) weaknesses in **performance measures** enabled the fraud to be easily concealed. There was poor budgetary control and budgets were not monitored closely. The fraudster hid debits in expense captions where the budget holder was known to be weak. Balance sheet management was poor. The fraudster was therefore able to hide debits against incorrect credit balances in the purchase ledger, in unnecessary provisions and in suspense accounts;

(c) there was no **risk assessment** process to profile the specific fraud risks in the payments process;

(d) there was no **fraud response** plan and no fraud reporting channels for staff to raise their concerns. As a result, staff who had concerns did not report their suspicions; and

(e) there was no overall **fraud strategy**, pulling together all the measures which the company should have had in place to combat fraud.

As regards the business environment:

(a) **people** factors were important. There was a low level of fraud awareness amongst management and staff. There was no training to highlight critical controls;

(b) the **management structure** also played a part. The company had moved from a hierarchical to an empowered management structure without realising that the nature of control needed to change. Virtually all finance responsibilities had been devolved to divisions. Group finance did not review the quality of controls in divisions and there was no internal audit.

How could the fraud have been picked up?

The fraud could have been picked up in a number of ways during the first month. The most direct ways are as follows:

11

What to look for

- spot check where authentication devices are actually kept

- check that passwords are not written down in obvious places, such as on guidance booklets, on stickers and in unlocked pen trays in drawer stacks

- check for manipulation of bank reconciliations – it is easy to flip over to the spreadsheet formulae and review for obvious anomalies in key cells

- set up a simple program to match employee and payee bank account numbers to pick up fraudulent payments to employees

Case study 2: purchasing fraud

This case study involves both accounts manipulation and purchasing fraud. The accounts manipulation provides the perfect cover for the purchasing fraud. Internal and external collusion are involved.

SAVING FOR A RAINY DAY

Marketing managers in the UK subsidiary of an overseas multinational siphoned off £5 million through a variety of purchasing frauds. Actual expenditure was significantly below budget but rather than report a favourable variance against budget they decided to hang on to the budget surplus by accruing actual to budget in the monthly management accounts and by putting through forward purchase orders and entering into collusive pre-invoicing with suppliers around the year end.

The manipulation of budgets provided the cover for a number of purchasing frauds including collusive over billing from suppliers with kickbacks to the marketing managers and bogus invoices from suppliers in which the managers had a personal interest.

Once again the elements highlighted in Chapter 1 are present:

(a) **pressure** – in this case there was extreme pressure in certain areas and lack of pressure in others, which made it easy for manipulation and fraud to go undetected;

12

(b) **escalation** – the manipulation gradually increased over a period of two years;

(c) a **disaster waiting to happen** – several aspects of the company helped the fraudsters to commit the fraud.

What enabled the fraud to occur?

The company had grown significantly in recent years, with turnover increasing 10 times. The aim had been to increase market share aggressively. 'Units sold' was therefore a key performance measure. Sales revenue was second priority while bottom-line profit was the lowest priority.

The result was little downward pressure on costs. For example, the total budget for advertising, marketing and promotion, which was a significant area of spend, was simply based on a percentage of budgeted sales. It was not developed on the basis of the business's strategic needs or specific marketing campaigns, events and initiatives. Elaborate spreadsheet analyses by month and by general ledger code were prepared but this was merely number crunching. There was poor linkage between the budgets and underlying planned events, campaigns and initiatives. There was a lot of slack in the budget. Provided the budget was not exceeded, no questions were asked.

Actual advertising, marketing and promotion expenditure was significantly below the budgeted figure. Marketing managers did not want to repatriate the surplus to head office. Initially, they wanted to hold on to the excess as a kind of 'slush fund' for use in future years when the overall budget granted by head office might be much lower. The gap between reported actual and 'actual actual' spend is shown in Figure 2.2 on page 14.

The manipulation undermined a critical high level control, the budget/actual comparison. Within the hidden zone, the shaded area in Figure 2.2, the managers could get away with what they wanted and not be found out.

Figure 2.3 on page 14 highlights the problem areas.

Figure 2.2 Gap between reported actual and 'actual actual' in case study 2

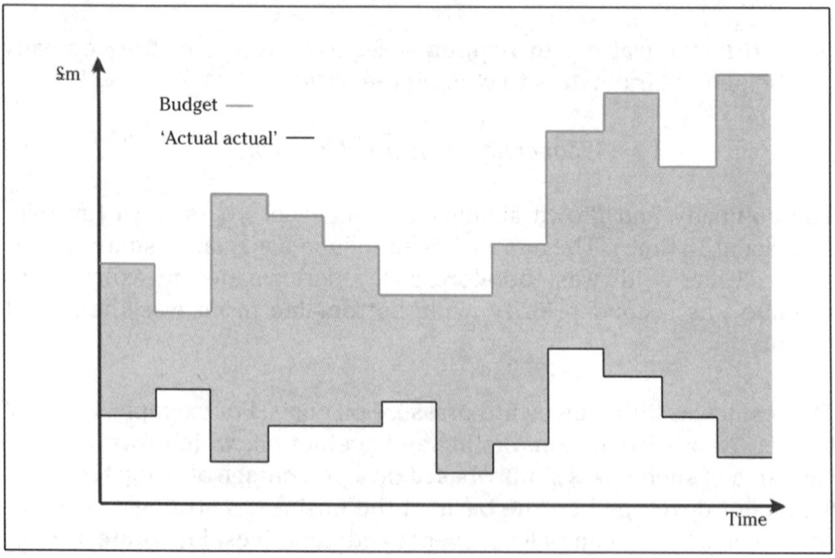

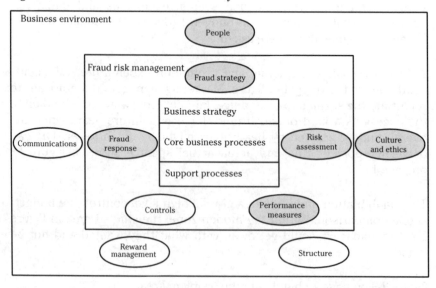

Figure 2.3   Problem areas in case study 2

As regards fraud risk management, the problems were as follows:

(a) as noted above, a key **performance measure**, the budget/actual comparison, was undermined. The budget setting process was weak and the actual figures were accrued to the budgeted level by putting through accruals in the monthly management accounts. At the year end, forward purchase orders were put through in place of the accruals. There was also collusive pre-invoicing with suppliers;

(b) **risk assessment** was weak. Given the company's strategy, it was important for senior management at both group and business unit levels to assess the risks inherent in the strategy of aggressively building market share;

(c) the lack of **fraud response** plans meant that staff with concerns did not report them.

As regards the business environment, **culture** played an important part. The subsidiary had an aggressive sales culture. Sales and marketing managers were the 'heroes' of the company. They were good at keeping finance off their patch. The board did not want to upset the marketing people by questioning them too closely on how they were spending the company's money, providing they remained within the overall budget.

How could the fraud have been picked up?

Effective **fraud response** plans may have encouraged staff to report their suspicions earlier. But the problem could easily have been picked up if business unit management, group management or internal audit had asked the right questions. The following series of linked questions and checks would have uncovered the manipulation quickly.

What to look for:

- Where are the pressures in the profit and loss account? Rank the relative pressures. This would highlight very low focus on the level of costs.

- How is the budget set? What is the linkage between budgets and underlying events campaigns and initiatives? This would identify slack in budgets.

- Does the company accrue actual to budget in the monthly management accounts? This would provide the first indicator of manipulation.

- If so, ask what happens at the year end. Check the year end period for forward purchase orders.

- Where there are forward purchase orders there will usually be collusive pre-invoicing. Check out invoices near the year end. This reveals considerable manipulation of budget and actual figures.

- Where there is collusive pre-invoicing there are likely to be other irregularities on the relevant supplier account – for example, no contract, no competitive tendering, no clear basis for pricing, poor documentation, prices agreed informally after work completed, lavish entertaining, etc.

- Where these problems exist it is likely that there will be some form of purchasing fraud.

Case study 3: accounts manipulation

The third case is a classic accounts manipulation fraud. There were eight different forms of accounts manipulation going on.

£20 MILLION 'BLACK HOLE'

A financial controller had some stock differences which he needed to look into. He had not had time to investigate them and with the year-end audit coming up, he decided to raise some false sales invoices on dormant sub-accounts to cover up them up. He intended to reverse the invoices and to look into the matter once the auditors had signed off.

But when that time came there were other pressures and he gradually became involved in several other forms of manipulation. He manipulated intercompany accounts which were poorly controlled and smoothed various revenue and expense captions in the profit and loss account so that results appeared to be in line with budget. After three years, what appeared to be a £10 million profit in the subsidiary concerned was in fact a £10 million loss.

He was regarded as a high flier and initially had not wanted to attract increased scrutiny from head office and the auditors due to the unresolved stock differences. The fraud was eventually picked up when the auditors showed an apparent confirmation from head office of an intercompany balance which in fact had been forged by the financial controller.

As with the previous two examples, the elements highlighted in the opening chapter are present:

(a) **pressure** is a key factor, this time pressure to perform and to maintain a promotion path. Once the financial controller is on the spiral the pressure increases because it is difficult for him to come clean about the initial cover up;

16

(b) **escalation** – this case does not start from an intent to commit fraud. The financial controller simply has some stock differences which he needs to look into;

(c) a **disaster waiting to happen**. A combination of factors within the company enables the fraud to occur.

The main problem areas in this case are illustrated in the following chart.

Figure 2.4 Problem areas in case study 3

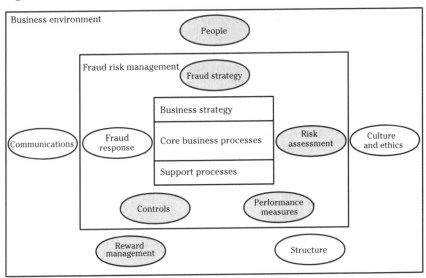

Once again there is an interplay between fraud risk management and the business environment. As regards fraud risk management:

(a) there are a number of weaknesses in **control**, in particular poor control of intercompany accounts and stock;

(b) one of the key **performance measures**, the budget/actual comparison, was undermined by manipulation;

(c) there was no fraud **risk assessment**. In particular at business unit board level and at group level, the potential for accounts manipulation was not recognised. There was total trust in the figures being reported.

In the business environment:

(a) as regards **culture**, there was great pressure on business units to deliver results. The culture did not encourage openness. If there was a problem, local management tended to cover it up, in the hope that they could resolve it without head office being any the wiser;

(b) **reward structures** had a big impact on behaviour. Promotion was closely linked to performance. The financial controller is regarded as a 'high flyer' and he is desperate to maintain that perception.

How could the fraud have been picked up earlier?

Group management needed to recognise the implications of the particular culture and reward structures and think through the most likely types of accounts manipulation. They needed to watch out for possible indicators of manipulation. For example, the business unit was performing extraordinarily close to budget, all the way down the profit and loss account. This was just too good to be true. If a few profit and loss account captions had been probed, excessive journals and adjustments would have been identified. What is the support for such journals? If some indicators emerge then this should trigger more detailed examination.

In the **controls** area, it was well known that intercompany accounts were poorly controlled. The implications had not been recognised. These accounts were used extensively by the financial controller to conceal unresolved differences and to facilitate accounts manipulation.

Summary

The above case studies are relatively straightforward and show how three common types of fraud happen in practice. The combination of factors which has enabled the frauds to occur is different in each case. Other causes of fraud are discussed in more detail in the following chapter and accounts manipulation, electronic banking fraud and purchasing fraud are dealt with in Chapters 5 and 6.

Why people commit fraud

Fraudsters operate at different levels within and outside a company and in a wide variety of business circumstances. Each has his own motives and opportunities.

In simple terms, people commit fraud when a motive coincides with an opportunity. The motive may be greed, lack of cash, revenge, a sense of ownership of the stolen property or of having earned it. The opportunity may arise because there is no real deterrent or little chance of discovery or because there are grey areas in the rules.

Over time the number of people who may commit fraud in a company is large. In many cases, the fraudsters are long-standing, trusted managers who for a range of reasons gradually become embroiled in dishonesty and deception. They may go on to commit similar frauds at other companies. This is why recruitment screening procedures are so important. Some fraudsters may join your company 'fully-trained'.

Pressure to perform

As already noted, pressure to perform is a key factor in a wide range of business situations. Here are a few examples:

(a) a managing director increases the profits forecast of a subsidiary to boost the apparent growth trend of the group immediately prior to a proposed acquisition;

(b) a managing director falsifies a company's financial position to obtain a rights issue;

(c) in the final year of an earn-out a management team realises that they are not going to meet their earn-out targets when the signing of a contract is delayed so they create a fictitious customer and contract and manipulate the cash flows so that the 'profits' may be brought forward into the current year;

(d) the chairman and finance director of a company inflates the company's worth to raise substantial equity and loan finance.

Sometimes the perceived pressure is at some time in the future. Management may have met their targets for this year and decide to tuck away some of the profit for future years when trading conditions may be less favourable. For example, in a dealing context, a dealer misvalues his positions (especially those where it is more difficult to obtain independent valuations) because he has already met this year's bonus threshold. He wants to carry forward the excess to next year when he may have more difficulty reaching the threshold.

Personal pressures

We saw in case study 1 how personal pressures can create the motivation for fraud. The fraudster had a serious gambling habit and mounting gambling debts. His need for large amounts of cash provided a powerful motivation to commit fraud.

Personal relationships can create pressure. For example, a solicitor who defrauded 19 building societies of £4 million had two mistresses whom he flew around the world, spending hundreds of thousands of pounds on them. He had two houses in Florida, a villa in Spain and drove a Jaguar and a Cadillac. The fraud came to light when one mistress found out about the other. Other problems might include large debts and expensive divorce settlements.

It is more difficult to pick up on personal pressures. Staff in a company may hear on 'the grapevine' about personal problems. Fraudsters are not good at keeping quiet about their new found wealth. Maybe, they claim to have come into a large inheritance.

Beating the system

Perhaps the most common image of a fraudster beating the system is that of a lonely and alienated hacker breaking into a company's computer system. But the challenge to beat the system features in many other frauds. For example, a highly paid operations manager in a London bank fiddled his expense claims not because he needed the money but because he got satisfaction from breaking the rules.

Unfortunately, this may lead to other types of fraud. In the above case, the manager had responsibility for procurement of computer hardware and software and, over a period of years, took kickbacks in the form of cash, holidays, free computer equipment for personal use and payment of school fees. Similarly, it is not uncommon to find that directors' expense claims include unauthorised expenditure. One director funded household maintenance and service expenditure through his expense claims.

Another long-standing director partly funded his son's school fees through expenses. In that case part of the problem was a mindset that the company's resources were his own to use as he thought fit.

Greed

Greed is a common motive but is usually driven by some secondary factor. In the purchasing fraud in case study 2, the marketing managers believed that their remuneration did not fully compensate them for the contribution that they had made to the UK business. They were reluctant to repatriate the profits to the overseas head office. They therefore found ways to cream off an additional 'bonus'.

Another example where management did not feel they had been suitably rewarded involved directors at a bank. Certain Swiss banks paid commissions to another bank for the introduction of substantial client funds for discretionary management. The directors who had arranged the introductions believed that they personally, rather than the bank, should benefit from the commissions and with management collusion the commissions were paid on receipt to personal accounts of the directors.

Boredom

Not all frauds involving large amounts of cash are motivated by greed. In one case a fraudster who had recently been released from prison, embarked on a plan to defraud banks of £1 million. He did not smoke, drink, gamble or own a car, despite having 10 driving licences. He created nine different identities with 11 banks and opened 90 accounts. For each identity he took a driving test to get his licence. He had a sophisticated card index system, with each identity having its own reference divided into different colours for each bank account. He could see at a glance how much credit he had on cards and accounts and how much room for further loans. The fraudster became known to the police as the 'pipe and slippers fraudster' so staggeringly boring was his life.

Revenge

Revenge is a factor in certain types of fraud. It may be due to perceived exploitation of employees, frustrated ambition, demotion of individuals following a reorganisation or take-over or low morale due to a redundancy programme.

21

Behavioural characteristics

Fraudsters use a wide range of techniques to perpetrate and conceal fraud. The first clue may be some unusual aspect of behaviour. Picking up on these aspects is crucial, it may be the only clue. The following profiles illustrate some of the more common types of deceptive behaviour. No single factor indicates fraud. Several together may indicate deception or dishonesty.

Table 2.1 Common aspects of deceptive behaviour

Boaster

- Boasts about having all the right contacts
- Talks over-optimistically about business prospects
- Gives the impression of being wealthy and successful
- Entertains or is entertained lavishly
- Flatters people to make them feel important

Manipulator

- Manipulates timetables and deadlines
- Carefully controls access to personnel, customers and suppliers
- Deals with certain accounts personally outside the main system or which would normally be delegated
- Blinds people with science. Exploits ignorance
- Plays off various staff and advisers against each other

Deceiver

- Says as little as possible unless confronted with the facts
- Answers different questions to the ones put
- Uses delaying tactics – always about to go to an important meeting
- Passes the buck to someone else
- Goes on the attack when questioned closely about matters he would prefer not to discuss

---

- Does not allow anyone to see the full picture

Loner

- Never takes a holiday
- Seemingly very conscientious
- Keeps people off his patch
- If absent, ensures that all problems are left for him to sort out on his return

How people respond to questions is often as important as what is actually said. It is easier to conceal than to falsify. It is easier for the fraudster to say nothing, because the right questions are not asked, than maintain a story under close questioning.

Common indicators and risk factors

Introduction

Before I look at more complex aspects of fraud in the following chapters, it is perhaps valuable at this point to highlight some common indicators and risk factors. It is not intended to be a comprehensive checklist. There is much more to understanding fraud risk in a business of any complexity but it is useful to keep in mind a few common indicators as well:

- autocratic management style
- mismatch of personality and status
- unusual behaviour
- illegal acts
- expensive lifestyles
- untaken holiday
- poor quality staff
- low morale
- high staff turnover
- compensation tied to performance

- results at any cost

- poor commitment to control

- no code of business ethics

- unquestioning obedience of staff

- complex structures

- remote locations poorly supervised

- several firms of auditors

- poorly defined business strategy

- profits well in excess of industry norms

- mismatch between growth and systems development

- poor reputation

- liquidity problems

Autocratic management style

Companies take their character from the chief executive or board. A corner-cutting approach to business by senior executives may lead to a superficial approach to financial controls throughout the organisation.

As is well known, in certain major reported frauds, overriding dominance by a chairman or chief executive has been an important factor. But does strong leadership and charisma necessarily lead to a problem? The lack of such qualities may itself be a cause for concern. The key is how such power is exercised. Situations which may cause concern are:

- transactions which are known only to one or two directors

- no meaningful debate of business issues at board level

- frequent override of senior managers' authority and

- obsessive secrecy where such behaviour is not justified

A related problem arises where a sole director has exclusive control over a significant part of the business, for example certain overseas operations, with little or no independent review of those activities by anyone else at board or senior management level. This might occur where a group finance director is prevented from probing the activities of certain overseas subsidiaries, the review of those operations being handled almost exclusively by another director. Problems also might arise where the managing director of a business unit is the former owner.

Similar problems may occur at divisional or departmental level in a company. A head of department may see himself as the driving force behind the business and start to behave more as owner than manager.

Mismatch between personality and status

There may be a mismatch between the planned and actual power structure or hierarchy. A forceful person in charge of a department or division exerts authority and influence disproportionate to his or her status. This allows controls to be overridden or unfavourable information to be suppressed: conditions essential to the concealment of many frauds.

COOKING THE BOOKS

An aggressive manager in charge of a major development project ruled his department by fear. The project was delayed and required substantial extra resources. At his instigation, reports to management outside the department were falsified by his staff to show a more favourable position.

Unusual behaviour

As already noted, anything surprising about the behaviour of individuals usually deserves further enquiry: for example a manager who keeps tedious responsibilities he would usually delegate, a supplier dealt with outside the purchasing system or abnormal levels of entertaining of one or two contacts out of line with normal business practice.

Unusual business events or situations may also be warning signs, for example, unusual volumes of credit notes or bank reconciling items, accounting breakdowns or abrupt withdrawals of suppliers or customers.

To detect the unusual you need to know what is usual. As the example over shows, this is not always easy.

SELF-SACRIFICE

A small overseas subsidiary always returned results exactly in line with its unchanging budget. During several years of high inflation none of the staff asked for or received any pay increases. In fact, the entire management and staff were colluding to steal all the profits in excess of the budget and had no need for pay increases.

Obsessive secrecy should be regarded with suspicion. A High Court judge once described secrecy as the 'badge of fraud'. Situations which may cause concern include:

(a) information only provided when pressed for;

(b) the true nature of a transaction revealed only when it becomes clear that you already have most of the details; and

(c) transactions and structures which do not have a clear business purpose.

SHUT DOOR POLICY

Staff at a company became suspicious when the finance director was the only director or manager to start shutting his door. They became even more suspicious when he had his office sound proofed. He was later charged with fraud.

Illegal acts

Blatant acts of an illegal nature will inevitably cause concern. Other apparently less serious breaches of legal requirements, or attitudes to such requirements, may be significant. Attitudes to Companies Act requirements regarding directors' interests or dealers' attitudes to position or counterparty limits may indicate something important about the culture of a company, its control environment and the integrity of individuals within it.

Expensive lifestyles

Lifestyles not commensurate with earnings are a well-known indicator. In one case a manager used to buy his staff champagne every Friday afternoon. In another, a manager used to change his Jaguar every year. His story was that his wife was extremely wealthy.

Certain companies make lifestyle checks on employees. Whether or not companies wish to do this is a matter of policy. Whenever a company becomes aware of a significant mismatch between lifestyle and earnings, scrutiny of the transactions handled by the employee is advisable. Maintaining an expensive lifestyle may provide the motivation to commit further fraud.

Untaken holiday

Concealing fraud is not easy. Workaholics and staff who do not take holidays may be trying to avoid the risk that their replacements may bring their fraud to light.

Many frauds come to light when a fraudster is absent unexpectedly. Enforcing a minimum of two clear weeks holiday is a simple but effective fraud prevention measure. However, ensuring proper cover during holiday absences is equally important.

Poor quality staff

A company is often judged by the quality of its people. Inability to attract high calibre personnel may say something about its reputation, its position in the marketplace, how it treats its staff and the culture of the company. Internal controls are only as effective as the people operating them.

Low morale

Low morale is conducive to fraud. Demotivated staff are less likely to operate controls effectively and may cut corners. Where a major redundancy programme is in progress or a site is to be closed, staff may avenge themselves at the expense of the company.

High staff turnover

High staff turnover may indicate disquiet at fraudulent activity or the way the business is managed and a reluctance to continue working under such conditions.

Temporary staff should be used selectively and not entrusted with valuable assets. Companies should ensure that the screening procedures of recruitment agencies for temporary staff are consistent with their own.

A DISHONEST MANAGER

During an investigation staff who had recently resigned were interviewed. Several commented adversely on the character of their immediate manager: one stated that he was unwilling to work for a dishonest manager and provided evidence of specific frauds.

Compensation tied to performance

Where remuneration is closely linked to financial performance it is important for checks to be made on the nature and quality of the profits generated by individuals remunerated on this basis.

Problems in this area have occurred in dealing rooms where high levels of bonus have been achieved by individual dealers based on the apparent profits which they have earned. Senior management may be reluctant to ask probing questions when dealers appear to be making a great deal of money for the company. It is possible that unauthorised position taking, false deals or misuse of client accounts underlie the apparent profits.

Results at any cost

Setting goals is an essential management tool but management may become so concerned with reaching financial or operational targets that this becomes the overriding aim at the expense of long-term productivity or efficiency. In such cases management may be inclined to manipulate results to ensure achievement on paper.

Earn-out schemes and bases of remuneration which are closely linked to performance may increase the risk of fraud.

BOOSTING AN EARN-OUT

The managing director of a recently acquired business manipulated profits to increase payments to him under an earn-out by paying certain expenses himself and over-charging customers.

Poor commitment to control

In certain companies there is general hostility to controls, regulation and audit. This may derive from lack of commitment to these matters by directors or senior management. It may also be linked to other cultural factors such as too much emphasis on short-term financial targets. Whatever the reason, these attitudes have a significant effect on the company's ability to protect itself against fraud.

Such attitudes may manifest themselves in hostile attitudes to internal audit or inspection staff, such as attempts to restrict the scope of the work and restrictions on access to individuals or documents.

No code of business ethics

The culture and tone of a company should be seen to be honest and opposed to fraud. Management at all levels must lead by example and ensure that rules are not bent, that business practices are above board and there are no hidden perks. It is important to avoid grey areas in the rules, for example concerning entertainment, gifts, commissions or conflicts of interest. One way in which companies may make clear their views on such matters is by having a code of business ethics.

Problems may occur in larger groups which have grown mainly through acquisitions. Variations in the business ethics may occur. For example, in one group three divisions each have a different code of business ethics and a fourth has no code at all.

A related problem is where groups of staff in a business have worked together before in a company or country with poor ethics. They are likely to carry on working in the same way. This may weaken the apparent segregation of duties or result in undue levels of trust being placed in particular individuals with inadequate review of their work.

Unquestioning obedience of staff

Staff may follow procedures by rote. This often occurs where there is an autocratic management style in a company or division. Sometimes this occurs where there are significant numbers of overseas staff and they are reluctant to return to a lower standard of living. In these circumstances staff may be more likely to acquiesce or collude in fraud or malpractice by their superiors. Scenarios include:

- staff are passive, showing no initiative;
- staff are in awe of their superiors;
- questioning of business decisions is not encouraged.

Complex structures

Many of the major reported frauds in recent years have involved the use of 'parallel' organisations – private companies under common ownership surrounding a 'public' or 'regulated' group. Typically a director or senior officer of the company, who is often also a significant shareholder, owns private companies which indirectly undertake transactions with the public or regulated group. The existence or ownership of the private companies is not disclosed.

Any suggestion of such structures should cause concern. Even where there are plausible explanations, for example tax reasons, this does not necessarily reduce the risk of fraud if the extent of such companies and their activities, and their relationship to the public or regulated group, is not fully understood by all the directors of a company and by those who advise it.

Remote locations poorly supervised

Fraud is most likely to occur where supervision and control is least effective. Remote offices, warehouses and factories located far from central management may need more autonomy to enable them to operate effectively. This can be abused if they are not regularly monitored and visited.

The same risk applies to activities which are regarded as peripheral to the main business, such as management of company car schemes, disposal of fixed assets and repair of goods under warranty.

Problems may occur in relation to newly-acquired subsidiaries where the management style or business culture may be different to that of the acquiring group.

BLACK MARKET SALES

A remote and seldom-visited subsidiary made black market sales to unlicensed customers. Some of the extra profits were recorded in the books to improve margins. The balance was pocketed by the managers and staff. Without the unlicensed trade, the subsidiary was unprofitable.

Several firms of auditors

The use of several firms of auditors within a group always increases risk and in certain circumstances may facilitate the concealment of fraud, especially where the auditors rarely communicate with each other. No one firm may have a proper understanding of the group's activities. Where there are a significant number of transactions between group companies and/or branches/divisions in different countries, fragmentation of the audit may be a particular problem. The problem is compounded where there are parallel organisations audited by different auditors, with different year ends.

Poorly defined business strategy

Matters of corporate strategy and policy are crucial to developing a corporate culture which inhibits fraud. Poorly defined strategy, while not usually the direct cause of fraud, is often one of the key aspects which defines the environment in which fraud may thrive. Symptoms include low morale, high staff turnover and an inability to attract good staff or an undue emphasis on short-term targets.

Profits well in excess of industry norms

Businesses which achieve results far in excess of industry norms should always be regarded with some suspicion; for example, rapid growth in sales, abnormal levels of profitability or an unusual ability to attract depositors or investors. These trends may indicate something about the nature of the product, the way it is sold, the customer base or the source of funds. Alternatively it may indicate that the company is overtrading and is heading for a liquidity crisis, which in turn may provide the motivation for fraud.

TOO GOOD TO BE TRUE

The vendor of an acquired business who remained with the company post-acquisition conspired with an employee of one of his major customers that they should accept invoices for 30 per cent more than were supplied. In return, the vendor paid personally for home improvements at the employee's house, foreign holidays and other luxuries. The acquiring company became suspicious when the company achieved margins 20 per cent above any other in the industry and the amount due under the earn-out clause of the acquisition contract appeared to be excessive.

Mismatch between growth and systems development

Disparities between growth or changes in the type of business and the associated accounting systems have been a particular problem in the financial sector where financial controllers have struggled to keep up with rapid developments in financial instruments such as derivatives. Similar problems have been experienced where growth is achieved by acquisitions which are not assimilated so that the group outgrows its command structure.

Poor reputation

The views of other participants in the market are always important. Market reputation usually indicates something about the company's products, its people or its way of doing business. The characteristics identified by outsiders may highlight a factor which undermines the apparent defences of the company against fraud.

Liquidity problems

Tight liquidity may increase the motivation for fraud. A number of the examples considered in Chapters 5, 6 and 7 were motivated by the need to meet regulatory limits or to give a more favourable impression of financial soundness.

Conclusion

This chapter has provided a 'helicopter view' of fraud. It is important to keep the big picture in view. Remember what typically motivates the fraudster. Watch out for the unusual and for the common indicators and risk factors.

But tackling fraud risk in a business of any size depends on much deeper understanding of what frauds are committed and what is driving fraud risk. The next chapter looks at the causes of fraud in greater depth.

3

Causes of fraud

Introduction

Huge changes in business have occurred during the last two decades but internal controls have stood still in many companies, based on structures developed in the 1950s. This chapter begins by looking at some of the factors that define today's fraud arena: globalisation, technological change, empowerment, downsizing, delayering, matrix management, outsourcing, new management styles and continuing change.

The main part of the chapter examines the impact of a company's business strategy and internal business environment – people, culture, ethics, management structures, reward structures and communications – on fraud risk. I explain how deep-seated weaknesses in these areas create abnormal levels of risk. The chapter concludes by highlighting typical failings in fraud risk management.

Today's fraud arena

I highlight below some of the main factors that contribute to risk.

Globalisation

While there is now said to be a global marketplace, in fraud risk terms the world is still a vast and complex matrix of markets, cultures, organisational factors and people. Every organisation must drill down to the local operational level before it can truly appreciate the fraud risks it may be running.

As has been shown in the financial sector, relatively small outposts can expose a business as a whole to potentially catastrophic risks. Cultural differences and practical factors such as shortage of jobs may mean that local employees will be loyal solely to the local managers and will carry out their instructions, whether improper or not. Lack of locally qualified or experienced personnel may quite simply mean that it is not possible to attract the calibre of people necessary to achieve effective control.

Technological change

Computer fraud and abuse is now a global issue. The increased use of the Internet means that companies must be alert not only to computer fraud and abuse trends in the home country but also to those in other countries. Of course, not all hackers are out to defraud, steal or damage their victims. Many are breaking into systems for the challenge. Unfortunately, they frequently advertise their successes on Internet hacking bulletin boards which are monitored by those with malicious intent. If a weakness is discovered in an organisation's computer security by an outside hacker, the information may become available to the rest of the world within hours.

While technology opens new avenues for business and sophisticated software enables complex processing, these improvements also create opportunities which are exploited by disgruntled employees and the criminal fraternity. The Internet has removed the traditional safety net previously provided by physical boundaries and replaced it with an information and communications 'free-for-all'.

The 'job for life' ethos has disappeared and, along with it, the traditional loyalty to the firm. IT departments are increasingly staffed with high numbers of contractors or are outsourced altogether. There are many cases of computer systems being infiltrated by the criminal fraternity acting as contractors.

Empowerment

Companies have moved from hierarchical to 'empowered' structures and cultures. Business units now have much greater autonomy to manage their activities and deliver performance. High levels of reward and incentives may be linked to that performance.

Linked to empowerment is a high level of trust. Group management may be reluctant to question closely the results reported to them in fear of undermining this new trust. The move to empowerment also takes much longer than senior management expects. Structures and cultures do not change overnight merely because top management say they must change. In the interim there may be cultural confusion. This confusion creates volatility because the nature of risk management and control needs to be fundamentally different in an empowered environment compared to a hierarchical one.

Downsizing and delayering

Technology has removed the need for many staff. Whole layers of middle management have been removed and costly head offices and divisional structures cut in size or eliminated altogether. Many of these changes were of course essential to the continued existence of the companies concerned. However, some companies have not recognised that a radical reallocation of responsibilities and the development of new skills is required among those who are left.

For example, in one large international group the head office has been cut by 60 per cent and the group's finance department has been almost completely outsourced. There is an internal audit department of three where there used to be 10. In that situation it is imperative that the business heads who visit and monitor subsidiaries become more alert and acquire the skills to pick up on the early warning signs of manipulation and fraud. If they do not, no-one else will.

Matrix management

Matrix management structures are common today. A number of financial disasters have been caused in part by confusion about responsibilities within these structures. For instance, there may be confusion between regional and functional reporting lines in an international group.

Companies are also reorganising traditional 'silo-based' functions such as sales, purchasing, production and finance, around key elements of the 'value chain'. As a result, many staff from central functions such as purchasing and finance may be re-located in business units and in multidisciplinary project teams, reporting primarily to local business unit or project managers with a 'dotted line' to their functional head.

Although the board may think that the dotted line reporting to the group purchasing or finance director is still strong, the reality can be quite different. The local business unit or project manager will have much more influence, taking hiring and firing decisions and setting 'pay and rations'. There are many cases of local purchasing or finance managers being drawn into manipulation of results when a business unit is under pressure and unlikely to meet targets.

The dynamics of internal control will also be different in this new environment. For the buyer who used to sit in a central purchasing department of 300 staff, it was easy to ensure that group purchasing procedures were followed. He had many expert colleagues nearby with whom he could consult on more difficult matters. Relocated in a project, he may find that the team members from other disciplines do not understand the reasons for many of the purchasing controls. The controls may be seen as unnecessary bureaucracy that impact the profitability on which the project team's bonuses are based. The procurement manager in the team may come under pressure to reveal sensitive procurement information to non-procurement professionals in the project team, such as the prices of other bids. So the purchasing procedures that the audit committee and group management see on the shelf in their offices may be compromised in practice.

Outsourcing

Companies are increasingly focusing on their core activities. Day to day activities which can be detached from the business such as transaction processing are being pulled together into shared service centres. Some companies are then outsourcing these activities under service level agreements that meet the organisation's needs in terms of cost, accuracy and timeliness.

Activities such as computer operations, finance and other services that were previously performed in-house are typical candidates for outsourcing. Some organisations have discovered that outsourcing has opened up new fraud risks. Not only is power to award contracts being given to new areas for the first time, but operations in these areas are also often highly specialised. As a result, it may be very difficult in the case of those responsible for control, to assess whether value for money is being achieved. Furthermore, while buying processes may be well developed in mainline purchasing departments, there may be few such controls in these new areas.

Control, cash management and similar activities are increasingly being managed throughout the business. Non-finance staff are expected to take control responsibilities, for example, a salesperson may be required not only to negotiate payment terms and discounts but also to manage the credit risk, traditionally something done by finance. In the strategic area, business managers increasingly need financial awareness to understand the financial implications of strategic business issues. Many companies underestimate the training required to develop the necessary skills among line business managers.

Management style

The new business leaders are bolder in their actions and less comfortable in steady state organisations. Decisions are made quickly and rely on simple measures of success. There is a desire to control organisations through culture, often linked to personalities. The business leaders often demand total commitment to the principles of the organisation with the culture firmly based on clear values.

The new leaders are often less interested in detailed financial information and comparisons. They need a simple, immediately available view of the business and its success. They expect control to be exercised through tight, computerised information and a clear value-based culture. They will have little time for analysis and prevarication.

In theory many of these changes ought to be positive. But the demand for commitment does not necessarily lead to deep-seated loyalty among staff. The traditional employee loyalties of the 1960s and 1970s have long since been dismembered and are not recreated overnight by issuing corporate values statements and briefings. Assessing risks in a structured way may run counter to this new management style. Taking account of downside risks may be seen as negative. This is not conducive to the effective management of fraud risk.

Change and discontinuity

Many argue that the organisations which succeed over the next decade will be those that thrive on change. There is no reason to believe that change will slow down as the factors that drive it – technology, personal aspirations, global competition – continue relentlessly.

Many of the specific changes outlined above mean that traditional forms of control are already out-dated. Procedures manuals are often ignored by management and seen to be an irrelevance. In future control will increasingly need to be based on staff at all levels in a company having the skills to think in a structured way about fraud risk and to question the unusual.

Case study 4

To set the scene for detailed analysis of the causes of fraud, let's now look at a more complex case study.

MAKE OR BREAK

A British-based multinational decided to expand its business in South East Asia. It operated a range of business divisions through a chain of subsidiaries overseas. The Australian subsidiary appeared to have just the person to develop the business in South East Asia: John Brown, a secondee from England with 20 years' experience with the group. He was at that time the finance director of the Australian subsidiary.

The Australian CEO was told by the British head of division that the South East Asia business would continue to be booked in the Australian subsidiary, but that John Brown must be allowed a free hand to develop the business, in line with the new policy of empowerment being introduced throughout the group.

Unfortunately, this policy of empowerment backfired:

(a) John fell in with corrupt local business practices, resulting in him approving concealed payments to bribe local officials;

(b) his response to empowerment was to do business at all costs, breaching company limits and controls and exposing it to significant financial risk; for example, he gave hidden undertakings to the local government concerned to fund projects in return for lucrative contracts that later fell through;

(c) the Australian CEO had apparent and legal responsibility for John's activities, but when told by the British head of division that John must have a free hand, he took the view that head office had in effect taken responsibility. Meanwhile, the head of division assumed that the Australian CEO was keeping John under control.

The problem areas in this case are summarised on the following chart.

Figure 3.1 Problem areas in case study 4

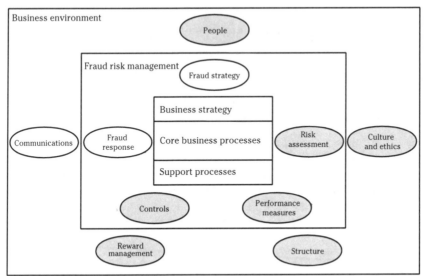

In the business environment the main issues were as follows:

(a) the matrix **management structure** created confusion over who was responsible for monitoring John Brown's activities. As noted above, the head of division in the UK thought that the Australian CEO was still keeping and eye on John while the Australian CEO thought that the head of division in the UK had now taken responsibility. The result was that no-one was monitoring John;

(b) there were important issues to do with **people, reward structures and performance measures**. It is never said, but the sub-text is that if John Brown succeeds, he is bound for senior management but if he fails he has reached his limit. There is an important human dimension: it is John's last chance for the top. It is therefore a 'make or break' situation;

(c) **culture** plays a part. As regards national culture, in the country in which John Brown was operating few foreigners speak its language. There are very few local professionals. There was considerable corruption among officials in institutions that John Brown was dealing with and also among many of the other foreigners seeking to do business there;

(d) as regards the **commercial culture** in the company, it had apparently changed to one of empowerment but the real culture was still relatively paternalistic and hierarchical, trusting of long-standing colleagues. John's colleagues were prepared to approve transactions on the basis of his word and authority without any effective questioning of the rationale for them. Culture does not change merely because senior managers say it must;

(e) the vast majority of staff will take considerable time to assimilate change and in the meantime, many of the **controls** that management thought it had over their newly empowered staff may be entirely ineffective. If empowerment is to be introduced, controls over those empowered must be much more rigorous;

(f) there was no fraud **risk assessment**. Given the planned strategy of expanding into emerging markets, a wider risk assessment by the board and senior management would have paid enormous dividends. The business risks relating to markets and distribution channels were assessed but the impact of wider issues in the business environment were not recognised.

Business strategy

We saw at the beginning of the chapter some of the wider external forces that are defining today's fraud arena. These forces are influencing corporate strategy and in turn impacting fraud risk. At a more detailed level, what the company's strategy is, how well formulated it is, who is involved in devising it and how well it is communicated can also affect fraud risk. Plans to introduce risk management structures sometimes fail to recognise these more deep-seated weaknesses in a company's strategic management process. If there are problems, it is virtually impossible to introduce sustainable risk management. The following two case studies illustrate the point.

Case study 5

CUTTING MATERIAL COSTS

A company wanted to cut its material costs by 40 per cent. Such costs represented a significant part of its cost base. This had been a strategic objective for the previous two years.

It was included in the group strategy document as one line. Although implementation of this objective affected all business units it was only included in one of the strategy documents for the individual business units. There were no implementation plans setting out how this major change would take place. It was therefore not surprising that little progress had been made.

From a business risk point of view, the proposed strategy has significant implications. It involved:

(a) rationalisation of the company's supplier base;

(b) renegotiation of many of its contracts;

(c) significant changes in the operation of contracts, for example relating to timing of deliveries and payment of invoices;

(d) staff and organisational changes; and

(e) development of improved purchasing skills.

The strategy also changed the fraud risk profile:

(a) the re-tendering and renegotiation of contracts increasing the likelihood of purchasing frauds such as bid rigging, bid fixing and kickbacks;

(b) the new contracts might include large discounts and rebates. There are fraud issues concerning the possible diversion of rebates and discounts as well as the potential for hidden contract terms, with the rebates taken to profit but conditional on future levels of turnover with the supplier;

(c) inadequate negotiating skills may make the company more vulnerable to suppliers agreeing non-standard terms, for example, manipulating more favourable payment terms to compensate for low prices submitted to win the bid.

In the following example the problem is lack of strategy, lack of business vision.

Case study 6

STRATEGIC DRIFT

XYZ Limited is a major equipment leasing company in mainland Europe. A few years ago it had significant financial problems and over the last few years the strategy has been about digging the company out of that hole. Management were incentivised with highly-leveraged reward structures. Those problems were resolved some time ago but the company has not put in place a clear business vision for the next few years.

People in the company made the following comments.

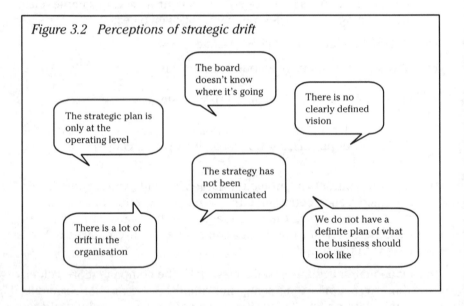

Figure 3.2   Perceptions of strategic drift

A number of high calibre staff were likely to leave because there were no challenges left. But a significant drop in the quality of people employed by the company would have an impact on quality of control.

The lack of vision created strategic drift. Sales and commercial managers who are still on highly-leveraged reward packages were migrating into new business areas which were not part of the company's strategy, without board approval. Some of these deals were more risky than those traditional areas of business. Such deals were not going through normal deal approval committee procedures. They involved counterparties hiding behind complex offshore structures. Face-to-face meetings with the counterparties, if at all, were held in hotel rooms and there was an unexplained urgency to complete deals. The company was being drawn into a more sinister world.

The above two case studies show why strategic management processes are inextricably linked to fraud risk management.

People

Introduction

People commit fraud, not business or systems. Starting with people rather than processes is important in considering fraud risk management. Management and staff can unwittingly disclose a great deal about a company often within the first few minutes of a meeting.

Figure 3.3 sets out some comments made during the first few minutes of a meeting with a financial controller.

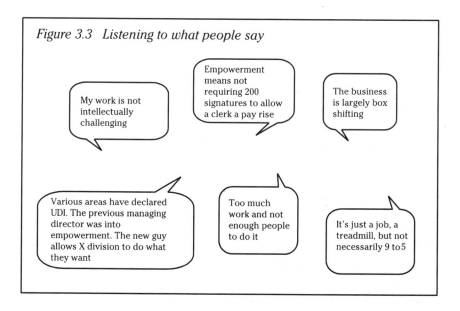

Figure 3.3   Listening to what people say

These comments give pointers to how the individual feels about his job, how he is treated by senior management, his workload, level of job interest, management tensions and how empowerment is perceived. All of these issues are highly relevant to fraud.

Recruitment screening

Many fraudsters are long-standing, trusted employees who, because of some business or personal pressure, become involved in a fraud. But some join as 'fully-trained' fraudsters, or display a tendency to lie at the time they apply to join the company.

Many screening checks are straightforward but are not properly performed. The following example is typical.

HAT-TRICK

A credit controller committed the same fraud at three companies in succession. She claimed to be a qualified chartered accountant. In fact, she had never taken an accountancy exam. Furthermore, she had spent time in jail in between jobs. None of the companies checked one simple matter: whether she was listed in the Institute of Chartered Accountants' register of members. The check is free, can be done by phone in less than two minutes and would have saved the companies £800,000. None of the companies probed the employment gaps in her CV effectively. Telephone calls to her previous employers were not made.

If someone is prepared to lie on their CV it is more likely that they may lie about other things once they have joined the company.

Screening procedures may be overridden when a director or senior manager already knows the applicant.

GOOD CHAP

A divisional finance director defrauded his employer of £300,000 over a two-year period. In fact, he had committed a similar fraud at his previous employer. The group finance director used to work at the same company and had come across him there. Some years after joining the company he recommended that the financial controller should be offered a job with the group, not knowing that he had subsequently committed a fraud at the other company. No references were taken and most of the usual recruitment procedures were not carried out.

A company may have sound procedures for permanent staff but comparable procedures may not be used by its recruitment agencies. Unquestioning reliance is too often placed on such agencies. The following example shows how weaknesses in this area enabled a cheque fraud gang to infiltrate a company.

GANGSTER'S GIRLFRIEND

A company employed a temporary bought ledger clerk. Unfortunately, the clerk's partner was a member of a cheque fraud gang. She was systematically placed in companies to obtain cheques. Cheques awaiting signature, or which had been signed and were awaiting despatch, were often left on desks by managers during long lunches. The clerk exploited this and stole cheques. Payee details on the stolen cheques were then amended.

The company became aware of the fraud when the police turned up at their door, having arrested the gang on an unrelated matter. In their pockets were two of the company's cheques. The company had not previously identified the fraud because it was six months behind with its bank reconciliations.

Similar risks arise with contract staff.

TAKEN TO THE CLEANERS

Contract cleaning staff in a company carried out a number of cheque frauds. They picked up cheques awaiting signature which were often kept on desks overnight in special colour-coded transparent wallets. Cheque books were kept in unlocked cabinets. They also identified cheques in post-out trays because the envelopes were semi-transparent and the cheques could be seen inside.

Prior business relationships

If you take a company's organisation charts and highlight those staff who have worked together before at a former employer, an interesting pattern may emerge. Sometimes it will highlight situations where controls may not be as effective in practice as they might first appear.

For example, two members of staff may be placed either side of an important segregation of duties. Perhaps they used to work for a company with an entirely different business morality. It is likely that they will continue to operate as they did before. Whatever the apparent segregation of duties, the reality may be different.

Another situation is where, for example, a head of credit joins a bank and sometime later he brings in a number two who used to work with him at his previous employer. The head of credit may put undue trust in his deputy or the deputy may not question transactions recommended by the head of credit. Sometimes the number two is brought in deliberately because it is known that he will be compliant and be a willing accessory to some planned fraud.

Sometimes a whole team may join a company, as in the following example.

CRONY SUPPLIERS

The procurement department in a company was brought in from a competitor and given complete autonomy to run a centralised purchasing function following significant losses caused by the previous decentralised operation.

It turned out that five members of the new procurement department simply brought all their old 'crony' suppliers with them and while there was an apparent tender process, it was always the same winners. Invitation letters to other contractors that were on the company's files were either never sent or the crony suppliers would beat the competitors who did tender but the subsequent over billings always meant that their projects were uneconomical. The director of procurement had shareholdings in two of the suppliers which had been introduced.

If the company had checked a little further they would have discovered that the former employers had suffered a similar fraud at the hands of this team.

Nepotism

Nepotism can be rife in certain companies or departments. For example, in one company the head of procurement had a deputy manager who was the son-in-law of the board director to whom he reported.

This 'meat in the sandwich' situation makes it difficult for the head of procurement to perform his duties. For example, if the head of pro-

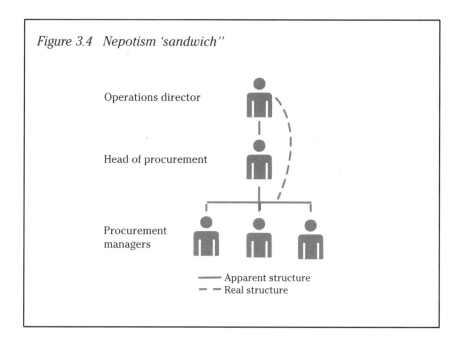

Figure 3.4 Nepotism 'sandwich''

Operations director

Head of procurement

Procurement
managers

——— Apparent structure
− − Real structure

curement suspects that the deputy manager is involved in some sort of
fraud it may be more difficult for him to raise his concerns. He may be
seen as a mischief-maker and he may feel that his own position is
vulnerable.

Certain departments may be particularly prone to nepotism and
conflicts of interest. For example, in a maintenance department a
number of close relatives were employed. There was a lack of objectiv-
ity in assessing whether in fact they were the best people to do the job.
Work was given to contractors who were connected with members of
staff.

Skills gaps

Key skills gaps can affect the ability of staff to manage fraud risk.
For example, poor negotiating skills and training in a purchasing
department may not only put the company in a weak negotiating
position with its suppliers but also increase exposure to manipulation
of the bid process by suppliers.

Courses on risk and control issues are rarely included in corporate training programmes. For example, account managers in a Training and Enterprise Council, responsible for managing suppliers of training services, received training on products and services, equal opportunities, IT packages, sector awareness, media, customer care and contract training. But their training did not include guidance on:

- risk profiling of suppliers;
- how to assess vulnerabilities at particular suppliers;
- guidance on good account management;
- monitoring and probing skills.

Career moves

The 'Make or break' case study earlier in this chapter illustrated the part career moves can play in risk management. It is not uncommon to find that staff are moved to positions for which they have little relevant experience, training or skills.

For example, in one case a financial controller had problems with a warranty calculation. The individual concerned had come up the sales side of the operation, was not a qualified accountant and had no specific guidance from group level on the calculation to be performed. Having made mistakes in the early months of handling the calculation, rather than coming clean that he was out of his depth, he tried to cover up his earlier mistakes with further mistakes.

Low risk alertness

As noted in the opening chapter, given the trend of escalation in many fraud cases, the trick is to stop things in the very early stages. Alertness to fraud in the organisation is crucial to protecting a company against fraud. Many companies have made the mistake of introducing more and more control to combat fraud. Usually the opposite is necessary: less bureaucracy would assist the management of fraud risk. There needs to be a balance between controls and risk thinking and awareness.

In practice, fraud awareness is low. Few companies have a fraud awareness training programme, although they are more common in the USA. Sometimes there is a focus on certain types of fraud risk but there are significant 'blind spots'. A few years ago I ran a workshop on fraud for risk managers at a major bank. At the beginning of the workshop I asked them how they saw the top 10 risks of fraud facing their bank. The chart below shows how they ranked the various risks.

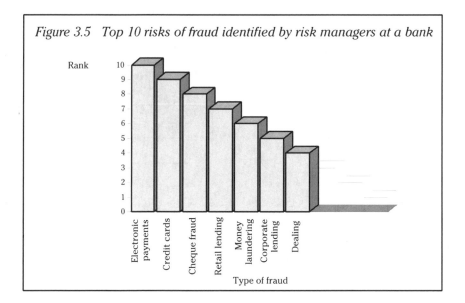

Figure 3.5   Top 10 risks of fraud identified by risk managers at a bank

The responses revealed the following issues:

(a) they only managed to identify seven fraud risks;

(b) the main focus was on the external and more visible frauds such as external payment frauds, cheque fraud and credit card fraud;

(c) the main risk in the credit area was seen to come from customers in the retail lending area. It was difficult for the group to face up to the possibility of management fraud, for example, in the corporate lending and dealing areas;

(e) none of the more general types of fraud, such as purchasing fraud, which can affect any organisation, were mentioned. The bank had a purchasing spend in nine or 10 figures.

Levels of alertness can be ascertained quite quickly. Ask the question: 'how do you see the key risks of fraud facing your company?' Staff who are alert to fraud risk and have addressed the issue should be able to quickly list eight or 10 key risks. Figure 3.6 sets out some typical comments made during fraud reviews.

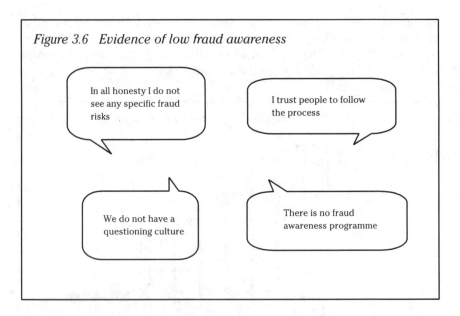

Figure 3.6 Evidence of low fraud awareness

A fraud awareness programme is an effective way of launching a number of related initiatives relating to ethics, risk management and control. I shall return to this issue in the concluding chapter on managing fraud risk.

Morale issues

Wider morale issues may be corrosive to the business and provide fertile ground for fraud. A number of organisations conduct employee attitude surveys to help them identify and address such issues. These are useful to a degree but the questionnaire-based approach can give a rather superficial result. Deep-seated morale issues sometimes only come out through careful interviewing of employees during counselling or other sessions.

Examples of situations which can lead to fraud include:

- low levels of job satisfaction due to high levels of drudgery and routine work resulting from inefficiencies and disregard of key processes;

- lack of intellectual challenge;

- low perceived status of the department and poor career progression prospects;

- unresolved conflicts within an organisational structure;
- dissatisfaction with how management treat staff.

Lifestyles and untaken holiday

Lifestyle issues and untaken holidays were highlighted in the previous chapter. Many frauds come to light when the fraudster is called away unavoidably as illustrated in the following extraordinary case.

MIRACULOUS RECOVERY

A long-standing employee at a bank who had not taken a holiday in years unfortunately had a car accident. This induced a minor heart attack and he was rushed to hospital. His colleagues were surprised when, the next day, he discharged himself from hospital and returned to work.

In fact, he had been committing a fraud for 15 years, keeping his extended family supplied with funds.

Management style and high staff turnover

Autocratic management styles were noted in the previous chapter as having been a factor in a number of frauds. High staff turnover may indicate unhappiness among staff at how the business is conducted, oppressive working conditions or disquiet concerning the activities of a manager in the company.

Culture and ethics

For the purposes of this book, I adopt a straightforward definition of commercial culture:

> A company's values, how a company does business, its management style and how it treats its employees, customers, suppliers, and other stakeholders.

There are then of course the national cultures within which the group operates. The interplay between these two aspects of culture produces many different variants of culture in a group. It is easy to assume that the commercial culture of a company will be adopted in all locations. As discussed earlier in this chapter, in fraud risk terms the world is still a vast and complex matrix of cultures, despite increasing globalisation.

One way of picking up on the hallmarks of a company's culture is to ask employees which adjectives describe what it is like to work there. This may provide an initial insight into whether the culture supports or works against effective control. There may be positive messages, there may be negative ones. Frequently, there is cultural confusion. That is the most volatile situation.

Ethics is closely linked to culture. Defining what is acceptable and what is not is important. There are a thousand shades of grey. It is often not clear to employees where their employer draws the line.

Cultural confusion

As discussed earlier in this chapter, there has been a move from hierarchical to empowered structures and cultures. Many organisations talk about empowerment but do not 'walk the talk'. Meanwhile, there may be cultural confusion.

For example, people in one organisation made the comments set out in Figure 3.7.

The confusion causes concern because the nature of control needs to be different in an empowered environment. Where greater autonomy is given to business units to deliver results, manipulation risk may increase. There needs to be greater scepticism concerning the results reported and new ways of monitoring, without undermining trust. There need to be clear accountabilities.

Staff may have new buying authority in relation to outsourced contracts. Poorly defined accountabilities may leave staff vulnerable to accusations of fraud or impropriety, for instance if they have not documented how and why a particular supplier was chosen.

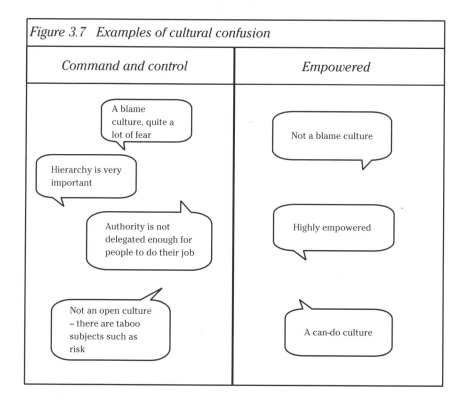

Figure 3.7 Examples of cultural confusion

Cultural pressures

Performance measures and targets are a necessary part of business life. But they may become unrealistic and overly aggressive. Where there are excessive pressures, this increases risk.

In one company people made the comments shown in Figure 3.8. The perception of unrealistic targets encouraged staff to give the appearance of achieving targets.

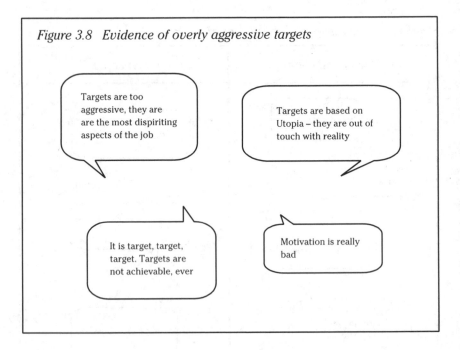

Figure 3.8   Evidence of overly aggressive targets

Targets are too aggressive, they are are the most dispiriting aspects of the job

Targets are based on Utopia – they are out of touch with reality

It is target, target, target. Targets are not achievable, ever

Motivation is really bad

Need-to-know culture

Some companies or divisions may operate a 'need-to-know' culture. Such a culture facilitates the concealment of fraud. Some of the behavioural indicators referred to in Chapter 2 are worth repeating here:

- does not allow anyone to see the full picture
- says as little as possible unless confronted with the facts
- answers different questions from the ones put
- uses delaying tactics – always about to go to an important meeting
- passes the parcel
- goes on the attack when questioned closely about matters they would prefer not to discuss
- carefully controls access to certain personnel
- deals with certain accounts personally outside the main system
- manipulates timetables and deadlines
- keeps people off their patch

Entities not assimilated into group culture

Problems can occur where staff of a local entity are not assimilated into the group culture. This is most likely to occur where the business unit is in the nature of a joint venture, has been recently acquired or has been purchased from existing management.

It can also occur where the local culture is fundamentally different to the culture of the home country, for example, the local culture is hierarchical or there is unquestioning obedience by staff. I shall return to these aspects when discussing management structure issues later in the chapter.

Poor ethical code

Business ethics is a big subject. For example, it includes policies regarding use of labour in third world countries and environmental issues. I deal here only with aspects directly relating to fraud.

Typical problems with development and implementation of ethical codes include:

(a) a 'cut and paste' approach to developing the code, that is taking parts of another company's code and quickly just changing the names. This rarely works as the language used in such documents and the specific ethical issues will very much depend on the company's culture, management style and business strategy;

(b) staff may be just required to give an annual sign-off. There may be no other communication of key messages, for example integrating messages into regular corporate briefings;

(c) there may be inadequate reporting channels or a discussion forum for staff to discuss ethical dilemmas;

(d) there may be no guidance on the specific circumstances or types of situations which staff might typically face;

(e) there may be no guidance on the business's attitude to integrity of reporting and financial information.

Ethical dilemmas

In most multinationals the range of ethical dilemmas which staff may face is huge, working in cultures with different business moralities. The scope for conflicts of interest is considerable. It is important that clear guidance and examples are given indicating the company's expect-ations. Workshops and 'cards on table' sessions that simulate more difficult circumstances are also useful.

The acid test is: 'if there was an article on this transaction in a national newspaper tomorrow, what would be the reaction of the board? What would be the impact on shareholder value and management credibility?'

Examples of ethical dilemmas include:

(a) sales of assets to a company in which a member of management, or one of their close relatives, has an interest;

(b) failure to declare an interest in a supplier;

(c) the need to pay commissions or undertake illegal practices to do business in certain regions. Despite ethical policies set by the board, sometimes there is a lack of transparency and the board is not fully aware of what is entailed in doing business in certain countries. The business practices may be in direct conflict with stated group policies and ethical codes; and

(d) only one or two members of the board may be fully aware of what commissions are being paid to whom to win contracts. Whether or not such commissions are paid is a matter for each company to decide. It is essential that all members of the board are fully aware of what is happening so that all such transactions are authorised and the implications fully considered.

Management structures

Structural risk is perhaps the least understood aspect of the corporate business environment. Structures are nevertheless the foundation of internal control. The structure defines the roles, responsibilities and reporting lines on which controls are based. Problems with structure may therefore completely undermine apparently good controls.

It is common to find that following a reorganisation, management believe that the new structure reflects how things are operating in practice. When one talks to people down in the organisation the reality may be completely different.

All structures carry risk. The key is to understand the risks inherent in the particular structure. The following case study shows how complex structural issues can create abnormal risk.

Case study 7

DOUBLE WHAMMY

A board director and the head of a division in an overseas multinational understated forecast revenue from certain remote overseas locations by US$100 million and overstated the funding needed for various overseas projects, also by about US$100 million.

The manipulation gradually increased over two years. The division always appeared to be achieving much better than budget/forecast and was highly regarded by the group.

Figure 3.9 shows in simplified form the board and divisional structure. I highlight below the key issues and questions.

Degree of collective responsibility

To what extent is their collective responsibility among the executive directors? Do all of the directors have insight into all the divisions of the group, for example into division Z? Or are the activities of division Z only known to director Z? What sort of information is shared/not shared?

In the actual case, director Z had almost sole insight into the activities of division Z. There were special reporting arrangements whereby division Z did not report through to group finance in the normal way. These arrangements were historical. Director Z had a close relationship with the directors and management of division Z prior to its acquisition.

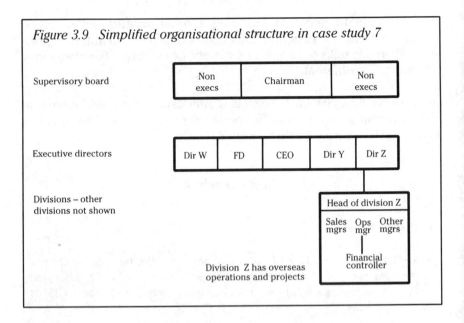

Figure 3.9 Simplified organisational structure in case study 7

Role of the chief executive

How much authority does the chief executive have over his fellow directors? Is he regarded as a team leader or is he just 'another director'? In this case he lacked authority over the other directors, in particular director Z.

Dominant personalities on the board

Who are the dominant personalities and what implications does this have on the effectiveness of the board? In this case director Z was a dominant personality and was good at keeping people off his patch.

Interaction between chairman and chief executive

What is the division of responsibilities between the chairman and chief executive? How are their roles perceived by people in the group?

In this case the non-executive chairman had previously been a long-standing executive chairman of the group. He quite frequently dealt directly with members of management and management still saw him in an executive chairman/chief executive role. This undermined the chief executive's position.

Director Z/head of division relationship

To what extent does director Z act in a quasi non-executive role in relation to division Z? How close is the relationship between director Z and the head of division Z? In this case they worked closely together and there was an extreme 'need-to-know' culture. Many things were only known to them.

Relationship between head of division and division staff

To what extent are strategy and business objectives communicated to staff in the division? How widely is information about the business shared? To what extent do staff understand what their colleagues do?

As indicated above, there was an extreme 'need-to-know' culture. In fact there was no communication of strategy and business objectives to staff in general. Staff had a poor understanding of what their colleagues did in other departments, and sometimes even within departments. When they were given schedules which helped to prove that the revenue forecast was understated, the member of staff concerned was disciplined by the head of division and told that he would be 'cut out of the loop' in future. There was unnecessary secrecy over routine matters.

Status of finance

What authority does finance have? What is its ability to probe? How do divisional finance managers interact with other members of the management team?

In this group finance had relatively low status and in division Z, partly for historical reasons, the financial controller was on the third tier of management rather than being a member of the divisional board. Finance's role in the division was very much 'bean counting'.

Remoteness of the non-executive directors

How close are the non-executive directors to the business? What authority do they have?

The supervisory board structure in this group tended to increase their remoteness from the business. While individually there were some high calibre directors, the other structural issues referred to above made it very difficult for them to exercise their powers effectively.

Dysfunctional board

How the board or divisional board is perceived by staff is not always readily apparent. The group board's standing amongst City analysts and institutions may be more apparent but this does not necessarily extend to divisional boards.

Perceptions of a divisional board in one group included the following.

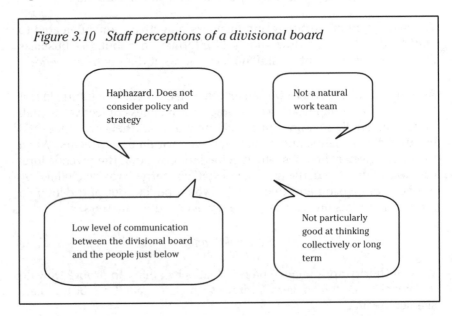

Figure 3.10   Staff perceptions of a divisional board

The board was seen to lack authority, was not sure where it is going and lacked vision. Where this is the case it is unlikely that the board and the management team will focus effectively on key risks.

A more complex situation may develop where the division or subsidiary is located abroad where, for example, expatriate management occupy the managing director and finance director roles. Sometimes, in these situations there is a sort of double structure. Problems may be compounded where the expatriate staff do not speak the local language particularly well. This is illustrated in the following case.

DOUBLE STRUCTURE

In a large UK subsidiary of an overseas multinational the managing director and finance director positions were occupied by senior personnel from the home country, both on three-year secondments. There was a deputy managing director and a senior financial controller who with the business division heads, for all practical purposes, ran the UK business.

Perceptions included the following:

(a)   the managing director and finance director played too low a profile in the company;

(b)   other board members and members of staff felt that there was an inadequate decision-making forum at which key issues affecting the company as a whole and conflicts between different parts of it could be resolved;

(c)   there was relatively poor communication and liaison between divisions. This was exacerbated by the managing director and finance director not giving sufficient lead and getting the company to pull together as one team;

(d)   the finance director had very little involvement in the activities of the finance department and so was regarded as rather ineffectual.

Clearly, these issues have business impacts. They are not conducive to effective fraud risk management.

Role of chairman and chief executive

In case study 7, we saw how a chairman still acting as chief executive can seriously undermine the authority of the current chief executive.

Another situation that can lead to problems is where a subsidiary chief executive, who is a high flyer and moving up the group rapidly, is acting in a quasi non-executive role having delegated many of his day-to-day responsibilities to another board member. This can lead to confusion in responsibilities, lack of a clear team leader at board level and a board which is not structured to look at risk issues effectively.

Matrix management

Problems with matrix structures have underpinned many financial disasters. Such structures are not inherently more risky. They simply involve different risks and those risks are not always recognised.

Loyalty to a local business head rather than the functional head

In a matrix management structure, loyalty may be to the country head or local head rather than to the product division head at group level. The board's intention, and assumption, is that the main reporting lines are functional. The problem is exacerbated where the local culture is hierarchical. For example, in certain developing countries tax will often dictate that country heads have responsibility for local operations to avoid 'mind and management' problems for tax purposes.

Incentives not aligned with structural responsibilities

Incentives are sometimes not aligned with structural responsibilities leading to conflicts of loyalties and creation of unrecognised reporting lines outside the structure. Business units may fill positions with loyal supporters. Pay and conditions may be determined by the local head rather than functional head. This may not be obvious from looking at the organisation structure or personnel department records. Hire and fire decisions may be taken locally rather than by the function head.

Special arrangements

Units or individuals may be allowed special arrangements outside the normal management structure or access may be restricted. Reasons may be historical, for example, a subsidiary was purchased and the local managing director was allowed to report to the group managing director directly. The entity may be 'the chief executive's baby' and no other members of management may be allowed real access.

There may be formal or informal management agreements which create misalignment, for example an acquired subsidiary where the management is told that they need not introduce group control systems provided they continue to meet budget. An individual may be regarded as a 'star' or 'difficult' and is allowed to operate outside the normal structure.

Lack of relevant expertise to operate a new structure

There may be lack of relevant expertise to operate a new matrix structure. New structures may need new skills which must be in place before the structures are changed: there are no 'parallel runs' with management structures as there usually are when implementing new computer systems.

Local entities may not have the infrastructure or skills to comply fully with requirements of the structure. Operations may be too small to warrant expenditure on the necessary functions or quality of skills.

Structure impedes implementation of risk management procedures

In decentralised groups, central management may not be able to implement and monitor risk management processes effectively relating to key objectives. For example, group management may wish to monitor product liability risk in business units but this cuts across normal reporting lines leading to the risk that adverse test reports may not be passed up to group level.

Business unit defensive

Where a business unit is at risk of closure or disposal, the unit may not report in line with the management structure resulting in a 'them and us' attitude to higher levels of management.

Status of 'front office'

'Front office' functions may take precedence over other functions. The result of a 'front office heroes' culture may well be to downgrade the importance and ultimately the quality of other functions. For example, in advertising, marketing and promotion in large brand-driven groups, the 'heroes' will be the 'creatives' coming up with the latest advertising campaign. Finance may have particularly low status and normal purchasing controls may be largely ignored.

Conflicting business objectives

Effectiveness of functions in the matrix may be impacted by other business objectives or strategies. For example, cost reduction programmes and delayering may mean that functions cannot operate as originally envisaged.

Conflicts between business units and central functions

Conflicts may arise between customer-facing business units and centralised functions. Business units may try to become completely self-sufficient contrary to the planned structure. For example, buyers in the business unit may not liase effectively with buyers in other business units to maximise group purchasing power. Buyers may also ignore group purchasing guidelines and become involved in corrupt purchasing practices.

Management structure undermined by reward structure

The apparent structure may be undermined by disparities in pay levels relative to market rates, resulting in significant differences in competencies of interfacing departments or low morale.

Case study 8

At a more detailed level, changes in matrix structures can have unforeseen changes on the dynamics of control. The following case study illustrates how changes to the organisation of purchasing activity had wider implications than at first appreciated.

PURCHASING MATRIX

XYZ plc is involved in major projects. The company reorganised its purchasing activities. Historically, most major purchases for projects were made by a central purchasing department.

The new structure was designed to make each project a mini business unit with its own profit and loss account. Many purchasing staff in the central department have relocated to the projects and sit in multi-disciplinary project teams. Most project purchasing will in future be done at project level.

The role of central purchasing will be to ensure quality of purchasing processes and controls across the group and to define the major suppliers from which projects may select; monitor competing demands between projects, for example as regards project scheduling where more than project is using a particular supplier, and to coordinate skills development issues. Local purchasing staff will report to the project purchasing director who in turn reports to the project director. Purchasing directors have a dotted reporting line to the group purchasing director but these dotted lines are not shown on the organisation charts.

The reorganisation outlined above is typical of changes that have occurred in many purchasing and finance departments in recent years. While there are strong business reasons for adopting this type of structure, it is important to recognise that the dynamics of internal control in the new structure may have fundamentally changed.

Typical problems include:

(a) apparent bid procedures may operate quite differently in practice. A comment by a purchasing manager in one of the projects was as follows:

> Keeping price and other commercial information confidential during the bid process is seen as divisive by other team members, for example technical people do not understand why they cannot look at this information.

Poor control over price information during a bid process is one of the main causes of bid fixing and bid rigging;

(b) maintaining consistent procedures across the group will be more challenging. Comments included:

> There is a tendency to migrate to non-standard procedures. The project team may sanction something that previously central purchasing would not have allowed.

(c) overall management of supply relationships may become confused. There may be tension over projects being forced to use suppliers or conflicts where a number of projects want to use the same supplier at the same time. Different project directors may send different messages to the same supplier depending on their individual outlooks;

(d) roles and accountabilities may not be adequately defined. There is a tendency to believe that once the new structure has been designed and circulated that everyone will follow it. In fact often the new role and remit of the central purchasing function may not be well defined. Within the projects the role of purchasing may not be fully understood;

(e) skills development issues may frustrate the implementation of the new structure. There is a big difference between the old structure where 300 purchasing staff, all working in the same 'silo', were able to consult with each other and share expertise compared to the new structure where experienced purchasing resource is spread thinly across many projects. The average purchasing experience in each project will be low. This may impact effective negotiation of contracts and the ability of the group to protect itself against corrupt supplier practices. Often there is a disparity between the experience levels of purchasing staff in projects and their opposite numbers on the sales side of major suppliers who are up to all the tricks.

The key point is that before making such structural change, it is valuable to prepare an analysis of the risks inherent in the new structure. Failure to do this will expose the company unnecessarily to increased fraud risks.

Regional matrix

Similar issues can arise in a regional matrix structure as illustrated in the following example.

REGIONAL MATRIX

ABC Limited put in place a new regional and area structure. Staff were organised into areas, area managers reported to regional directors who in turn reported to the divisional director. There were also functional reporting lines to the heads of the various lines of business for the group as a whole.

Functional heads found it difficult to obtain information and manage the activities of their functions across the group, for example, as regards the basis and type of contracts entered into. They perceived that their functional reporting lines conflicted with the reporting lines to the divisional director.

Role definition

As noted in the introduction to this section, clear roles and accountabilities are the foundation of control. Problems here will mean that seemingly good controls are undermined. Internal control reviews can fail to pick up on these fundamental issues because the focus is more on the control infrastructure itself (i.e., whether a particular control is there or not) rather than how the control structure links into the management structure.

Problems include:

(a) the management structure has developed piecemeal and is a patchwork of reporting lines and historical anomalies;

(b) the structure was designed to fit the business a few years ago but strategy and objectives have moved on requiring a different structure;

(c) there are unnecessary reporting levels in the structure;

(d) individuals in the structure have more than one 'hat' and these compound roles are not understood by everyone in the structure.

A good way of identifying disparities between the actual and documented structure is to put the latter in front of a number of people in the organisation. I often find that interviewees start to re-draw the documented structure saying 'actually, this is how it works, X reports to Y with a dotted line to Z'. Sometimes there are three or four versions of a management structure with none reflecting the actual structure.

This may be just a problem of poor documentation but usually there are more serious business implications such as:

(a) confused reporting lines so that people do not receive the right information at the right time. As a result, management may not pick up on unusual trends that provide the first clue to fraud;

(b) cumbersome structures are worked around and in so doing segregation of duties is compromised;

(c) unnecessary fragmentation of skills and functions. For example, in a leasing company, skills which would normally be brought together in a portfolio management department were split between finance, customer services and other functions resulting in sub-optimal management of the lease portfolio;

(d) accountabilities are vague and it is difficult to apply effective performance measures.

Status of finance

From a fraud point of view, if the status of finance is low, it is unlikely that controls will work effectively in practice. For example, people might make the comments in Figure 3.11 about finance.

Where this is the case, certain areas may be poorly controlled especially where those functions, for strategic or other business reasons, have high status. For example, the marketing department in a

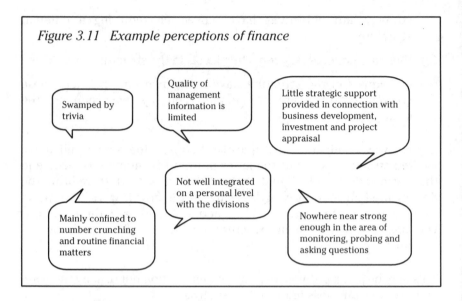

Figure 3.11 Example perceptions of finance

Swamped by trivia

Quality of management information is limited

Little strategic support provided in connection with business development, investment and project appraisal

Not well integrated on a personal level with the divisions

Mainly confined to number crunching and routine financial matters

Nowhere near strong enough in the area of monitoring, probing and asking questions

brand-driven business had few written contracts with suppliers, the basis of pricing was unclear, pricing was often only agreed long after the work had been completed, competitive tendering was rarely undertaken, there were very close relationships with suppliers and there was lavish entertaining. Finance had no oversight of the department.

Complex structures/multiple audit relationships

As noted in the previous chapter, many major frauds have involved unnecessarily complex company structures. Sometimes these organisations are located in jurisdictions where it is difficult to find out who is behind a company. Similarly, multiple audit arrangements have been a factor in a number of cases with no one firm being able to obtain a complete picture.

Reward structures

In case study 6, we looked at a company where highly-leveraged reward structures, which had been set when a business faced severe problems in the past, were not aligned with current strategy. Where the reward structures and the business strategy are misaligned, serious problems can result.

This section examines the impact on fraud of bonuses, earn-outs and other aspects of reward arrangements.

Bonuses

Performance-based pay is common in most industries. Linkage between these reward structures and internal control is less often made. For instance, internal audit departments of banks often do not have access to, or do not take account of, dealers' reward structures when assessing risk management and control in dealing rooms.

The following example illustrates why it may be crucial to understand the reward structures when reviewing the reported results of a dealer.

SAVING FOR A RAINY DAY

A dealer had made sufficient profit to meet his bonus threshold for the current year. He therefore depressed the year end valuations of his trading book so that he could carry forward some of his profits to the following year, when less favourable trading conditions might prevail and he might have more difficulty in reaching his bonus targets. Many of the products he dealt with were over-the-counter financial products and in emerging markets so it was difficult for the middle office to challenge the valuations.

Sometimes, the manipulation may be more subtle.

TOP SLICING

A senior dealer in foreign exchange in the London branch of a foreign bank was very successful. He produced significant profits for the bank. He had good contacts and he knew the market. On some days he produced exceptional profits so he decided to award himself an unauthorised bonus.

He could not go through the normal bonus system so he arranged a transaction at off-market rates. He was not able to deal with his own bank because that was not allowed under the internal rules. So he arranged through a foreign exchange broker to borrow the name of a Swiss bank so that the Swiss bank dealt with the London branch which employed him. He then dealt with the Swiss bank but at off-market rates.

He rang up his contact at the foreign exchange broker and arranged with the Swiss bank to set up a dealing line both for the London branch and also for himself personally. A transaction was then done whereby the London branch sold to the Swiss bank at 1.45. At exactly the same time, the Swiss bank sold to the dealer in his personal capacity at 1.46. So the Swiss bank made a small turn on the business. The dealer then sold to the market at 1.50, which was the market price. So both deals were not at market prices but the Swiss bank had made a small turn. The branch lost money because it had entered into transactions at off-market rates. The dealer got away with it because he chose days when he had already earned a large profit for the branch. He just took a slice off the top through his off-market deals which he took for himself.

When one looked at the profits he had been reporting, the days in question appeared to be some of his best days. He was caught because the Swiss bank eventually realised what had been going on.

The following chart illustrates the parties involved and the prices at which the deals were done (simplified for the purpose of illustration).

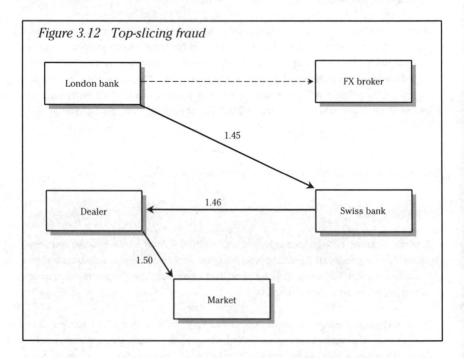

Figure 3.12 Top-slicing fraud

There are a number of ways this might have been picked up in the London branch:

(a) a screen could have indicated if there was a significant difference in the rate at which a deal was done and the last rate at which the particular financial product was dealt;

(b) reviews by a senior dealer might pick up such anomalies. In this case it would obviously not have worked because the senior dealer was the problem;

(c) the middle office risk management function may have picked it up. If, however, it is a small margin it is less likely to be picked up. If the financial product is one of the new more volatile products where there is a wide bid/offer spread, the price may well be somewhere in that spread but it may be difficult to determine whether the deal has been done at best price or not;

(d) internal audit might pick it up, but this is likely to be some months later.

The key is to look at the reward structures and the dealing trends together. If the middle office looks at prices at which deals are done or valuations in the context of the dealer's reward package, it may be possible to see unusual trends or activities occurring as the dealer reaches the bonus threshold.

Reward structures can sometimes undermine apparently good controls. For example, in a leasing business some form of deal approval committee, similar to a credit committee in a bank, will be usually be in place. This may appear to be well constituted and have deal committee minutes. The dynamics of the committee may be quite different in practice though as the following example illustrates.

DONE DEALS

Sales staff in a leasing business received highly-leveraged reward packages. This created immense pressure to close leasing deals. Situations arose where sales staff would become aware of crucial information about a new or existing credit shortly before deal closing. Rather than sharing this information with the head of credit it was suppressed until shortly before deal closing, when it was too late for the company to withdraw from the deal, or until after the deal had closed.

Earn-outs

The following examples show how earn-outs may be manipulated. The focus may be on arithmetical accuracy of the calculation rather than how the inputs may have been manipulated.

MISSED EARN-OUT TARGET

A management team who were in the third year of an earn-out realised that they were not going to meet their earn-out targets when a processing plant contract got delayed. So they created a fictitious customer, a bogus contract, and dummy suppliers. They manipulated cash flows to give the appearance of an actual contract so that they could bring forward some 'profit' into the current year and hence achieve their earn-out targets.

Sometimes the business may appear to be doing well, keeping its cost base under tight control. The reality may be quite different.

8-TIMES FRAUD

Directors and former owners of a company which had recently been acquired under an earn-out bore certain expenses personally. Given that the earn-out was based on 8 x profits, this meant that for every £1 borne personally the directors received back 8 times that amount in increased earn-out.

Disparities with market rates

Disparities in relative pay levels can undermine apparent controls. For example, in purchasing, there will be important interfaces between purchasing, technical, production, and projects. Any major equipment tender will involve the technical department developing a suitable specification which can be included in the tender documentation to be sent to bidders. The role of the purchasing department is of course to control the bidding process and to manage the overall relationship with the supplier.

Where there are significant disparities in relative pay levels compared to the relevant market rates of pay this may undermine the apparent processes and controls. The following case is an extreme example of this.

MONKEYS

ABC Limited had a purchasing department set up in a conventional way with the normal bidding procedures. However, there was a large disparity in pay levels relative to market between staff in technical and those in purchasing. Technical staff were bright graduates paid significantly above market rates whereas those in purchasing were low in calibre and paid below market rates for their job.

Purchasing staff had been moved into the department because there was nowhere else for them to go: purchasing was a 'dumping ground'. Staff in technical and other departments viewed purchasing staff as 'order placers' and sometimes in pejorative terms such as 'monkeys'.

In practice, purchasing had weak relationships with suppliers, rarely visiting their premises, and were often in a weak negotiating position due to poor negotiating skills. On the other hand staff in the technical department had extensive contacts with suppliers. They met new suppliers at trade fairs, established close working relationships with such suppliers, commissioned design work. Such suppliers would then become 'chosen' suppliers even though there were other suppliers in the marketplace equally able to provide the product.

Apparent tender procedures were followed with three or four suppliers being invited to bid. Sometimes the specification was based around the chosen supplier's product which imposed unfair criteria on the other bidders. Later in the process, suppliers would be eliminated with a one or two line memo indicating that the supplier was unsuitable on technical grounds. While there was an appearance of a bid process, the technical department was controlling the selection process.

Communications

Effective communication can contribute to a successful operating environment, by securing staff buy-in to strategies and policies and giving management early warning signs of issues which may have important business implications. Many of the examples given so far in this chapter have involved communication issues. Some further aspects are discussed below.

Poor organisational learning

Many businesses try to be 'learning organisations'. Unfortunately, the appetite for learning rarely extends to the fraud area. Incidents that have occurred in one division may not be known about in another division. There can be sensitivities about disseminating information but it is usually possible to modify the material so that the key lessons are learned.

Most larger companies now operate an Intranet. This is an ideal way to promote increased awareness of fraud warning signs and key lessons.

Learning from other businesses

Incidents affecting other businesses today can highlight problems that may affect your company tomorrow. For example, there have been numerous cases in the Medicare sector in the USA relating to inflated billings, services patients never received or multiple claims for the same services. These cases are directly relevant to private healthcare operations in the UK. There have been numerous fraud cases concerning the defence industry in the USA, involving substandard product frauds and manipulation of projects. A number of these cases are equally relevant to the UK defence industry.

Communication of fraud and ethics policies

Many companies have a policy on fraud and an ethical code. As noted earlier in the chapter, the problem is that they are not communicated effectively. Companies may require their employees to submit an annual return that they have read the latest update of the ethical code. In fact, most employees have never read the original version let alone the updates. Perhaps the code was not launched effectively and key messages from the code are not integrated into corporate communications.

Similarly, there may be a policy on fraud reporting. In one business, the company secretary managed to dig out a policy, having rooted around in his desk drawer for a few minutes. It turned out that only he and one other person in the company, the security officer, were currently aware of the policy. It was circulated when issued five years previously but had long since been forgotten by other staff. The pre-Christmas period may be an appropriate time to remind personnel about ethical codes as this is the time that excessive hospitality, entertaining or gifts are likely to be on offer by suppliers.

Fraud risk management

It is now time to examine how weaknesses in risk management enable fraud to occur. By way of introduction, Table 3.1 summarises some of the typical elements of fraud risk management in companies and what is missing.

Anti-fraud strategy

Many companies do not have an anti-fraud strategy. In others there is a strategy but it only covers certain aspects of fraud. For example, insurance companies may focus on claimant fraud but mis-selling on the underwriting side or other frauds, such as purchasing fraud, which can affect any organisation, may be overlooked.

The anti-fraud strategy should include:

- the company's stance on fraud and other breaches of the ethical code;

- what will be done and by whom in the case that frauds or other breaches are suspected;

- the key initiatives which the company proposes;

- who will lead these initiatives;

- clear deadlines and measures for monitoring effectiveness of implementation.

Table 3.1 *Typical missing elements of fraud risk management*

In place	Missing
• Business strategies at group and business unit level	• No risk analysis at group or business unit level, linked to the strategies
• Values charter	• Integrity value missing. Fraud issue generally suppressed
• Group risk management manual	• Out of date and gathering dust. Not launched effectively and not integrated with the management calendar. No fraud awareness programme or fraud risk profiling
• Code of ethics	• Annual sign off but messages not built into team briefings. No forum for staff to discuss ethical dilemmas
• Fraud policy and response	• Not known to most staff. Fraud reporting channels not clearly defined
• Group accounting manual	• Covers 'bean counting' and accounting policy issues rather than fraud risk
• EFQM and TQM models	• While valuable models, they do not cover fraud risk specifically
• Performance measures	• Provide few indicators of fraud or information on control quality
• Minimum control guidelines and procedures manuals	• Not linked to an assessment of fraud risk so difficult to assess whether all risks are covered
• Corporate governance manual	• Turgid with little coverage of fraud risk specifically

Typical findings in the area of fraud strategy are illustrated by the following comments encountered in fraud reviews.

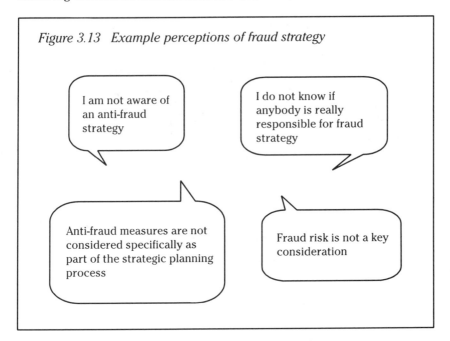

Figure 3.13 Example perceptions of fraud strategy

I am not aware of an anti-fraud strategy

I do not know if anybody is really responsible for fraud strategy

Anti-fraud measures are not considered specifically as part of the strategic planning process

Fraud risk is not a key consideration

Fraud risk assessment

In Chapter 2, I suggested that one way of looking at fraud is to see it as a shadow profile of the business risk profile. It is the darker side of life. Fraud permeates every area of business.

Typical findings in the fraud risk assessment area are set out in Figure 3.14. (See page 80.)

Problems include:

(a) no systematic process to assess fraud risk;

(b) no forum or time allocated in the management calendar to assess fraud risk;

(c) it is not an agenda item;

(d) overriding trust of employees;

(e) relying on the risk management function to identify all risks. Risk

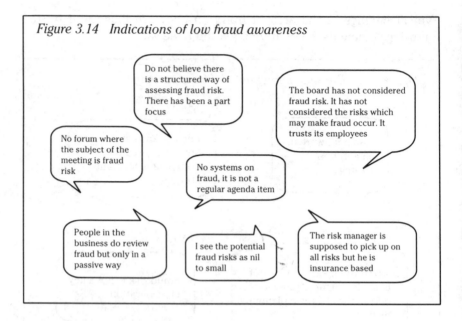

Figure 3.14   Indications of low fraud awareness

management departments often look at insurance cover, health and safety issues, fire risk, and business continuity planning and do not advise on wider business and fraud risk;

(f)   a tendency to see fraud risk as minimal.

Strategic risk assessment

The assessment of fraud risk needs to be considered at various levels in the group. Business risk reporting is often seen as an upward only process to be completed by business units. In other words, business units are required each quarter, or each year, to assess and record their business risks. These are then aggregated at group level and so-called 'interdependencies and accumulations' of risk are considered.

It is equally important that risks are assessed at group level and communicated to and compared with risks assessed by business units. Likewise at business unit level it is important that the business unit board or management team communicates its assessment of risk and compares it with detailed risk assessments performed by project teams and departments.

Fraud risk is often completely ignored.

Examples of strategic issues that might change the fraud risk profile include:

(a) entry into new overseas markets involving new distribution channels, agencies and intermediaries creating new risks of revenue being siphoned off by local management or by counterparties;

(b) a joint venture may be necessary to gain entry to a new overseas market. The other business interests of the joint venture partner may conflict with the interests of the joint venture itself. The joint venture partner may be involved in irregular business dealings in the local market or be perceived to have connections with people involved in such dealings; the joint venture partner may have power to let purchasing contracts to suppliers in which he has some interest;

(c) outsourcing of various operations combined with increased empowerment of business units may mean that a much larger number of people in the organisation have buying power. Unless staff are clear on their accountabilities purchasing fraud risk may increase;

(d) introduction of new accounting and payment systems in several parts of the group may open up gaps in the handling of electronic payments;

(e) changes in reward structures and increased autonomy for business unit managers may increase the risk of accounts manipulation.

Detailed risk assessment

Many procedures manuals and control guidelines are not linked to a detailed assessment of risk. Controls are therefore robbed of significance. Staff may not understand the reasons for the controls. Controls are perceived to be a burdensome bureaucracy yet important risks may be unmanaged.

For example, in the sales area typical control objectives are as follows:

- integrity of information on price master files is maintained
- orders are valid approved and promptly expedited
- deliveries are valid, complete and invoiced
- invoicing is complete and accurate
- credit notes are authorised and supported
- reconciliations are performed, documented and independently reviewed

These controls ensure completeness and accuracy of invoicing, correct processing of credit notes and related reconciliations.

In the credit area control objectives might be:

- credit vetting carried out for new customers and reviewed regularly for existing customers
- amendments to customer master files are authorised, accurate and complete
- debtor receipts are allocated to debtor accounts on a timely basis
- debtors are monitored and debt recovery procedures are followed
- doubtful debts are adequately provided for
- bad debt write-offs are authorised
- the accounts receivable ledger and reports are reconciled and reviewed monthly

Internal audit work often involves checking whether the controls are there or not or seeing that management have completed an internal control questionnaire (commonly known as an ICQ), a form of self-assessment. The work may not ask the more fundamental question: how well do these controls manage fraud risk?

There is a mismatch between the above control objectives and typical fraud risks in the sales and credit control areas.

Set out Figure 3.15 are some of the typical sales frauds and manipulations. Most of these frauds are not addressed by the above control objectives. I shall discuss these in more detail later in the book.

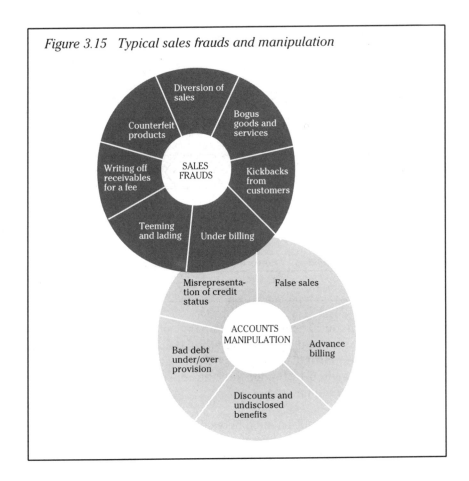

Figure 3.15   Typical sales frauds and manipulation

The key is to profile the key fraud risks in each main business process, then match controls to risks.

Some areas may be over-controlled. For example, in one company I found no fewer than nine signatures on each purchase order, each person signing because the person before him had signed. Other risks may not be controlled at all.

Sometimes controls start half way through the process. In one company the procedures manual started where the computerised purchasing system started, at the purchase order stage. The system was strong from purchase order through to payment but there were no formal procedures for the whole of the 'front-end' of procurement: vetting, selection and contract award. Unfortunately, that is where the biggest

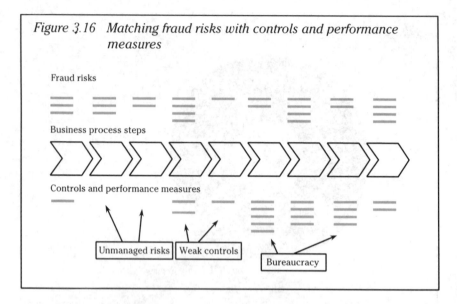

Figure 3.16   Matching fraud risks with controls and performance measures

problems are in purchasing. The company let some very lucrative contracts. It was not surprising therefore that there were slack bid procedures with particular suppliers being favoured, inappropriate suppliers being invited to tender and the reasons for suppliers being selected or deselected unclear.

The key is to get the right balance between risk and control, to manage risk to enhance business performance, not to be obsessed with risk and over-controlled nor ignorant of risk and unduly exposed.

Traditional approaches to risk assessment involve the following steps:

- risk identification;
- assessing impact of risks;
- assessing likelihood of risks crystallising;
- prioritising risks;
- deciding whether to eliminate the risk (exit the particular activity), transfer the risk (for example, by changing contractual terms), insure against the risk or to accept the risk; and
- agreeing actions to manage residual risks and assigning responsibilities.

Theoretically, this a sound approach. Where do things go wrong?

As regards **risk identification**, the mainstream commercial risks facing the business may be well covered: for example, risks associated with the company's markets, distribution channels and competitors, but fraud risk is ignored. Brainstorming of risk may be superficial.

Assessment of **impact** and **prioritisation** may be inaccurate because there is:

(a) a low level of fraud awareness. Unlike other business risk areas, fraud is remote from the day-to-day experience of many managers. Fraud awareness training is essential before undertaking detailed risk assessment;

(b) a tendency to net off controls against risks. For example, management in one company did not believe that they had any substandard product fraud risk. It became evident that this was because they believed controls were totally effective. In fact, they were exposed to huge risks in this area (for example, bogus aircraft parts). The effectiveness of controls had been compromised due to changes in the supplier profile and organisational changes.

Likelihood is often assessed on a 'gut feel' basis: high, medium or low. Even where more gradations are used, the problem is that the factors that increase risk may not be taken into account. For example, a business risk assessment may come up with a number business risks such as 'failure to satisfy customers' or various health and safety risks. But the process may not examine what may make it more likely that these risks actually crystallise. This is the most crucial aspect. Management in a business unit may be under significant pressure to deliver results otherwise the unit may be closed down or manufacturing capability transferred to another plant. This may lead to cutting corners on quality aspects. For instance, in a US case a company submitted false certifications on gearboxes supplied for use in fighter planes when it was under severe financial pressure.

A useful technique is to identify 'soft' spots in the profit and loss account and balance sheet, the places where it is easiest to hide fraud. To illustrate the point, let us go back briefly to case study 1 in Chapter 2. You will remember that this case involved an accounts supervisor who managed to get £1 million out of a division with profits of £1.5 million. The following chart shows some of the 'soft' areas of the profit and loss account and balance sheet where he was able to conceal the fraud.

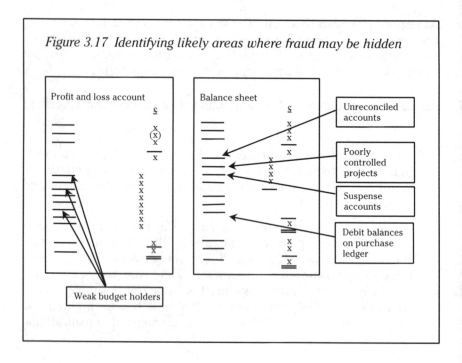

Figure 3.17 Identifying likely areas where fraud may be hidden

Performance measures

Performance measures, or 'key performance indicators' (KPIs) as they are often called, are essential to monitoring business performance. Great reliance is placed on such indicators. The integrity of the underlying data is not always questioned. All KPIs are capable of manipulation. The motivation may be higher where:

- there is pressure to deliver results and/or highly-leveraged reward structures;

- overemphasis on certain KPIs so that other areas receive too little focus.

An example of the latter situation is illustrated below.

EYE OFF THE BALL

A financial controller in a division of a European rental group stole £500,000 over a two year period through the electronic banking system. The payments were just beneath a higher approval threshold. He debited some of the amounts to a little-looked-at hire purchase control account. Management's main focus was on rental asset control and completeness of rental income. There was little focus on the liability side of the balance sheet and therefore an unusual debit balance on the control account was not picked up.

Some common KPIs and typical fraud issues associated with them are as follows.

Table 3.2 Typical fraud issues relating to performance measures

Key performance indicator	*Typical fraud issues*
Actual sales versus forecasts	False sales, advanced billings, discounts advanced or delayed, misrepresentation of credit status
Net sales per salesperson	As above but at salesperson level
Trade promotion spending	Hidden promotions in next period
Number of deductions, credit notes	Credits hidden in price manipulation, discounts to be credited later
Number of unresolved customer issues	Suppression of customer complaints, kickbacks to customers
Supplier quality performance	Bribery of quality inspectors, false quality certificates, manipulation of quality data
Material unit cost trends	Inflated costs through bid fixing built into budgets and forecasts
Material usage versus planned	Padding of estimates, bribery of experts providing completion certificates
Capacity utilisation	Misallocation of time between projects, running private business within the business

We have already looked at a number of situations where budgets and actual figures are manipulated. Other problems which may undermine the budget and forecasting process and facilitate fraud include:

(a) budgets rolled forward from year-to-year, plus or minus a percentage;

(b) no zero-based budgeting, with poor linkage between the budget and underlying planned activities;

(c) poor accountability and ownership of budgets;

(d) unauthorised transfers between individual budgets in the year;

(e) procedures which allow the budget holder to authorise expenditure up to the total budget amount. For instance, the budget holder may only have spent 30 per cent of his budget by period 11 then spend the remaining 70 per cent in one transaction in period 12. Even if the transaction is not fraudulent, it may mean that normal purchasing procedures have been bypassed and the expenditure unnecessary. It may be indicative of collusive pre-invoicing;

(f) failure to monitor other unusual trends in budget utilisation and actual figures. For example overspend from the previous financial year may come through in excessive first quarter expenditure.

Direct controls

We have already seen in the sales area how there can be a mismatch between the fraud risks and controls. Let us now look at purchasing to see how direct controls typically fail or are abused.

The starting point is to understand the profile of the purchasing function, including:

• the nature of the purchasing spend;

• the reasons for using particular suppliers;

• the nature of suppliers;

• types of contracts;

• skills of purchasing staff;

• how the critical controls are perceived.

As regards the **nature of purchasing spend**, it is often difficult to obtain basic analyses, for example, an analysis of spend showing for each product the relevant suppliers. This may indicate poor overall management of the supplier base. There may be 20 suppliers for a particular product where four would do.

But there are also implications for fraud:

(a) the large number of suppliers may indicate weak account opening procedures. Sometimes virtually everyone in the company has power to open a new supplier account. The first that finance knows about the need for a new supplier account is when the invoice comes in;

(b) suppliers may be recorded on the system several times with slightly different spellings. An alphabetical listing of suppliers may reveal that there are several branches or dummy branches set up on the system. This may be due to inefficiency and lack of communication, for example someone did not realise that the supplier was already set up on the system, or it may be that a fraudster has set up a dummy branch on the system, with his own bank account details as payee, knowing that the payment is much more likely to be approved if it appears to be a legitimate supplier;

(c) there may be connected suppliers on the system. For example, staff in the maintenance department may have opened suppliers in which they or their close family have an interest.

As regards **the suppliers used** one may find that:

(a) a supplier is used for 'historical reasons' or 'because we used them last year'. Alternatively, a supplier may be used because there is some form of corruption or because it is connected to management in some other way;

(b) a particular type of supply may apparently be 'single source' but in fact there are a number of suppliers who could supply the item. The reasons for the single sourcing may not be documented or the reasons for suppliers being deselected during a bid process may be poorly documented;

(c) in many engineering and project-based companies, the customer may have apparently selected the supplier as part of the sales process. While certain sorts of equipment may understandably be a customer selection, there may be other components where it is much less likely that the customer would have specified a particular supplier. Staff in sales or procurement may be manipulating the supplier selection process to favour a particular supplier in return for some form of kickback;

(d) the supplier base may include a number of suppliers who are intermediaries or agents. The reason for these suppliers, their status, what they deliver and the basis of the pricing may be unclear. For example, in one case a print buying intermediary company owned by the procurement manager was interposed between the buying company the underlying print suppliers, adding a 100 per cent mark up to the underlying cost of supply. In another case, a bogus leasing intermediary was interposed, owned by the financial controller, to apply a similar mark up.

As regards the **nature of suppliers**, it is often possible to make straightforward checks of public domain information at the initial supplier vetting stage which may indicate that further investigation should be carried out for example, relating to the suppliers' directors, where the supplier is located (for example, a remote supplier used for routine services), and how long the supplier has been trading.

Contract types can have a big impact on the fraud risk profile. Highly-leveraged contracts involving rebates and discounts carry different risks to other contracts. Diversion of rebates to management, manipulation of the timing of rebates and hidden contract terms such as the rebate being conditional on future levels of turnover may be issues.

Consistency of contracts is important. In one company, purchasing staff had an excessive amount of discretion in negotiating contract terms so that non-standard payment terms were granted to certain suppliers who had quoted a lower price to win bids. In some areas, contracts may not exist, or may be poorly prepared. In advertising, marketing, and promotion, supplier contracts are often not in place and the basis of pricing and other important matters may not be clear.

As regards the **skills of purchasing staff** and how they see **critical controls**, earlier in this chapter we looked at how people issues can have a fundamental impact on fraud risk management. There may be important skills gaps. There may be no clear focus on the key fraud risks. Staff may be unclear what the critical controls are.

Problems with control guidelines and questionnaires

In recent years many companies have introduced control guidelines or internal control questionnaires. These are listings of control objectives and control requirements. Business unit management is often required to sign off periodically that they have complied with the guidelines.

This may give head office management a false sense of security because:

(a) the control guidelines may not be linked to an assessment of risk and therefore key risks may be unmanaged;

(b) the specific controls at local level may vary considerably in practice between business units;

(c) the business profile, and the related risks, may have changed since the controls were designed;

(d) business unit management may sign-off with little assessment of how controls are working in practice.

Control guidelines and questionnaires may be introduced without training or a communications programme.

How controls are undermined

Many groups appear to have good controls. The key question is how seemingly good controls are undermined. Some of the weak spots in a bid process are highlighted in the table below. No single weakness will lead to fraud. When reviewing purchasing files one often finds several warning signs. The example which follows the table shows how some of these factors came together in an actual case.

Table 3.3 Some common weak spots in a bid process	
Step in bid process	*Typical weak spots*
Initial need and budget setting	• Project budgets based on historic prices or informal quotations

Specifications	• Specifications biased towards a particular supplier or a supplier's name even appears on a specification
	• Contact with suppliers by design or technical departments without purchasing being involved or informed
	• Late specifications or unrealistic timescales for purchasing
Solicitation process	• No formal criteria regarding the bid list from which suppliers are drawn
	• No data showing the suppliers canvassed on each occasion, the other suppliers in competition and the results, price and other data on performance
	• No set minimum number of bids required for particular values
Invitation to tender and selection criteria	• No standard invitation to tender package
	• Selection criteria not set in advance of the bid process
	• Invitation packages do not set out the penalties for attempted bribery and fraud or a person (outside the purchasing department) to whom complaints should be addressed
	• Suppression or withdrawal of qualified bids is possible
	• Specifications or other terms may be changed and the changes are not advised to all suppliers
Receipt of bids	• Bids are not opened at the same time in the presence of two or more authorised personnel
	• Bid compliance schedule regarding the format and quality of bids received is not enforced
	• Bid information, including prices, is copied to personnel outside the purchasing function. Prices and the identity of bidders is made known to other bidders on occasion

	• No formal reporting channels whereby staff can declare that they have been offered a bribe or excessive gift or hospitality during the bid process
Evaluation of bids	• Basis of the decision to award the contract is not clearly documented.
	• Selection criteria are not used
Negotiation	• Negotiations take place with a favoured supplier at a late stage in the bid process without documentation of the matters negotiated and the basis
Award of contract	• No formal management review of the purchasing process, monitoring that all key controls have been followed

MAJOR EQUIPMENT CORRUPTION

Four companies, A, B, C, and D, were invited to tender for two pieces of major equipment. A brief review of the file revealed the following:

(a) the technical department first met the chosen supplier at a trade fair. Shortly afterwards they had detailed discussions with the supplier and asked for a quotation. The purchasing department was unaware of this;

(b) the bid process was subsequently organised by the purchasing department and bids were sent out based on a one-page outline specification produced by the technical department;

(c) terms relating to the contract were not specified at this stage as the group preferred to negotiate detailed terms late on in the bid process. Closing dates for bids were specified;

(d) supplier D asked for an extension of one week and this was granted;

(e) bids were received from the four companies as follows: supplier A £1,200,000, supplier B £1,100,000, supplier C £600,000 and supplier D £1,080,000;

(f) copies of the bids from suppliers A, B, and C were circulated to various senior managers and staff in the procurement and technical departments and the bid from supplier D was circulated one week later when it arrived;

(g) two months later the company sent out detailed specifications to the four companies and asked for definitive quotations. All confirmed their previous prices

> apart from supplier C who indicated that their model of equipment did not meet the detailed specifications. They therefore withdrew;
>
> (h) the bids were evaluated but unfortunately there were no schedules showing how this was done and the criteria adopted. There was a note on file from technical department briefly indicating that companies A and B were not acceptable for technical reasons;
>
> (i) supplier D was awarded the contract.

Sometimes a control may appear to be in place but it takes place at the wrong time. For example, in one company financial viability reports on suppliers took place too late in the annual retendering process. Quite often the contract had been signed before the financial viability report was received and it was too late to withdraw. Even though it was technically possible to withdraw there would have been a significant cost in changing supplier at such a late stage. It may also be impossible for another supplier to step in at such a late stage.

Fraud response

Staff in a department where fraud has occurred often knew or suspected that fraud or malpractice was taking place. However, it is often not clear to whom those with suspicions should talk and what the protections are for them. It is essential that companies pick up on this front-line 'intelligence'. It is also crucial that once suspicions have been reported, they are followed up in an appropriate manner.

Fraud reporting and response arrangements should include the following:

- the company's policy on fraud;
- the person to whom and the ways in which suspicions of fraud could be reported;
- protections for employees reporting suspicions;
- actions to mitigate further loss;
- the criteria for evaluating suspicions, assessing the credibility and motives of the whistle blower and the quality of available evidence;
- capture and protection of relevant evidence including IT-based records;

- consideration of further fraud problems linked to the matter reported;

- a clear process for setting up an appropriate investigation and the personnel, both internal and external who should be potentially involved;

- dealing with publicity issues;

- giving appropriate rights to the suspect and ensuring the company complies with its disciplinary procedures and with employment law;

- insurance issues;

- police liaison;

- follow up of the fraud incident so that appropriate lessons are learned in all relevant parts of the business.

Clearly, the requirements of the Public Interest Disclosure Act need to be taken into account. The UK charity Public Concern at Work provides guidance on this legislation and on whistle blowing more generally (see the charity's website on http://www.pcaw.demon.co.uk).

Conclusion

This chapter has covered a wide range of factors which may increase the risk of fraud. Table 3.4 summarises the main issues. (See page 96.)

Table 3.4 Fraud Watch chessboard

STRATEGY	Nepotism	High staff turnover	Ethical dilemmas not dealt with	Structure conflicts with risk management framework	Complex structures	Poor learning from other businesses	Overly aggressive targets
Weak strategy	Skills gaps	**CULTURE AND ETHICS**	**STRUCTURE**	Defensive business units	Multiple audit relationships	Poor communication of fraud and ethics policies	Core business processes not clearly defined
Poor implementation plans	Inappropriate career moves	Cultural confusion	Dysfunctional board	Front and back office skills and status mismatch	**REWARD STRUCTURES**	**FRAUD RISK MANAGEMENT**	Gaps in processes and controls not identified
Poor communication of strategy	Low morale	Cultural pressures	Confusion between chairman and chief executive roles	Structure does not fit strategy	Impact of bonus and other structures not recognised	No anti-fraud strategy	Low focus on areas most vulnerable to fraud
Strategic drift	Low level of fraud awareness	Sub-cultures	Confused reporting lines	Centre and business units in conflict	Risks relating to earn-outs not managed	Fraud implications of business strategy not assessed	**FRAUD RESPONSE**
PEOPLE	Untaken holiday	Need-to-know culture. Concentrations of power	Management structure not aligned to reward structures	Poor role definition	Relative disparities in pay to market rates	No fraud risk profiling	No fraud policy
Weak recruitment screening	Lifestyles inconsistent with salary	Business units not assimilated into culture	Special reporting arrangements	Responsibilities for managing fraud risk poorly defined	**COMMUNICATIONS**	Fraud risks not matched with controls	Poor fraud reporting channels and protections
Prior business relationships	Autocratic management style	Weak ethical code and values	Lack of expertise to operate structure	Low status of finance	Poor organisational learning	Performance measures manipulated	No fraud response plan to follow-up fraud incidents

4

Computer fraud and abus

Introduction

As noted in the previous chapter, computer fraud and abuse is now a global issue. The increased use of the Internet means that companies must be alert not only to computer fraud and abuse trends in their home country but also to those in other countries. Whilst technology opens new avenues for business and sophisticated software enables complex processing, these improvements also create opportunities which are exploited by disgruntled employees and the criminal fraternity. The Internet has removed the traditional safety previously provided by physical boundaries and replaced it with an information and communications 'free-for-all'.

Attitudes of need-to-know are being replaced with need-to-share. The 'job for life' ethos has disappeared and, along with it, the traditional loyalty to the firm. IT departments are increasingly staffed with high levels of contractors or are outsourced altogether. And users have an increasing knowledge of IT, particularly at the more junior level, increasing the divide from senior management still proud of the fact they cannot even turn on a PC – and unfortunately, because of this, too naïve to realise the new threats this sophisticated technology has brought.

Whilst computers are often only a medium for fraud, there is no doubt that the opportunities for abuse are increasing from many directions. Whereas the employee was normally the perpetrator of a fraud, the advent of viruses, hackers, and cyber criminals has now complicated the picture. Employee-generated crime is unlikely to decrease and fraud and abuse from the outside can only increase.

The changing technology brings many advantages but also a number of problems including:

(a) a total or heavy dependence on IT systems for operational as well as accounting and management information systems;

(b) open systems and networks, particularly to support electronic commerce, which bring added risks of hacking and illegal access;

(c) systems integration which is pulling down the 'ring fences' around different computer applications, improving efficiency, but increasing the potential impact of any problems and the importance of good controls over access;

(d) the prevalence of small networks under the control of end-users, who often have little understanding of the threats and necessary counter measures, which has increased many organisations' exposure to fraud; and

(e) the increasing complexity of technology which makes it more difficult to check that all major loopholes in controls are closed.

Finally, there are the external influences forcing changes such as legislative and regulatory requirements. Change is also being forced on the businesses from customers and consumers who increasingly expect to receive service via faster electronic communications replacing the traditional postage system and personal service.

MISSPENT YOUTH

A dedicated freephone line provided for field engineers of a US company was compromised so that access was possible straight into the company's UNIX server. Trap and trace facilities finally established that the attacks came from a UK-based youth. The motivation was the ability to spend long periods of time on the Internet without the expense or the knowledge of his parents.

People issues

Technology cannot provide all the controls necessary in today's environment. There remains a high reliance on staff and the application of manual controls. However, the role of the individual in the organisation is changing. This has led in many cases to a change in the attitude of staff towards their organisation with loyalty harder to develop and retain.

Added to this is the modern culture which is quickly moving towards the 'something for nothing' attitude. An increasing number of employees, given an opportunity, will defraud. Whether this is through an unjustified claim of sexual harassment or theft of data and resources, the result is losses to the employing firm.

SENSE OF HUMOUR FAILURE

An organisation paid out several hundred thousand pounds when employees complained of sexual harassment. A number of women objected to a joke explaining 'why beer is better than women'. The organisation had no clear documented policies on e-mail usage.

Employees are now more IT aware, with PCs on almost every desk. They learn IT at school, many have PCs at home, and employers provide training to help them work with IT more effectively. In addition, there is greater access to knowledge as companies develop their Intranets and make process and procedures manuals available to a wider audience (either purposely or without thinking).

The computer programming environment is also changing. More packages are used reducing the need for large system development staff. As IT departments get smaller, segregation of IT-related duties becomes more difficult to impose. There is also a greater dependency on end-user developed spreadsheets and databases which often contain accidental (or malicious) errors.

Attacks from dishonest or disgruntled employees will always remain an issue. The use of the Internet may enable them to continue their attacks from outside the physical boundary of their company.

HOAX HEADLINES

A disgruntled ex-employee of a financial service information provider gained access to a deserted news room and, using an old account which had not been disabled, created a number of false and mischievous flash headlines on the news system. The potential damage to the victim company in loss of credibility, customer confidence and future sales was enormous.

Outsourcing provides an opportunity for fraud from an external source and can lead to a lack of control or gaps in the control process. Outsourcing also provides opportunity for conflicts if contracts do not clearly define what level of service is expected and the ownership of developed software.

MAFIA MAKEOVER

A Mafia-backed software firm was closed and employees arrested when it was found that they were building unauthorised codes into applications which needed updating to cope with the year 2000. The code would have enabled unauthorised financial transactions to take place without detection.

Extent of computer fraud and abuse

The term 'computer fraud' is often used to describe any fraud in which a computer has been involved. Such involvement will normally fall into one of two categories:

(a) computer-assisted fraud, where the computer is used to process a fraudulent transaction. In computer-assisted frauds, the computer is functioning exactly as it should;

(b) genuine computer fraud is, for instance, where the computer generates a fraudulent transaction – in other words, the computer has been tampered with so that it does not function.

The identified instances of genuine computer fraud are probably low because of the specialist IT knowledge normally required for the fraud to be committed.

'Computer abuse' is normally used to describe activities which can result in either corruption or loss of software and data, or interruption of computer processing. Some types of abuse can be used to aid fraud or extortion. Common types of abuse include hacking, viruses, pornography and e-mail chain letters.

Many studies and surveys have been done in the UK and abroad to estimate the levels of fraud and abuse. Whilst several seem to indicate the number of fraud cases are levelling out, the value of these frauds has generally increased. Opinions vary as to the reason for this. A common view is that fraud is going undetected in environments which have downsized to the extent that management control is no longer able to prevent and detect, resulting in smaller frauds remaining undiscovered.

How computer fraud occurs

The easiest way to understand how computer fraud occurs is to look at the typical path of transactions through a system. Fraudulent processing may take place at any of the key stages in computer processing. These are:

(a) input-related – usually computer-assisted fraud involving the manipulation of the data to be input into the computer;

(b) system-related – genuine computer fraud consisting of unauthorised changes to the programs or systems used to process the information; and

(c) output-related – the manipulation or suppression of computer output.

The diagram over gives a simplified overview of the main processes which occur in a typical computer system. The type and amount of equipment will vary enormously from one company to another, as will the way it is linked together, but the processes are consistent.

Each of these categories is discussed below.

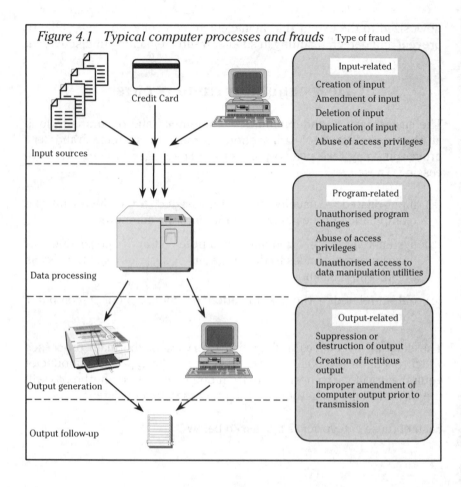

Figure 4.1   Typical computer processes and frauds   Type of fraud

Input-related

Creation of input
Amendment of input
Deletion of input
Duplication of input
Abuse of access privileges

Program-related

Unauthorised program changes

Abuse of access privileges

Unauthorised access to data manipulation utilities

Output-related

Suppression or destruction of output

Creation of fictitious output

Improper amendment of computer output prior to transmission

Credit Card

Input sources

Data processing

Output generation

Output follow-up

Input-related computer fraud

Input-related fraud is the most common (70 per cent of reported frauds in the Audit Commission's 1998 'Update, The Ghost in the Machine') and easiest to commit form of computer fraud. It does not normally require any sophisticated understanding of technology to perpetrate.

Where it is possible to amend or alter input, prior to or during its capture by the computer systems, there is the potential for fraud. Accordingly it is important that adequate controls should exist over the input sources to prevent or detect the unauthorised alteration, addition, deletion or duplication of input.

Input-related computer fraud requires knowledge of how the information is input into the computer system and the supporting clerical and approval processes. For example, what steps are required to add a new supplier or a new employee to the system and whether there are any controls to highlight the change.

A brief description and examples of the various input-related frauds which are set out below.

Creation of input

This involves the creation of input in the correct format and type to be included with existing input (or submitted on its own) without detection. This could be as simple as inserting an additional expense requisition into an existing batch or the direct entry of a sales order into a sales entry system. There may be no paper copy of the input as many modern systems allow direct on-line entry of data.

The creation of false input is one of the most common and simple ways of perpetrating a fraud, particularly when carried out in conjunction with a related change to standing data.

PEEKED PASSWORD

A payments clerk in a bank discovered his supervisor's password which made it possible for him to prepare, authorise and send a payment instruction for £10 million. The attempted fraud was detected because staff at the receiving bank realised the instruction was unusual and queried it with the originating bank's management.

Amendment of valid input

Amendment of existing input involves making a fraudulent change to the original input after the item has been approved but before its input to the computer system, for example, increasing an expense claim or changing the name and address of a loan applicant.

PERSONAL INTEREST

A data entry clerk reduced the interest rate on specific personal loan application forms when entering them into the bank's computer. In return the applicants paid the clerk 50 per cent of the value of the interest saved.

103

Deletion of valid input

The deletion of input prior to its entry or capture into the system could be as simple as the removal of an item from a batch of records or the deletion of the entire batch.

GHOST EMPLOYEES

A payroll employee regularly destroyed employee termination notices and then changed the bank account details for the payment of salary. The fraud was not detected until he was taken ill.

Duplication of valid input

Duplication of input is a simple but effective way of having selected information (for example, request for payment or stock shipment) processed more than once with the extra transaction being channelled to the credit of the perpetrator. The process of duplicating input may involve copying input and submitting both the original and the copy or simply re-inputting the original document in a later cycle if there is no cancellation of processed items.

REWARDING RESEARCH

A university employee responsible for the approval of applications for university tuition funds fraudulently obtained over US$4.1 million by creating and submitting false applications for work.

Abuse of access privileges

Whilst most input fraud is carried out through the use of applications software, it is also possible for data to be input or altered directly by using the same system utilities used for correcting accidentally corrupted data. Data which is input or changed in this manner may escape detection, bypassing the normal reporting functions (for instance, a payee name and bank details can be altered without this being reported in an audit trail).

A GREAT CREDIT

A data entry clerk processed valid credit notes twice to a particular customer. A friend of the customer would claim a refund for the excess credit and forward a share of the refund to the clerk.

What to look out for:

- lack of segregation of duties and responsibilities over the computer systems

- apparent problems with processing which continually require fixing by a particular member of staff

- high levels of customer and supplier queries and complaints

- extensive use of adjusting and other specialist input types to keep accounts in balance

- unusual transactions occurring on reconciliation suspense reports

- sharing of passwords

- failures in reconciliation checks across systems (e.g., for integrated packages where one input transaction may need to generate several system transactions affecting a number of ledgers)

- passwords not changed regularly/deleted when people leave

- clerical and supervisory staff with excessive levels of access (usually justified as required 'just in case something goes wrong')

It is important to distinguish between the alteration of the different types of input as the risks associated with each may be considerably different, requiring different levels of controls to prevent and detect. The alteration of standing data input is typically more difficult to detect as the source of the fraud is a single act rather than the recurring action required to alter transaction data alone (for example, fraudulently increasing the hours worked on a weekly time sheet).

The table over provides examples of the alteration, addition, deletion and duplication of both standing and transaction data.

Table 4.1 *Examples of standing and transaction data frauds*

Fraudulent procedure	Standing data examples	Transaction data examples
Creation of invalid output data	Creation of a bogus employee	Creation of a fictitious invoice from a supplier
Amendment of existing input data	Changes to a customer's discount percentage	Increasing the discount offered to a customer on a one-off order entry form
Deletion of valid input data	Deletion of a valid notice of death of a registered shareholder to enable diversion of dividends	Deletion of a stop payment instruction on a cheque already written but not backed
Duplication of valid input data	Duplication of new insurance policy details (to inflate new business statistics)	Duplication of an invoice for services (as no check against goods received)

It should also be noted that the more complex the system, the more important it is that reconciliation checks are made across systems. Twenty-four-hour processing may limit the opportunity for 'cut-offs' which enable an organisation to balance across all systems. Although many integrated packages have sophisticated facilities for identifying transactions which may have failed part way through an update (for example, an order is filled and stock levels are reduced but the sales ledger is not updated) a surprising number of packages do not, providing an easy way of illicit data manipulation without detection.

Program- or system-related computer fraud

Program- or system-related frauds involve the illicit manipulation of computer programs or computer operations. Unlike input- or output-related frauds, system-related fraud requires a thorough understanding of the information being processed and a sound knowledge of the computer systems involved. Not surprisingly such frauds only account for a small percentage of reported frauds.

Examples of program-related computer frauds include:

(a) tampering with a computer program so that it only generates despatch documentation and does not record any entries in the financial records when goods are delivered to a particular customer;

(b) inserting processing to take the value of 'rounding-off' and add it to a special account;

(c) changing the computer programs so that sales commission is calculated on the basis of gross sales figures before credits notes have been applied.

Whilst specialist knowledge may be needed for the alteration of traditionally programmed computer systems, it should be noted that an increasing number of end-users have become proficient in the design and development of sophisticated spreadsheet and database applications (for example, a spreadsheet application may be used to verify or cast expense claim calculations). Such applications, once checked as working correctly, may not be protected from unauthorised change in the same way as other applications.

BUSY TRAVEL AGENT

An employee of a large international hotel chain used his computer knowledge to devise a system where he could fool a networked computer booking system into thinking that hotel reservations all over the world had been made by a particular travel agent, who could then collect a 10 per cent commission.

ROUNDING DIFFERENCES

A bank's computer programmer inserted code into an interest calculation program so that interest income generated from rounding down on any account would be directed into one of five accounts previously created. Over £120,000 was stolen in the four months before the fraud was detected.

What to look for:

- changes to programs are poorly controlled
- little or no user involvement in testing program changes
- high volumes of program changes
- no quantitative controls over file contents
- lack of physical security over access to computer facilities

Output-related computer fraud

Computer systems produce output in many forms. These range from a screen message to hard copy reports or electronic payment instructions transmitted across international borders.

A fraud involving the misuse of output typically involves suppression, fraudulent creation of misleading output or the theft of output which can be used to create value. Like input-related computer fraud this type of fraud does not normally require a detailed knowledge of the actual computer systems involved but does require a detailed knowledge of the flow of information and the supporting clerical and approval processes (for instance, who receives the exception reports or which printer generates the pre-signed cheques).

Examples of such misuse include the following:

(a) suppression of specific entries on a report highlighting non-performing loan customers at a bank;

(b) creation of a report containing fictitious or duplicated insurance policies to support inflated new business claims;

(c) amendment of payee details on BACS payment tapes between preparation and transmission (for example, by unauthorised access to computer libraries);

(d) theft of computer generated cheques.

COVERING TRACKS

A bank's computer operator was given access rights to the journal entry screen so that banking staff would not need to be called in if end-of-day transaction postings did not balance. The operator used the facility to post cash to his own account and suppressed the audit report showing his activities.

What to look out for:

- sharing of passwords may be common practice. Therefore password users are not accountable for their activities

- staff may have excessive levels of access, usually justified as essential when someone is absent or something goes wrong, but again raising the question of accountability and division of duties

- apparent problems with processing may continually require fixing by a particular member of staff and therefore are not checkable by others

- staff may make unusual use of computer resources, for instance by accessing the computer systems out of hours

- unusual use of dial-in lines to the computer without proper investigation

- large volumes of items or unusual transactions occur in reconciliations or suspense accounts, a common location for hiding irregular transactions

Fraud on the Internet

In essence, the Internet is a group of inter-connected computers, but now on a massive scale with millions of computers linked. Historically, academic institutions dominated the global club of owners. Lately, the apparent business benefits have encouraged a large number of commercial organisations to participate. But the collaborative nature of the system means there is no single responsible governing body.

The Internet is robust, but its strengths are also its potential weaknesses. It will route messages whatever way it must to get them through, so anything sent from one computer could be run through one or more other computers, potentially in different countries, before reaching its final destination. Security is all up to the user.

Although the Internet has been in existence for several years, it is only with the creation of the World Wide Web (the web) in 1992 by Tim Berner-Lee that businesses started to exploit the major potential for Internet-based electronic commerce. Financial transactions taking place over the Internet are already measured in billions with exponential growth expected over the next few years. The Internet and the web are powerful tools for business but can be equally powerful for the criminal. Threats include:

- unauthorised disclosure of information – it could be research, sensitive results, or customer databases;

- unauthorised access and illegal use of information – the perpetration of major fraud;

- loss of information integrity – unauthorised changing of web pages or tampering with reports;

- system failure – viruses, malicious hacking, or e-mail bombs (multiple e-mails to block a system);

- theft – from stolen software to unauthorised use of computers.

HACKED IMAGE

Following an air disaster, ValueJet changed its name to help improve its image. However, its web page was hacked to show a picture of a burning plane alongside the caption 'so we killed a few people, big deal'. So wide was the coverage of the hacked site that the example is frequently used by security presenters all over the world to promote the implications of website abuse.

Despite these threats, the potential benefits to businesses, particularly through electronic commerce, is overwhelming. Suddenly, regardless of size, the reach of the organisation is international. Small businesses are able to compete on a like-for-like basis with international organisations.

Messages can be sent quickly to anywhere in the world without the overheads of postage or telecommunications or the difficulties of time zone restrictions. Because orders can be captured and processed electronically, costs for input operators can be reduced. Reductions in human intervention mean fewer transcription errors and less chance of misinterpretation.

With multimedia, the marketing messages can be versatile and interesting. Catalogues are easily linked to pictures, product descriptions, video clips or independent product reviews. The costs of keeping catalogues and marketing messages is reduced as costly reprints are avoided whilst the speed of updating is increased.

Overall, some healthy cost reductions are possible so long as the volumes of transaction justify the cost of technology. Even so, the proliferation of service providers means that even a small business can gain access to technology without overwhelming costs.

However, with commercial growth comes growth in fraud. Oft quoted is Willie Sutton, the bank robber, who said when asked why he robbed banks, 'Because that's where the money is'. Not surprisingly, the Internet is also recognised by the criminal fraternity as an area for exploitation.

Not only does the Internet allow electronic communications from and to virtually anywhere in the world, it also allows these communications to be made anonymously or in secure encrypted form thus creating the perfect environment for criminals and mischief-makers to create havoc in relative safety. Even if detected, the lack of a sufficient global legal framework will, in the eyes of the perpetrator, improve the chances of not being prosecuted even if caught.

Cyber criminals are the underground of the Internet world and come in many shapes and forms, from the major organised crime rings now in operation around the world to the man on his own working from the back room. A cyber criminal may be after information which can be sold on, he may be looking for ways of making extortion demands or for ways of defrauding a company. For instance, whilst the Internet will enable trade around the world, verification checks may become more difficult and will certainly need to change. Fraudsters will increasingly be looking for weaknesses in company procedures which will allow them to take advantage.

To date, the majority of Internet-related fraud is directed at the end consumer. As this trend increases some consumers will no doubt become more wary, but evidence so far indicates Internet purchasing is unlikely to stop and business will in fact continue to grow. Businesses who decide to sell or purchase via the Internet should be aware of these frauds and the implications they may have on their own business or on their targeted customers. Amongst the more popular frauds are:

(a) levying charges for services that were supposedly free or payment for services that were never provided or falsely represented;

(b) sale of business opportunities promising big profits for little work;

(c) sale of goods which are either not delivered or have been misrepresented in their advertisement.

Another growing problem is the use of 'copycat' sites where a customer may be tricked into believing he is dealing with a reputable and well-known company whereas he is actually dealing with a fraudster selling an inferior product. A similar situation may be created if an organisation

111

Figure 4.2   Common forms of Internet-related fraud

End consumer	Company
False charges to credit cards	Industrial espionage
Misrepresentation of goods/services	Denial of service attacks
'Copy-cat' sites	E-mail bombing
Blackmail	Website hacking
	Extortion
	Cyberwar

---

has purchased their Internet domain name but has not registered it to a specific Internet provider address (i.e., a search on their name does not lead to their selected website) or is not actively using the name. In this case a criminal could forge a letter to the registration authority reallocating the domain name to an IP address which is under their own control.

Whilst the majority of fraud is currently aimed at the end consumer, most other types of abuse are targeted at organisations. Industrial espionage is a growing field made easier by the Internet. Many organisations would be surprised to discover the amount of information that can be gleaned simply by perusing websites, news feeds and electronic discussion forums.

The information available from internal Intranets is even more valuable. These contain information on processes, manufacturing methods, research results, procedures, authorisation lists, holiday rosters and a myriad of other useful information that is now being openly shared within the organisation. Unfortunately, it may also be being shared with a cyber criminal. Unauthorised access may not even be necessary as many organisations make their Intranet sites freely accessible to contractors and consultants along with e-mail and other office automation technology. Once obtained, the information can be quickly transmitted by e-mail to anywhere in the world.

Activists are also becoming more IT-literate. Whilst demonstrations, blockades and criminal damage are unlikely to disappear, activists are discovering the benefits of using IT to disrupt and destroy. A common method is a 'denial of service' attack on a firewall. The firewall is pelted with thousands of messages over a period of time such that:

(a) the firewall shuts down, unable to cope, completely severing the business from the outside world;

(b) the firewall shuts down but leaves all communications continuing without firewall security, leaving the company more vulnerable to hacking attacks; or

(c) normal business communications are significantly impeded because of the extra transactions the firewall must filter. A successful denial of service attack on a firewall could cost an organisation thousands of pounds.

DENIAL OF CHRISTMAS

A large Internet Service Provider suffered a denial of service attack resulting in 3,000 of its customer's websites being unavailable for 40 hours during the Christmas shopping rush.

Similar attacks may be made on e-mail servers using e-mail bombing techniques. Again, the attacks may result in the e-mail server failing due to overload. Additionally, there is the potentially time-consuming task of efficiently deleting the unwanted messages whilst retaining those that are needed.

Activists are also hacking into and altering company websites, replacing original messages with the activist's own message and images. Often the images are pornographic. They also use their own websites to publicise their messages often providing links to the sites of those organisations they are targeting. Activists also use the Internet to organise public disruption of business.

Extortionists may use some of the same techniques as activists. In this case, however, the targeted organisation may be forced into paying off their attackers.

Not surprisingly, governments are also using the Internet as a means of spying on each other and obtaining sensitive information. Although military secrets are the obvious target, there is much that can be deduced from the information created and used by the business community, particularly for developing nations. Hacking and changing websites can also be used to provide counter-propaganda against companies and governments. Evidence of this has already been seen in the UK with successful attacks on both the Labour and Conservative party sites.

X-PLOIT

A group of Mexican hackers defaced a government Internet home page and announced plans to break into and publicise official bank accounts, cellular phone conversations and e-mail addresses. The group, which calls itself X-Ploit, claimed its actions were being carried out to expose the 'endemic corruption' of the Mexican government.

Terrorist groups are also likely to be using the Internet. Imagine the value, for instance, of the travel plans of a CEO or eminent person. In the USA, Pentagon officials revealed that cyber terrorists were launching sophisticated, coordinated attacks – as many as 100 a day – on Pentagon computers.

Hacking

Hacking is the term commonly used to describe unauthorised access to computer systems. Although the problem for most firms is still most likely hacking by employees or other insiders, there are also increasing reports of hacking by outsiders.

Many terms are used for hackers including crackers, phreakers, and cyberpunks. They are not all out to defraud, steal or damage their victims. Many are breaking into systems for the challenge. Unfortunately, they frequently advertise their successes on Internet hacking bulletin boards which are monitored by those with malicious intent. If a weakness is discovered in an organisation's computer security by an outside hacker, the information may become available to the rest of the world within hours.

Surprisingly, many firms believe that the hacker problem is over-hyped. They believe that hackers are only after big companies and governments. Such firms believe they are safe in obscurity. This is naïve. There are many types of hackers and some will hack at anything they happen to find. What is more, the number of hackers is increasing.

Computer literacy is no longer restricted to only a few and 'hacking tips' are becoming more prevalent. Many IT departments take steps to ensure software is installed to detect and report hacking attempts. Most fail to check the reports or notify senior management of any problems.

PLASTIC OVERLOAD

A man was arrested after being found with an encrypted CD-ROM disk with approximately 100,000 credit card details on it. He had arranged with an undercover agent to sell the disk for US$260,000. The credit card details were captured by hacking into the computers of businesses doing credit card transactions with their customers.

Hackers gain access to systems using a variety of methods. Packet-sniffers, also known as LAN analysers, are devices which can be used to record any information sent over a network. These were originally developed as tools to help identify data flows as well as check for unauthorised traffic throughout networks. However, such a tool can also be successfully used by hackers as included in the information captured may be user IDs and passwords which can be then used to gain unauthorised access to systems.

Many organisations invest heavily in security hardware and software only to be compromised by a user with an unauthorised link to the Internet via an unsecured route. War-dialling software allows the systematic dialling of telephone numbers and is useful for finding such links. Once a hacker gains access to an organisation's internal network individual servers and hosts can be targeted and compromised.

In a similar vein, port scanners are a valuable tool for hackers. Port scanners will test each port (rendezvous points where TCP/IP connections can be made) on a computer looking for one that may have been left open, for instance, from a failed operation or badly written software. A port left open for file transfer protocol can then be used by the hacker to gain access to other resources.

Password crackers are computer programs which literally work through dictionaries and other common word, name and numbers lists to try and match user passwords. They are commonly used for brute force attacks where an automatic program tries every conceivable password combination until one is found which works.

In a third of organisations using the Internet, there was no limit to the number of attempts to log on before the system locked the user out. Yet the

115

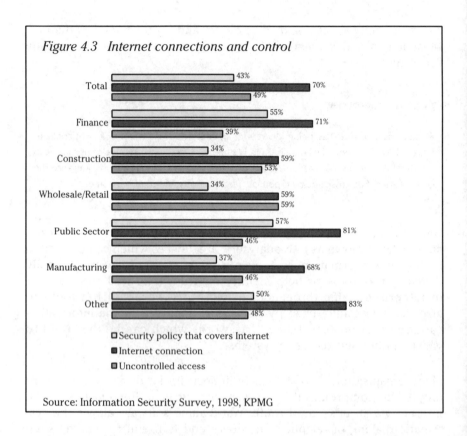

Figure 4.3   Internet connections and control

Total: 43%, 70%, 49%
Finance: 55%, 71%, 39%
Construction: 34%, 59%, 53%
Wholesale/Retail: 34%, 59%, 59%
Public Sector: 57%, 81%, 46%
Manufacturing: 37%, 68%, 46%
Other: 50%, 83%, 48%

☐ Security policy that covers Internet
■ Internet connection
☐ Uncontrolled access

Source: Information Security Survey, 1998, KPMG

easiest way to gain access to a system is by cracking the password – using easily available tools.

Information Security Survey 1998, KPMG

Keystroke recording programs can also be used to capture passwords as they are input by the user. The program, installed on a user's PC, will capture every key input by the user and stores the information in a file for later perusal. This gets over the problem of trying to decrypt encrypted data as the information is captured before encryption takes place.

Denial-of-service attacks may also be made on firewalls by the hackers in an attempt to make the firewall shut down. A badly configured firewall may shut down whilst leaving communications to the Internet open rather that closing them down completely. Worms and viruses may also result in organisations needing to sever their network connections.

MELISSA

In November 1998, the most famous computer virus (technically a worm) was introduced onto the Internet. The worm spread quickly infecting thousands of computers within hours. Many machines were infected with so many copies that their processing slowed down to a halt. Many sites had to cut themselves off from the network to protect themselves.

Often the hacker can exploit vulnerabilities in the software. For instance, patches to close up 'security holes' or programming bugs are frequently released by vendors but often not applied by their customers. A number of bulletin board sites have also been set up by security organisations. However, many organisations fail to monitor the bulletin boards and are unaware of the weaknesses in their systems.

Information on how to breach software weaknesses, where to get hacking software and other information on hacking techniques is available through the large number of hacking bulletin boards that can be found on the Internet. Hackers also run regular conferences where hacking techniques and software are freely exchanged. Many hackers will design and write their own hacking software which they then share with others.

Hackers, however, will often not need to be technically clever to break into systems. IT departments often instal new software without changing default passwords. For instance, an operating system may be installed with an account named 'Guest' with the password of 'Guest'. If this account has not been removed or the password changed, the hacker will easily gain access.

Once into a system, the hacker will explore the system file configuration settings to find out what areas of the server he is able to access. In many cases, these settings have been set up by the IT department to make their own job as easy as possible. Hackers may find that through trial and error they are eventually able to gain access to superuser facilities, if not access to the superuser account itself. The unauthorised accesses may be overlooked as the cause in the first place was IT staff too naïve to understand how such laxness can be exploited by a hacker.

Hackers may also place software onto a system, once initially accessed, which may enable valuable information to be captured. Such programs may not be noticed by IT staff, particularly if the program is disguised as something else.

Social engineering is also a common technique. Hackers may telephone users pretending to be help desks and trick the users into giving out their password. They may telephone help desks to ask for dial-in telephone numbers or, pretending to be a confused user, ask for other advice. It is rare for a help desk to verify the identification of a caller before giving out help and advice.

TECHNICAL DIFFICULTIES

A hacker created a program with a fake screen passing himself off as an ISP employee. He sent out a message saying that due to technical difficulties, users needed to immediately re-enter their passwords or lose their accounts. Naïve users obediently typed in their passwords.

Viruses, worms and hoaxes

A computer virus may be defined as a self-replicating computer program or code used to infect a computer. The virus or code is usually written and hidden within apparently normal programs or macros. It is spread by its introduction to the organisation on a disk or through a network, for example via an e-mail attachment. When the programs or macros concerned are used the virus is activated and runs. It could be as simple as displaying a rude message on the user's screen or as devastating as deleting or corrupting data or files.

A virus will be programmed to duplicate itself and can therefore affect many or all the computers linked together on a network. In some instances the virus may be triggered by a specific date (for instance, Friday the 13th Virus). In this case the virus lies dormant until the internal calendar on the computer system reaches the trigger date and the virus is then activated. A worm, although technically different, is similar in behaviour and can also cause considerable damage to an organisation.

The need for controls in relation to viruses in some businesses may be as important from the perspective of damage and cost as that of fraud. The media publicity from viruses can be particularly damaging.

Viruses are now easier than ever to produce as macros can be written by almost anyone with basic PC skills. They are also easier and faster to propagate through the Internet, via e-mails, through increased use of home working and home PCs, and the increase of information sharing in general.

Viruses are viewed seriously by most IT departments and prevention is much preferred to cure. But the protection available is often restricted to anti-virus software which needs constant updating, often to large numbers of PCs. Rules prohibiting the introduction of external disks and programs without appropriate safeguards, combined with the use of anti-virus software, appropriate reporting and help-desk procedures, and a comprehensive staff awareness programme, provide some level of protection.

Hoaxes and chain letters are equally prevalent and for many companies are resulting in as many 'incidents' as real viruses. Each hoax needs to be investigated and 'helpful' employees can clutter up e-mail systems by warning each other of the new threat. Again, strict policies and procedures for the reporting of viruses combined with good staff awareness programmes can help to prevent significant levels of time wasting.

EXPLOSIVE E-MAILS

A help desk was swamped with calls from concerned users who had received an e-mail claiming that a new virus could cause an electrical charge resulting in an explosion. The e-mail claimed that several users had already been injured by broken glass from the VDU screens.

Other computer abuse issues

Active content and Trojans

Active content is used by web page designers to enhance the presentation and use of the web page to the end-user. There are several types of active content, such as Java applets and Active X, each with differing functionality. Simplistically, however, they are programmable code that is embedded into a web page. When the page is accessed the code is automatically downloaded and executed on a user's workstations, often without the user's knowledge.

119

Although some active content has been designed with security in mind, this is not the case in all instances and businesses need to be aware of the risk of unauthorised code being executed on their user's systems.

Active code provides the ideal carrier for Trojan horses. A Trojan horse is a bit of software which appears to have one function whilst it is actually carrying out a completely different function. There is already evidence that Trojans have been developed which can enter a system and e-mail out all the information it finds. Users may not even be aware of what has happened. Combined with virus (self-replicating) abilities, the Trojans of the future have overwhelming destructive capabilities.

CHAOS COMPUTER CLUB

The German Chaos Computer Club, using an Active X program they wrote, proved that they could cause a PC running the Quicken financial software to transfer money from one account to another without the user's knowledge.

Pornography and impacts on the business

Pornography is widespread on the Internet and even with sophisticated filtering systems it is impossible to prevent employees able to use the Internet from gaining access to pornographic material. From there it is quite easy for the material to be downloaded and circulated throughout the organisation, an activity which could lead employer and employee to prosecution.

Whilst many organisations do not object to their employees making limited and sensible personal use of Internet access (similar to policies regarding telephone usage), it will clearly be costly and embarrassing if that privilege is abused by the handling of pornographic material.

E-mail

The Internet allows inexpensive e-mail contact and is now being extensively used by many organisations. However, few organisations have the same controls over their e-mail correspondence as they do over their traditional postal and fax communications. An e-mail sent by an employee using a domain name belonging to the employer arguably has the same legal status as a letter sent on letterhead paper. Because of this, it is possible for an employee to accidentally commit the company to a course of action through careless or misjudged use of the e-mail.

Because e-mail is in many cases easily spoofed (the e-mail looks as though it came from someone who did not send it), many organisations will now automatically add a disclaimer on to the tail end of every e-mail sent to external addresses. Whilst being helpful, disclaimers only have limited use: it is not possible to opt out of responsibility for everything in an e-mail message without also destroying its value as a communication tool. Disclaimers have also been known to be added to spoofed messages to appear more credible.

However, ignorance of the dangers of forged e-mails could result in embarrassment or inappropriate business actions or decisions.

NOT KNOWN AT THIS ADDRESS

A major international organisation found that an employee sent an e-mail to a number of external recipients, purporting to come from the Chairman, containing a joke of questionable taste. The incident was discovered when one of the e-mails was automatically returned as 'address unknown'.

E-mail is often used by employees for personal use, usually with the blessing of the employer. However, a lack of clear policies on what constitutes appropriate use can result in misunderstandings, particularly where an employee is suddenly unavailable and their e-mail needs to be viewed by another member of staff. Inappropriate e-mail usage may also lead to a risk of poor staff morale or potential harassment charges.

Software theft

Software theft is a criminal activity. The copying of computer software without authorisation violates the UK Copyright, Designs and Patents Act (1988). Software creates unique problems because it is so easy to duplicate. However, Copyright Law makes no distinction between duplicating software for sale or for free distribution. The law protects the exclusive rights of the copyright holder. Unfortunately, many people regard illegal copying as morally acceptable behaviour and these attitudes leave many organisations vulnerable to legal action under the 1988 Act.

Civil damages for copying unauthorised software can be substantial. Criminal penalties for the manufacture, possession, importation and distribution of illegal software include significant fines and imprisonment.

SOFTWARE LICENSING ERRORS

A large corporation faced claims of over £13 million for software licensing errors. These were calculated from the time of original purchase and included costs of the updates and audit programme. The claims were subsequently negotiated down to a six figure settlement, but a second exercise elsewhere in the organisation revealed the potential for substantial additional claims.

The software industry, represented by organisations such as the Federation Against Software Theft (FAST) and the British Software Alliance (BSA), are justifiably seeking to recover these revenues and help organisations to reduce the occurrence of illegal copying.

PIRATES

A company found out that one of its employees had been taking copies of software and selling it on to other companies. FAST agreed not to prosecute if the company under-took a complete inventory of their software to establish how much was properly licensed and implemented appropriate controls to prevent future occurrences.

Theft of data or resources

With the current trend for many firms to publish as much useful information as possible on Intranet sites, hacking is not always necessary to enable theft. Publication of such information on the Intranet not only makes it easily available to members of staff, but to anyone with access to the Intranet, including temporary staff and contractors who may also be working for competitors. The wide availability of such information also makes it easier for the fraudster to find out about how other parts of the organisation work and look for weaknesses which can be exploited.

SHARK-INFESTED WATERS

A man was arrested for stealing company information. It turned out that he owed money to a loan shark and had run into problems with repayments. The loan shark offered to clear the loan in return for valuable company information.

Theft of resources may also be costing organisations large sums of money. There is a difference between the employee who uses his computer for occasional personal use and who makes a living out of it.

'Phreaking' is the term given to the manipulation of telephone lines to avoid paying for telephone calls. The most famous case was that of the Whistler who had learnt to whistle at the right pitch required to connect telephone calls without having to make payment. There are many simpler techniques. Even telephone systems with international barring can often be overridden by employees dialling 141 before the international telephone number. Of greater concern is the increase in telephone charges though rerouting of calls without the user's knowledge. Many of the older telephone switchboard systems lack the sophisticated security controls necessary to prevent this abuse.

Voice mail systems may also create vulnerabilities. Codes for access to voice mail boxes may be easy to guess and could result in disclosure of sensitive messages. Detailed consideration of cellphone abuse is outside the scope of this book.

MOLDOVAN CONNECTION

A number of users faced huge phone bills when, unbeknown to them, after downloading pictures from a website, their telephone connection was rerouted through Moldova and remained connected until their PC was switched off.

IT security

Security management

Information security awareness and practices are now so important to today's business that they should be considered an integral part of the business manager's responsibilities.

Many computer auditors and security specialists will be familiar with the traditional 'onion-skin' approach to IT security. Computers and their data were protected in the core of the onion and surrounded by layers of physical, logical, procedural and organisational security. This approach was fine in an environment of dumb terminals, limited communication links and tightly controlled applications which restricted access and use of data.

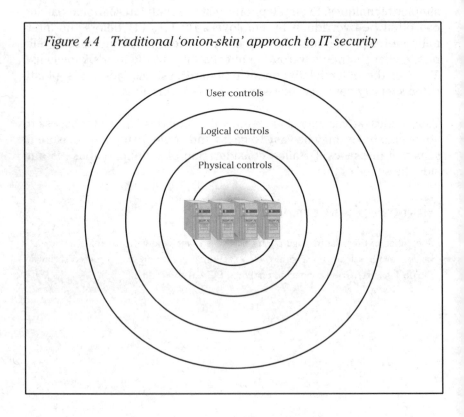

Figure 4.4 Traditional 'onion-skin' approach to IT security

User controls

Logical controls

Physical controls

In today's environment powerful PCs sit on the user's desk or are operated remotely from outside the business premises and most are capable of direct connections to the rest of the world via the Internet. Information is frequently downloaded and manipulated in user developed spreadsheets and databases. As a result, the days are gone when security could be viewed as an IT activity delegated to the IT department. Today, security practices need to be an integral part of the way in which every employee carries out their job.

Technology has made huge advances in the functionality and sophistication allowing information to be processed and manipulated, but corresponding technical functionality for security is lagging behind. Identification of the gaps these weakness create is a key part of security management and requires close liaison and good communication between IT departments and business management.

The security management function is reliant on good risk management practices to ensure cost effective protection. A typical representation of the security management life cycle will start with risk assessment and end with review.

Risk assessment allows the identification of threats and vulnerabilities, and estimation of the likelihood and value of losses or other impacts from security breaches. Once these are identified and understood, appropriate policies and controls can be selected and implemented. Operationally, an organisation will monitor, measure and audit to ensure the controls are working as they should with the level of effectiveness required. This information is then fed back into a review process which reconsiders risks and alters policies and controls as appropriate.

Within this framework are many areas where security review points are required including change management, systems development life cycle, incident management and help desk management. Each area either generates a change prompting a need to reconsider security, or reacts to a problem indicating a weakness in existing controls.

Selection of policies and controls must be made in the context of many factors including the level of risk an organisation is willing to accept, the culture of the organisation, the operating environment, the industry type, legal and regulatory requirements, and practicality. There are many good sources of guidance for security controls, most notably British Standard 7799 'Code of practice for Information Security Management'. BS 7799 was updated in 1999 to take account of the significant changes in IT over the last few years since its first publication in 1993.

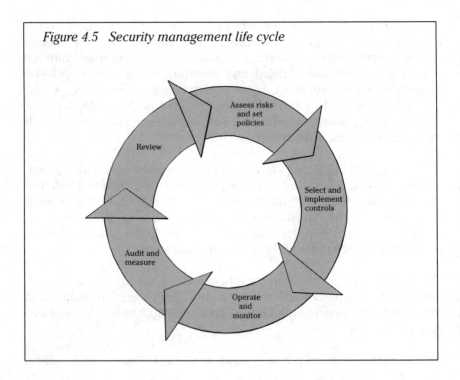

Figure 4.5 Security management life cycle

Software

It is common to set value parameters for transactions to reduce errors or impose authorisation limits, but there are other opportunities for IT to be actively used to help prevent or detect fraud or system misuse. For instance, by comparing each transaction against a set of rules, unusual activity can be identified and either stopped or reported. Special search and comparison programs may also be designed to find unusual data patterns or inconsistencies across systems.

As well as application software, the same tools used by hackers can be used by an organisation to test its own security. An example of this is SATAN which was developed in the USA but is free on the Internet. Software is also available to perform sanity checks on file permissions – reporting those which are suspect, to check the strength of passwords, identify unused user IDs and report on potentially weak configuration settings.

126

Penetration testing

Penetration testing has become a major tool for organisations looking for assurance over their security arrangements. The testing is normally carried out by an 'independent' (i.e., someone not involved in the design or development of the security infrastructure). Attempts are made to penetrate the system in one or more scenarios such as 'an unknowledgeable outsider', 'an unknowledgeable insider' or 'a knowledgeable insider'.

Good testers will use a variety of both technical and social engineering techniques to break into the system. For instance, an automated password cracking routine will commonly identify weaknesses in the selection of passwords. A bogus call to a user asking for their password, perhaps pretending to be the help desk, will often work just as effectively.

Digital signatures

Digital signatures are likely to become the most common method of verifying a user's identity in the electronic trading environment. Public key infrastructure (PKI) which allows digital signatures to be used anywhere in the world is growing as fast as electronic commerce. Not all of the security issues and concerns with the use of digital signatures have been resolved as yet, but they represent the most likely solution for secure commerce and their wide adoption will help to reduce vulnerability to and incidents of fraud.

Bulletin boards

There are a number of good and reputable bulletin boards available over the Internet which provide up-to-date details of software vulnerabilities and from which patches for common problems can be obtained or downloaded. Other bulletin boards give details of current viruses and latest hoaxes. Many IT suppliers also provide details relating to problems and fixes for their software along with FAQ information.

Conclusion

Information technology provides one of the most effective business enablers available today. However, failure to recognise and mitigate the associated IT risks may result in disastrous consequences. The process of identifying, understanding and addressing IT risks will only be accomplished effectively through the combined efforts of business and IT management.

Good security and people management are essential components of enabling technology. Integrating good security and management into systems helps to build the levels of trust that are necessary in today's technology dependent world.

5

Accounts manipulation

Introduction

Accounts manipulation is misrepresentation of financial or other important information required for management or statutory reporting, including information on the commercial risk in transactions. It may involve active manipulation of that information, suppression of salient information and sometimes forgery of documentation.

While there may be no actual theft of cash or other assets, the frauds can cause significant loss of value in terms of the company's market standing and management credibility. In some cases, there can be serious losses to investors who have invested on the basis of misrepresented financial or other information. There may also be indirect losses to the organisation as a result of management decisions made on the basis of incorrect information. Concealed risks in transactions may crystallise with potentially devastating consequences.

As organisations have become more decentralised and have incentivised management of business units and subsidiaries, there has been a significant increase in accounts manipulation. Most cases are unreported. But manipulation is a risk hardly recognised by many boards. It is missing from most risk management models.

It is an important risk for management at the centre of groups, or of major divisions, to manage. But the resources to do so may have been severely reduced as central functions have either been cut or devolved to business units. To make an obvious point, but one that is overlooked by many companies, managers are unlikely to assess their own units as being at risk of manipulation. The risks of manipulation must be dealt with by the management at the next tier above, working up to the board of directors addressing the risk of manipulation by senior executive management.

What drives accounts manipulation?

Factors that increase the risk of accounts manipulation include:

- excessive pressure to achieve targets;
- fear of losing one's job or missing out on a promotion path;
- lack of openness in the culture, a blame culture;
- highly-leveraged reward structures;
- personal interest of management in the company's share price;
- history of preparing over-optimistic forecasts;
- cash flow problems, possibly involving breach of debt covenants;
- aspects of the profit and loss account based on a significant degree of judgement;
- history of untidy balance sheet management;
- revenue or profit growth out of line with the industry or inconsistent with the degree of risk, for example significant profits in products which are inherently low risk.

Key risks

Figure 5.1 summarises the main risks. I have put all the risks on one chart to bring out the linkage between the various forms of manipulation. There will usually be several different forms of manipulation going on.

Each type of manipulation highlighted in Figure 5.1 has many sub-categories and these are discussed in detail below.

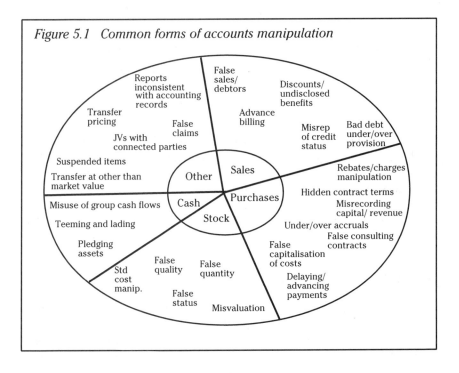

Figure 5.1   Common forms of accounts manipulation

Sales

False sales

False sales involve the generation of false invoices or the manipulation of prices or quantities to increase turnover or forecast turnover.

Common instances of this form of manipulation include a company which issued dummy invoices for stock which was old, on sale or return or on display, and profit was recognised although no payment was expected. Old invoices were redated so that they would appear as current on the aged debt report. Another company agreed to 'sell' goods to one of its distributors with an agreement to buy back the goods after the year end at a higher price.

Other examples are:

- issuing dummy invoices to fictitious customers;
- making sales to 'friendly customers', with an undisclosed agreement to buy back the goods at a later date;

- overcharging customers;

- kickbacks to customer staff to accept higher prices/quantities;

- misrepresentations about forecast sales or contracts and orders in the pipeline; and

- forged or suppressed documentation and/or audit confirmations.

The motivation for such frauds will be higher when market conditions are difficult. Excessive pressure on management to meet financial targets or tight liquidity may also increase risk, for example, where loan covenants may be breached if key ratios are not met.

The following two examples are more complex cases of false sales manipulation.

PAINTING A FALSE PICTURE

A managing director allegedly presented a false picture of a company's financial position ahead of a rights issue. A year after the rights issue the company's shares were suspended and receivers appointed, with its debts standing at over £100 million. The company had originally expanded under the Business Expansion Scheme which enabled it to increase the number of hotels it operated very rapidly.

The profit forecast included profits of over £1 million for consultancy services provided to two hotel businesses: there were no contracts. The search of the company's offices found forged documents in various stages of production as well as documents showing invented sources of income. In some cases the forgeries were detectable, with telephone numbers and company registration details omitted and identical headings on different letters.

The managing director forged a report which showed fictional management charges that were owed to the company for hotels that the group did not own but managed on behalf of another company. He faxed photocopies of the report signed by the directors of the company which had supposedly agreed to pay the company a management fee. The director's signature was superimposed on the bottom of each page of the report. He also fabricated bogus paying-in slips which showed the company to be earning extra fees from other businesses.

Forged documents were delivered late, with little time for the reporting accountants to check them. The managing director asked his bankers to send documents to his offices instead of sending them directly to the reporting accountants. For example, he changed a bank confirmation of assets and account balances to show that borrowings from the bank were nil. He then photocopied the tampered document to hide the alterations made to the original and faxed the new version to the reporting accountants. The original was never sent to the accountants.

RIGGED FORECAST

A small public company had grown rapidly by acquisition and had been successful at integrating the companies it had acquired with its existing businesses. The opportunity arose to make a very large acquisition, necessitating the issue of a circular and the usual reports on working capital and profit forecasts. There were several months to go before the end of the financial year at the time the bid was made.

When the preliminary projections were reviewed it was evident that the rate of growth in profits had slowed down, not an ideal platform from which to launch a bid. The group managing director had a close involvement with a number of subsidiaries which had formerly belonged to a small public company that he had managed and controlled, and which had been bought by his present company.

He increased the profits forecast by one of their subsidiaries to reinstate a trend of growth to the group. He and the managing director of the subsidiary claimed that the subsidiary was about to gain a substantial overseas contract. This would make a major contribution to profit as the margin earned would go straight to the bottom line. There was no documentation of the contract, which had not been signed, and no other documentation as it was claimed that the customer would be buying the company's standard products. The managing director referred to his previously good track record when asked to justify the inclusion of the contract in the forecasts.

In the event, the contract was not awarded and was probably fictitious. The outcome will never be known because the group itself was acquired by a hostile bid shortly afterwards and the business involved in the manipulation was disposed of. The managing director left shortly thereafter.

What to look for:

- unusual fluctuations in sales. High sales in the final quarter
- changes in activity levels inconsistent, for example, high sales in period but no change in distribution costs
- change in business pattern, such as entry into new, remote market
- shipments to new or unusual customers towards the period end

- cash recycling – payments or deposits coincident with receipt of funds from debtors
- unusual number of credit notes around period ends
- large number of journals and adjustments in sales ledger and/or bank reconciliations
- circularisation of particular customers refused/customer not replied to circularisation or balance not paid
- customer not generally known in accounts department. File for customer not in main filing. Account handled directly by senior manager, rather than accounts staff
- evasive answers re movements on particular accounts

Advance billing

Advance billing is the bringing forward of sales to boost apparent sales revenue and profits. Common techniques are as follows:

(a) sales recorded in breach of accounting polices;

(b) collusive pre-invoicing, advancing sales by routing transactions through connected intermediary companies;

(c) undisclosed sale and return transactions;

(d) stocks 'allocated' to a warehouse under the company's control or under the control of a compliant third party to give the appearance of apparent sale.

Sometimes advance billing involves misrepresentation of the completion of longer-term contracts or stages of those contracts, with a view to inflating turnover or profit. In one case a completion certificate was wrongly obtained in return for an undisclosed side letter to the contract customer confirming that certain outstanding contractual obligations would be performed.

SALES BEFORE DELIVERY

Branches of a retailing group allegedly recorded sales before products were delivered to customers, in contravention of it stated accounting policy. This resulted in profits being overstated. Apparently, the practice was widespread at the time of the company's flotation two years previously and involved planned collusion in the company. The shares were suspended and reopened, after an investigation into the company's affairs, at 15 per cent lower. The finance director and retail operations manager subsequently resigned. The practice was disclosed by a sales assistant.

COMPLIANT CUSTOMER

A major electronics manufacturer from the Far East had suffered a shortfall in sales in a particular product line. The product manager agreed with its UK distributor that a large shipment would be invoiced to the distributor in the month before the manufacturer's year end. A credit note would be issued several months later, when the manufacturer's audit was complete. The goods were supposedly shipped to a warehouse in the Far East.

PRE-INVOICING

A group involved in the manufacture of equipment overstated its results due to accounting irregularities. The group got into financial difficulties by overextending itself in difficult markets. It offered credit in Europe just as exporters were hit by a strong pound. The company also tried to get into new markets with a new type of equipment. The equipment developed problems and the company could not cover its costs. Managers tried to rectify the problems by pre-invoicing of sales, facilitated by the use of discounted bills of exchange and other financial instruments.

As the bills bounced, debtors for proper delivery of machines were lost from the accounting system, whereas false sales and sales relating to goods not yet delivered remained as debtors. The management accounts did not disclose the substantial use of bills of exchange or the extent to which funds were generated from dealer financing facilities in advance of the manufacturing of machines.

By omitting such financing from the balance sheet, the use of overdraft facilities was minimised, emerging difficulties were obscured and the full extent of the problem was disguised until such financing, and the bills of exchange in particular, resulted in financial loss on maturity, when the bills bounced. If equipment was not delivered or a customer was unable to pay on maturity, bills were rolled over to a future date. The management accounts included no recognition of the potential liability arising from the bills which were dishonoured.

What to look for:

- changes in pattern of business

- inconsistencies in trading pattern, for example delivery costs do not fluctuate rateably with deliveries

- reports from merchandising staff of high inventory volumes in distributors/ wholesalers/retail

- unusual changes in debtor ageing profile

- stocks 'allocated' to customer, but not delivered

- products shipped to unusual destinations (not usual customer addresses)

- unusual number or value of credit notes subsequent to year end

- change of pattern of trade with particular significant customers

Discounts/undisclosed benefits

Manipulating discounts and other benefits opens up more subtle forms of manipulation. Techniques include:

(a) discounts to be credited later or credits transferred to dummy accounts for write off later;

(b) credits given to customers in reduced prices in the current period rather than via credit notes, with correspondingly higher prices in the following period. This sort of manipulation may attract less attention and involve fewer people in the company than credit notes;

(c) taking back non-selling stock at full valuation; to avoid a write off in the current period; and

(d) hidden promotions in the next period.

What to look for:

- change in pattern of business with particular customers

- change in prices applied to particular customers around the year end

- unusual number or value of credit notes after year end

- agreement for special advertising or similar promotional deal in the following period, without increase in volume shipped

- extended periods of credit for particular customers

- customers dealt with outside main system, for example, no price information on standing data or file held outside main filing

- certain customers dealt with exclusively by a senior member of staff

- no independent review of prices and terms (or changes thereto) for particular customers

Misrepresentation of credit status

Manipulation in the credit area involves:

- suppression of credit information shortly before a sale or a deal is concluded;

- false information on credit status to induce agreement to sales to poor risks;

- bribery of credit control staff by sales managers.

What to look for:

- abnormal delays in obtaining routine information

- restrictions on access to proposed customers imposed by sales and commercial staff

- poor quality documentation, word processor produced references, hand written documentation, etc.

- use of 'accommodation' offices by new customers

- constitution of credit committee does not allow for ultimate veto by the head of credit

- concerns raised by credit staff about information not being shared with them by sales staff

- recurrent problems with new credits shortly after sales are concluded

Bad debt under- or over-provision

Manipulation of bad debt provisions includes over- as well as under-provision. In the following case the group concerned had already achieved the level of profit it wished to report and expected the following year to be lean. It therefore created reasons for substantial provisions in one of its subsidiaries knowing that their auditors focused on under- rather than over provision.

Other problems include:

- false representations by management concerning the status of particular customers;

- recycled funds to give the appearance that customer accounts are current;

- manipulation of the debtor ageing analysis.

PROFIT SMOOTHING

An international construction company had operations in many parts of the world, but had one particularly successful subsidiary the results of which had a material impact on the results of the group as a whole. In order to manage the reported profitability of the group, the stringency or otherwise applied to surveyors' valuations of work in progress varied with the profit that the group wished the subsidiary to contribute.

However, in one year a large proportion of contracts in the subsidiary were close to completion and there was little scope to create significant provisions in the contracts concerned. The group had already achieved the level of profit it wished to report and expected the following year to be rather lean, particularly as a result of the incidence of contract completion in the subsidiary. In order to create the necessary level of provisions, and hence to defer profits, the group established provisions against some of the subsidiary's contracts at head office level on the claimed basis that there was a significant risk that the main client for which a number of contracts were virtually complete would seek to 're-measure' many of the contracts and to seek significant price concessions.

What to look for:

- need for provisions suddenly disappears when large cash receipts are unexpectedly received shortly before provisions are finalised

- no independent check of the aged debtors analysis, sales ledger or bank reconciliations

- bad debt write-offs and recovery proceedings not consistent with provisions

- debtor ageing profile not consistent with proposed provisioning or unusual trends in profile of the report during the year

Purchases

Manipulation of rebates and discounts

Manipulation of rebates and discounts is a common problem and the incidence of such activity has increased in recent years with highly-leveraged supply contracts becoming more common as groups have rationalised their supplier bases and renegotiated contracts.

Common problems include:

(a) rebates taken to profit too early, perhaps conditional on levels of future turnover with the supplier. The conditions may not be included in the written contract. They may form part of some hidden contract terms or a side letter;

(b) extra charges suffered now against a rebate in the following period;

(c) postponed charges;

(d) misrepresentation or forging of confirmations and contract details regarding rebates.

What to look for:

- lack of openness about the negotiation process and the deal concluded

- restrictions on access to the supplier

- budgets utilised late in accounting period

- surplus stock levels on particular lines to trigger volume discounts

- significant increases or reductions in charges by suppliers in following period

- no checks on whether appropriate volume discounts received

- highly-leveraged supply contracts negotiated by one person or a very close team

- no independent review of the need for goods/services supplied

- deliveries taken at unusual times in year

139

Hidden contract terms

Hidden contract terms and side letters are used in many business areas. The following example shows how a side letter to a customer was used to manipulate the timing of completion certificates on long-term contracts.

TAKING PROFITS EARLY

Due to poor trading results, a company gave a side letter to a customer setting out certain undertakings, in consideration for the issue of a completion certificate. This enabled profit to be taken early on the contract even though certain contractual obligations had not been completed.

What to look for:

- unexpected completions ahead of schedule
- unusual trends in results in the period prior to the year end
- resistance to direct contact with supplier to agree account balances or terms
- late changes in allocations between capital and revenue
- supplier billing unusual items, for example, description of items changed to appear as capital items, when in fact revenue
- unusual leasing arrangements or lessors

Misrecording capital or revenue items

Misrecording of capital or revenue items is one of the better known forms of manipulation. As already indicated, it is common to find several different forms of manipulation going on at once. The following example involves misrecording of capital and revenue items, hidden contract terms, false capitalisation of costs, misvaluation of work-in-progress and producing reports that are inconsistent with accounting records. If evidence of any one type of manipulation comes to light it is important to probe further because it will usually be part of a wider cancer.

ACQUISITIONS IN WORK-IN-PROGRESS

The managing director and financial controller of an overseas subsidiary colluded to conceal certain transactions. There was pressure to maintain profits as there was a threat that the manufacturing activities would otherwise be relocated to the UK.

Over a two-year period the following accounts manipulation took place:

- secret purchase from a liquidator of a business which manufactured equipment used by the company to manufacture its own products. Know-how, drawings and certain assets were acquired and the company was also obliged to take over certain unfinished contracts on the order books. The consideration for the purchase was recorded in four different accounts within work-in-progress;

- the contracts taken over were very unprofitable. The design costs and consequent losses on these contracts were booked against profitable jobs within work-in-progress; and

- the management accounts were manipulated and did not agree to the underlying general ledger.

The following example involves a different mix of manipulation practices: this time misrecording rebates of a capital nature as revenue, recording credit notes as sales, capitalising revenue costs as capital, inflation of asset values and false claims to have sold assets.

INFLATED WORTH

The chairman and finance director of a company inflated its worth by over £250 million. A projected profit of £10.5 million was later reported as a loss of £23 million and the share price collapsed from £2.26 to 10p.

The group acquired companies in the UK and overseas. To buy a US company it had to raise substantial finance. It stretched the company to the limit and a worldwide recession also put great strain on the company. To maintain the image of success, and keep the share price high, the following activities occurred:

- inclusion of a rebate on the purchase price of a company as income (which in turn caused inflated profit expectations for the company in the financial markets);

- credit notes booked as sales, capitalisation of research and development and inflated valuations of the company's assets;

- false claims to have sold an overseas subsidiary.

What to look for:

- unusual trends on individual work-in-progress accounts

- evidence of operational difficulties or unknown counterparties when talking to operations staff in the business unit

- pressure to deliver results, especially when combined with some other factor such as impending closure, transfer of operations

- adverse economic or market conditions

- nervous or vague response when asked about detailed aspects

- underlying working papers relating to management accounts

- audit trail between management accounts and general ledger unclear or long-standing systems problems

Under/over accruals

Accruals are one of the easiest areas to manipulate. Given the visibility of accruals it ought to be one of the easiest forms of manipulation to spot. Evidence of over or under accruals may provide the first clue to wider problems.

Companies most vulnerable to this sort of activity are those where there is a poor linkage between budgets and the underlying activities. For example, where the budget for a particular caption is based on a percentage of turnover rather than on a bottom-up assessment of required spend based on the strategic needs of the business. Problems may be compounded where transfers between individual budget captions during a period are not closely controlled.

Other common problems include:

(a) accruing actual to budget in the monthly management accounts. At the year end this activity will usually be linked to forward purchase orders and collusive pre-invoicing with suppliers;

(b) concealed supplier invoices;

(c) cost of goods received over/under stated.

What to look for:

- change in creditor age profile

- change in purchasing pattern before and after year end

- 'soft' budgets based on a percentage of turnover with no zero-based budget

- transfers between budgets and actual figures to manipulate under- and over-spends

- virtually no budget/actual variances

- unusual trends on particular budget captions, for example significant under-spend up to quarter three with budget fully utilised by period end

False consulting contracts

Consulting and other service contracts provide the ideal opportunity for creating false costs as there may be little tangible evidence of the service provided. These contracts may be used by fraudsters to take money out of a business. But false consulting contracts relating to acquisition assistance, bid defence work, public relations, design, introductions to new markets and similar services are also used to manipulate reported results.

The costs may be simply accrued or paid to a connected or bogus counterparty for future use in the business or may be a way of cloaking unauthorised, illegal or corrupt activity.

What to look for:

- significant increase in consulting payments for which there is no apparent service received or related activity

- invoices with vague descriptions of services provided

- invoices from suppliers not previously known to the company and/or with status which cannot be readily verified

- other typical warning signs of bogus invoices (see dummy supplier frauds in the purchasing section of the next chapter)

False capitalisation of costs

False capitalisation of costs is closely related to misrecording capital/revenue above. Here though forgery or misdescription on underlying documents is involved. Examples include:

- forged or manipulated documents to support capitalisation criteria;

- costs misdescribed on invoices.

Sometimes the deception is elaborate and may involve collusion with a number of parties.

What to look for:

- evasive responses when requesting access to certain documents

- administrative details, which would usually be delegated, handled by a member of senior management

- delaying tactics

Delaying/advancing payments

Agreeing non-standard payment or other terms is a common way of shifting profits between periods. The suppliers concerned may be happy to comply as they may have temporary cash flow problems themselves or may be happy to oblige in return for a favour in the future.

Other problems include:

(a) non-standard payment or other terms agreed with suppliers to reduce or inflate apparent prices charged to the profit and loss account in the current or next period;

(b) misrepresentation of creditor ageing;

(c) 'teeming and lading' of suppliers.

What to look for:

- non-standard payment or other terms in contracts

- contracts bypassing normal negotiation or contract procedures

- oral evidence from accounts staff of advancing or delaying payments on particular supplies

- changes in the profile of the company's cash flow

- changes in pricing and margins around period ends

Stock

Misvaluation

Over-valuation of stock is another well-known form of accounts manipulation. Under-valuation is perhaps less well recognised as an issue. Where management have already achieved their targets in the current year and/or their bonus thresholds, they may want to tuck away some profits for use in a subsequent period when trading conditions may be less favourable. Such practices may be orchestrated from group level with 'required' profits levels being defined and then stock and other figures being manipulated to arrive at the chosen profit figure.

Such practices may be endemic yet there may be a sort of 'double-think' which denies that they go on. More seriously, these practices provide the perfect cover for other fraud.

Typical activities include:

- over- or under-valuation of raw materials;

- over- or under-valuation of work-in-progress;

- losses on unprofitable contracts credited against work-in-progress of profitable contracts.

The first example below shows how stock manipulation is used to cover up other problems in a business. The second case is based on a well-known retailer and shows how manipulation practices can become embedded in the culture of a group.

BLACK HOLE

Within a few months of joining a manufacturing company a new financial controller received intense pressure by top management to achieve budgeted results. This was despite the loss of a large contract which accounted for a quarter of the budgeted turnover.

An operations director indicated that he considered stock values to be on the low side. The financial controller began to overstate stock values, without seeking any substantive justification. Thereby, he increased gross profit margin and brought profit back on track with budget.

Half-way through the year the financial controller was tasked with handling the close down of a site and the related redundancies. The financial controller was under considerable stress during the redundancy programme and requested a bonus for all his hard work. This was refused and the financial controller decided to add spurious names to the redundancy list and used these to effect payments to himself and his family. By the year end the financial controller had overstated the profits of the business unit by approximately £5 million. He had also stolen about £25,000.

AVOIDING A VISIT FROM HQ

A retail group monitored on a weekly basis results, stock levels and stock write-downs from its numerous outlets. Any stock write-downs above a well-known norm resulted in a team from head-office descending on the outlet concerned for a detailed investigation and questions as to the manager's competence. As a result, stock write-downs were suppressed or lost as 'shrinkage' (i.e., theft of stock by customers).

What to look for:

- profit or bonus targets reached in latter part of the year with flat performance thereafter
- new explanations about saleability of stock and market conditions
- unusual trends in the valuation of particular stock lines or work-in-progress and/or margins

False status

Closely linked to the misvaluation frauds, where valuation numbers are simply changed, are practices involving forgery, misrepresentations regarding ownership and suppression of information linked of the value of stock. Activities include:

- forged/slashed information regarding the prospects of disposal or realisable values of stock;

- misrepresentations regarding ownership;

- collusion with a third party to borrow stock around period ends;

- stock sold or leased at the time of a stock count counted as unsold stock.

What to look for:

- new or unexpected explanations for realisable values

- obsolescent or slow-moving stock lines which miraculously find a new market – for example a distributor in an emerging market where the status of the counterparty and the distribution channel is clouded in secrecy

False quantity

Storage and packing arrangements may facilitate falsification of stock quantities. It may be difficult for stocktakers or auditors to verify whether multiple storage crates actually contain the goods represented.

Manipulating quantities might also include:

- forged quantities on stocktake sheets;

- inclusion in stock of items already sold to third parties; and

- other forms of cut-off manipulation.

The following example is a typical case.

FICTITIOUS STOCK

A listed group had performed extremely well on the stock market and its results had been growing rapidly. The structure was one of a lean head office with operating responsibility devolved to subsidiaries, but high pressure from the centre on those subsidiaries to perform.

Market conditions contributed to under-performance in an important subsidiary. In order to achieve internal targets, the finance director over valued stock. This he apparently achieved by increasing on stock sheets the volumes of certain lines of stock held at the year end which had not been counted by the auditors. To identify such lines of stock, he combined visits to certain subsidiaries with the stock-take, noting lines that the auditors selected and then ensuring that the lines that he increased were not amongst those that they counted.

When the fraud came to light, the resultant 'black hole' cast doubt over the whole of the group, its stock market rating fell significantly and there were changes of top management.

What to look for:

- close monitoring by management of which stock lines are being checked by auditors

- different handwriting on certain stock sheets which are part of a sequence counted by one person

- unusual trends in stock levels

False quality

Manipulation of quality data involves false documentation and suppression of information. Bribery of and collusion with internal or external quality inspectors will frequently be involved. Stock which requires expert valuation or which deteriorates over time is particularly susceptible to this form of manipulation.

Manipulation may also be linked to collusive substandard or bogus product frauds on the purchasing or sales side of the business. For example, substandard or substituted components may be obtained and incorporated in products which purport to meet quality standards.

What to look for:

- changes in quality inspectors used

- poor quality supporting documentation

- oral representations with delayed supporting documentation

Standard cost manipulation

Most manufacturing companies will use some form of standard costing system in the manufacturing system. These systems are prone to manipulation.

What to look for:

- late adjustments to standard costs
- change in standard costs inconsistent with changes in selling price/general costs

Cash

Some of the frauds to be discussed in the next chapter relating to cash and payments overlap with activities covered in this section. The activities discussed here though are more to do with moving funds around a group to inflate asset values and overstate sales whereas the cases in the next chapter relate to fraudsters taking funds out of a business for personal use.

Pledging assets

Pledging assets usually involves giving hidden pledges of assets in return for temporary cash flow which can be recycled in the group.

For example, in a banking context, a bank may place a deposit with another bank which in turn lends money to a nominated beneficiary against the security of the deposit. No record of the pledge or the contingent liability arising in respect of the ultimate loan is made, thereby not only concealing the credit exposure but also retaining the benefit of the deposit to satisfy liquidity reporting requirements. The proceeds of the loan can of course be channelled back to the bank, for example to give the appearance that bad loans are performing.

What to look for:

- deposits not consistent with business activity
- rollover of deposits with individual banks
- unusual counterparties

- change in pattern in receipts from debtors (debtors pledged and refinanced)
- unusual size of deposits

Teeming and lading

A well-known fraud in the sales area is 'teeming and lading'. This involves the theft of cash or cheque receipts on a sales ledger and the use of later receipts, or receipts from other customers, to settle the outstanding amounts. The fraudster conceals the unpaid amounts for as long as possible until he is able to repay the amount or, more likely until he disappears. These frauds are sometimes referred to as 'lapping' frauds. Similar frauds can take place on the purchasing side of a company.

Similar techniques can be used in the cash area to manipulate the financial position of a company, for example regarding cash in transit and the creation of unauthorised overdrafts. The following case involved the use of foreign exchange transactions to do this.

UNAUTHORISED OVERDRAFT

Directors in a company entered into foreign exchange transactions, requesting same day settlement. The transactions involved the purchase of sterling for dollars. The sterling was paid in by the counterparty into a nominated London account of the company before the dollars were expected to be received in New York, owing to the time difference.

The counterparty then discovered on the following banking day in London that the dollars had not been received. The directors then entered into another transaction using the funds received on the first transaction to settle the second transaction, again leaving an unsettled dollar liability on the second day. The directors built up a significant rolling overdraft of tens of millions of pounds in this way. The banks did not pick this up for some time as they did not consider credit aspects of such transactions because problems with non-settlement by a counterparty are rare.

What to look for:

- oral evidence from operational staff of settlement problems or banks chasing for settlement
- evidence of transactions or contracts with banks which do not form part of the company's treasury strategy

- transactions with numerous banks, in particular lower quality banks internationally

Misuse of group cash flows

Cash may be moved from one part of the group to give the appearance that debtors or loans in another part of the group are performing and therefore not requiring bad debt provisions. This sort of activity may be combined with other forms of manipulation such as suspending items in unreconciled intercompany accounts.

Associates or joint venture companies may be particularly attractive to the manipulators because the results may not be consolidated in the group figures. The following case is an elaborate case of such manipulation.

FICTITIOUS CONTRACT

Two directors in an acquired subsidiary were on an earn-out. In the final year of the earn-out the directors realised that they were not going to reach their earn-out targets because a long-term contract in their business got delayed.

They set up a fictitious contract in an emerging market. To make it appear real they created the appearance of receipts from the customer, suppliers and subcontractors to whom payments will be made. They set up fictitious suppliers using offshore companies and trusts, which in turn set up subsidiary companies in the supposed locations of the suppliers. Funds were transferred to the suppliers against invoices generated by the finance director, transferred to a bank account controlled by another dummy company set up for the fictitious customer and then returned to the company.

Since advance payments were normally expected from the customer in respect of the particular type of contract, the finance director used a 25 per cent joint venture company, which was in effect under their control through a management agreement. The company had a different firm of auditors and a different year end. The seconded general manager received funds from the company and returned the funds when instructed to the finance director with payment instructions through the correspondent bank that indicated that the funds had been received from the fictitious customer.

An intermediary was interposed between the company and the fictitious customer to facilitate the concealment and was explained as the local funding agency wishing it to appear that the contract was being carried out by a national rather than a British contracting company.

What to look for:

- large movements in cash through intercompany, associate or joint venture accounts
- transfers of assets through intercompany, associate or joint venture accounts
- large values of cash-in-transit
- unusual pattern of foreign exchange transactions

Other areas of manipulation

Transfers at other than market value

Transfers at other than market value have featured in many international accounts manipulation cases. Typical activities include:

- assets exchanged for shares at inflated values;
- values increased/decreased by moving assets around a group;
- assets acquired with concealed or understated liabilities.

INFLATED VALUES

An overseas financier owned a web of shell companies with one of his associates. The shell companies sold companies to the group's industrial holding company at inflated prices. When he was eventually dismissed the investigation found that the assets were overvalued by hundreds of millions of pounds.

What to look for:

- frequent movements of assets amongst group companies
- asset movements with no commercial/tax reason
- transactions in assets with offshore/tax haven companies

Suspended items

Suspending items in intercompany accounts is one of the more obvious forms of manipulation. So obvious in fact, that the implications of unreconciled intercompany accounts are often overlooked. Reconciling intercompany accounts is seen as a tiresome, routine task.

In case study 3 in Chapter 2 we saw how a financial controller hid unreconciled stock differences and other amounts in an intercompany account with head office which had not been reconciled for some time. Even where reconciliations appear to have been done this may simply camouflage irregular activity through intercompany accounts. It is therefore important to review the nature of transactions flowing through.

What to look for:

- significant reconciling items in intercompany accounts, branch accounts or joint venture accounts

- photocopied or faxed confirmations received from other group entities

- poorly documented reconciliations with the reasons for reconciling items unclear

- reasons for certain items going through intercompany accounts not known by accounts staff

Joint ventures with connected parties

Joint ventures and other alliances may be used to inflate or depress the results of either party for a period.

Sometimes a joint venture is set up specifically for this purpose as we saw in the 'Fictitious Contract' example above.

What to look for:

- new joint ventures late in period

- unclear reasons for joint venture

- joint venture not generally known to staff or handled in the normal way

- joint ventures with residential addresses, same address as another supplier, as an employee, his next of kin or an employee's former employer

153

Transfer pricing

Transfer pricing is used by some groups to shift profits around a group. This will often be tax-motivated but there may be other reasons such as compliance with debt covenants or keeping local regulators happy.

Activities include:

- liabilities assumed by a subsidiary or associate and under-/ over-valued;
- profits or losses taken by a subsidiary or associate through manipulated transfer pricing.

What to look for:

- transactions with other group companies/associates/joint ventures for no apparent commercial reason
- pricing of transactions not at normal intercompany prices
- prices fixed after deliveries

Claims

A less visible form of manipulation relates to claims against a company. Management may suppress information regarding a claim or some adverse finding in respect of the progress of a claim. The manipulation may also involve false or forged information relating to the status or impact of such a claim. This form of manipulation may impact a wide range of contracts and activities in a company from commercial disputes involving breach of contact and loss of profits to environmental and public liability claims.

What to look for:

- conflicting information from operational staff, from third parties or public domain information
- difficulty in obtaining answers to relatively straightforward questions about the claim. Delaying tactics
- information controlled by one individual who tries to restrict access to other parties

Reports inconsistent with accounting records

This is perhaps one of the most basic forms of accounts manipulation. It will feature in some form in many of the manipulations discussed above.

The seeds for such manipulation may lie in poor systems, for example it is difficult to reconcile the management accounts with the general ledger system. Perhaps the general ledger system is not able to cope with the analysis required for management reporting purposes. This may encourage, or sometimes necessitate, the inclusion of estimates to produce management accounts. In that environment, extreme time pressures for 'flash' reports encourages slack practice. Active manipulation of the management accounts is then only one small further step, and of course differences or lack of audit trail can easily be blamed on the systems or analysis problems.

What to look for:

- inconsistency between the management accounts and general ledger
- inconsistency with apparent levels of activity and normal cost/operational relationships
- poor quality management information
- poor skills of staff preparing such information

Conclusion

This chapter has covered a wide range of accounts manipulation problems. The tables on the following pages summarises the detailed forms of manipulation discussed.

Table 5.1 Accounts manipulation

Sales

False sales/debtors	Advance billing	Discounts/undisclosed benefits	Misrepresentation of credit status	Bad debt under- or over-provision
• Dummy customers • Sales to connected parties • Kickbacks to customers • Overcharging customers • Forged documents • Forged/suppressed confirmations	• Sales recorded in breach of accounting policies • Collusive pre-invoicing • Undisclosed sale or return • Stocks 'allocated' to warehouse under control	• Discounts to be credited later • Credits hidden in pricing manipulation • Stock taken back at full valuation • Hidden promotions in next period • Credits transferred for write off later	• False information on credit status to induce sales to poor risks • Suppression of credit information • Bribery of credit control staff	• Misrepresentation of credit status • Recycled funds to give appearance account is current • Manipulation of debtor ageing

Rebates/charges manipulation	Hidden contract terms			False consulting contracts
• Rebates taken to profit too early • Extra charges against rebates later • Postponed charges • Misrepresentation or forgery of confirmations re rebates	• Hidden conditions and terms that impact results • Side letters to advance or delay income or expense recognition			• Costs or revenues concealed/created via false consulting contracts

Purchases

Misrecording capital and revenue items	Under and over accruals
• Allocating costs in contravention of accounting policies • Hiding capital items in revenue • Costs billed and recorded to conceal their true nature	• Accruing actual to budget • Forward purchase orders • Concealed supplier invoices • Costs of goods received over/understated

False capitalisation of costs	Delaying or advancing payments
• Forged or manipulated documents to support criteria • Costs misdescribed on invoices	• Non-standard payment terms to compensate for reduced or inflated prices • Misrepresentation of creditor ageing • Teeming and lading of suppliers

Stock

Misvaluation	False status	False quantity	False quality	Standard cost manipulation
• Over/undervaluation of raw materials • Over/undervaluation of WIP • Losses on unprofitable contracts credited against WIP on profitable contracts	• Forged information re prospects of disposal • Misrepresentations re ownership • Collusion with third party to borrow stock • Stock sold or leased but included in count	• Third party stocks already sold included in stock • Forged quantities on stocktake • Cut-off manipulation	• False document re quality of stock • Suppression of quality data	• Standard cost changes inconsistent with changes in selling prices or general costs

Cash

Rebates/charges manipulation	Hidden contract terms	Misrecording capital and revenue items
• Recycling fund through associates joint ventures and group companies	• Teeming and lading cash in transit • Teeming and lading, creating unauthorised overdrafts	• Hidden pledges in return for temporary cash flow

Other

Transfer pricing	JVs with connected parties	Suspended items	Misrecording capital and revenue items	Claims	Reports do not agree to accounting records
• Assets exchanged for shares at inflated values • Values increased or decreased by moving assets round group • Assets acquired with concealed or understated liabilities	• Joint ventures with connected parties to inflate or depress profits	• Cost or revenues left unreconciled in intercompany and branch accounts	• Assets exchanged for shares at inflated values • Values increased/decreased by moving assets round group • Assets acquired with concealed/understated liabilities	• Suppression of information • False/forged information relating to existence, status or value	• Invented or partially invented management accounts

6

Fraud in manufacturing and services

Introduction

This chapter deals with the main risks of fraud affecting manufacturing and service companies. Many of the frauds which affect these companies also affect companies in the financial sector but there are many more specialised frauds in that sector too. These are dealt with in the next chapter.

Clearly, the precise way in which many frauds occur will vary from industry to industry and company to company. The aim is to provide a clear briefing on the more common frauds. This should form a good basis for more detailed risk profiling. The areas covered are as follows:

- purchasing
- sales
- stock
- cash and payments
- other areas

Some of the frauds are similar or overlap with the accounts manipulation practices covered in the last chapter. The distinction is that most frauds covered in this chapter involve the fraudster directly or indirectly taking value out of the company for personal benefit.

Purchasing

Introduction

Purchasing fraud is one of the most insidious forms of fraud. Many frauds involve kickbacks that are 'off book', the backhander going

159

straight to a manager or employee of the buying company rather than through the company's books. Many frauds are about how much less the company would have paid if corruption was not built into the cost base. The difference will not necessarily be visible in the variances between actual and budget as inflated estimates may be included in the budgets.

Even though total purchasing spend may be material to the results of a company, it is common to find that finance do not have much insight into the purchasing cycle. Heads of purchasing usually report to an operations director or to the head of a business unit rather than to finance. The result is that finance do not monitor fraud risk and control issues in the purchasing area. Finance may coordinate budgets, open up new supplier accounts and match invoices received to orders and other documentation prior to making payment to the supplier. They may also undertake reconciliations of the purchase ledger and to statements from suppliers. The problem is that this will rarely detect purchasing fraud.

The biggest problems in purchasing occur at the vetting and selection stages. The likely forms of fraud will depend on the purchasing profile: the types of supply, the nature of suppliers, the form of contracts and how purchasing is organised.

For example, a company involved in contract catering with large, highly-leveraged supply contracts with major food companies will have a very different fraud risk profile to a sales subsidiary of an electronics group. In the contract catering company, with high levels of rebates and overriders based on levels of turnover (or future turnover) contracts are likely to be negotiated by a small number of senior people. Hidden contract terms may feature or part of the rebates due may be diverted to the board member or senior manager concerned.

In the sales company, a significant part of the non-product purchasing spend may relate to advertising, marketing and promotion. Here contracts frequently do not exist or may be poorly prepared. There may be informality in most aspects of the purchasing process. How, why and when particular suppliers came to be used may be unclear. A wide range of people in the company may be able to initiate supplier relationships and open supplier accounts. The most likely frauds here may involve kickbacks and lavish entertaining to maintain supplier relationships, supplies by companies connected to marketing staff or billing for services not supplied.

160

The main phases in the purchasing cycle are as follows:

- selection of the supplier and ordering the goods or services;
- receipt of the goods or services;
- receipt and recording of the supplier invoice; and
- payment of the invoice.

The most common problems in each phase are shown in the following chart.

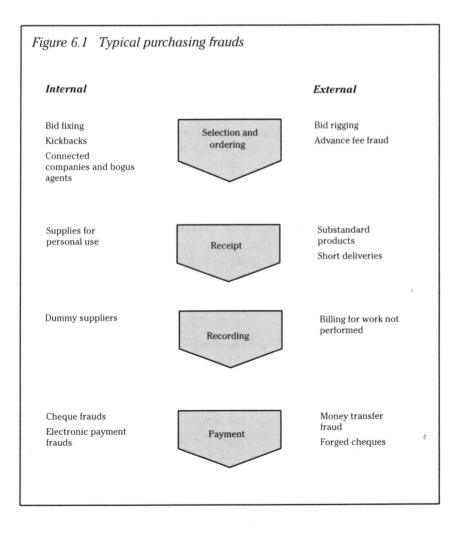

Figure 6.1   Typical purchasing frauds

Internal

Bid fixing
Kickbacks
Connected companies and bogus agents

Supplies for personal use

Dummy suppliers

Cheque frauds
Electronic payment frauds

Selection and ordering

Receipt

Recording

Payment

External

Bid rigging
Advance fee fraud

Substandard products
Short deliveries

Billing for work not performed

Money transfer fraud
Forged cheques

In the **selection and ordering** phase, the key concerns are that suppliers of appropriate status and capability are invited to bid. Issues include who is behind the supplier, their capability to deliver and financial viability. There should be a truly competitive selection process and only properly authorised orders should be processed. Internal frauds in this phase include bid fixing which involves the release of confidential information by employees of the buying company. Connected companies or bogus agents may be invited to bid or may otherwise join the supplier base. External frauds include bid rigging and advance fee fraud, whereby companies are persuaded to part with an up-front fee or deposit with the promise of future delivery, the fraudster then disappearing without trace.

In the **receipt** of goods or services phase, the main concern is that goods or services of the correct quantity and quality are supplied. Internal frauds include work done or goods supplied for private purposes, so the goods are never delivered to the company at all. External frauds include short deliveries and the supply of substandard products.

On receipt and **recording** of the supplier's invoice, the first concern is whether the supplier invoice is genuine. The second concern is whether the prices and quantities on the invoice are correct. Internal frauds include the creation of dummy suppliers and the misuse of credit notes, rebates and volume discounts. External frauds include billing for work not performed and over-billing.

At the **payment** stage, the main concern is that payments are only made in respect of authorised invoices and that proper security is maintained over cheque-books and the use of money transfer systems. Frauds in this phase of the cycle are discussed under cash and payments later in the chapter.

Internal purchasing frauds

Bid fixing

In bid fixing, bidders obtain inside information, usually in return for a kickback paid to an employee of the purchasing company. The information may relate to the selection criteria, technical specifications or the prices of other bids. The effect is that the purchasing company pays more and obtains less favourable terms than it would have done had a truly competitive process been in place. In certain cases the specifications for an entire project may have been compromised as equipment inappropriate to the company's needs may have been purchased. This has happened for instance on several major computer installation projects.

In larger contracts, so-called 'information brokers' may act as intermediaries between employees of the purchasing company who divulge the confidential information and tendering companies who wish to buy such information so that they may obtain lucrative contracts. The brokers make it more difficult to trace the source of the leak. Payments of kickbacks may also be concealed by the brokers, using front companies in offshore locations and/or numbered bank accounts in countries with strict bank secrecy laws.

The examples of bid fixing below illustrate the wide range of situations in which this type of fraud occurs.

NEW SIGNAGE

The directors of a sign company which was to install new signage at dealerships and showrooms of a major car manufacturer bribed the corporate identity director, who was responsible for negotiating contracts with suppliers, so that the company would be awarded a £6 million contract. The directors paid for expensive refurbishment work to be carried out at the home of the corporate identity director. The fraud was picked up when internal audit noticed an unusual movement of funds during the bid process.

AMMUNITIONS

A purchasing director was found guilty of taking bribes over an eight-year period from European defence suppliers in exchange for awarding contracts. Although he was only on a modest salary, police found evidence of several million pounds passing through his bank accounts. The bribes or 'commissions' were paid by one of the suppliers through two Swiss companies and a third company. The director had nine houses both in Britain and abroad and several luxury cars. The organisation's vetting arrangements failed to pick up his extravagant lifestyle. Officials had visited his home but had not considered anything strange. He was known to have money but it was explained by his wife being a medical practitioner. The frauds were only discovered five years after the director had retired. Police went to his home initially because it was thought he had classified information there. They then noticed documents relating to payments to Swiss banks.

INFORMATION BROKERS

Employees in a major civil engineering company passed inside information to 'information brokers' who in turn passed it to one of the bidders for a large contract. The information related to the selection criteria being used by the purchasing company and the prices of other bids. The information enabled the supplier to pitch its bid 10 per cent (£20 million) higher than the price it would otherwise have submitted.

SHIP REPAIR CONTRACTS

An employee responsible for ship repair contracts at a major oil company allegedly accepted bribes as an inducement to send more vessels from the company's fleet for repair at a particular shipyard. The shipyard had been hit by declining margins.

What to look for:

- abnormal prices or terms (specifications which can only be met by one supplier)
- prices of bids close together
- well-known suppliers not asked to tender
- pre-qualified suppliers
- small supplier/large contract. Supplier small relative to size of purchasing company
- location of supplier unusual: for example remote supplier used for routine services or supplier providing services outside normal range of business
- tenders accepted after closing date
- high level of extras/claims by particular suppliers
- changes to the specifications or price soon after the contract is awarded
- a large number of invoices for particular supplier just beneath approval threshold, thereby avoiding more formal tendering procedures

Other clues are the use of particular brokers or consultants in the bid process, common names, addresses or solicitors between various bidders, waivers of normal business terms and conditions and procurement staff being unduly defensive when questioned about particular contracts. Other relevant matters include whether or not vendor complaints are handled independently and whether former suppliers or unsuccessful bidders are debriefed.

Kickbacks and inducements

Kickbacks and inducements are used in many types of purchasing fraud to induce employees to favour particular suppliers, for example the installation of computer equipment, office refurbishment, maintenance, design and consultancy contracts. This purchasing may take place outside the central purchasing department.

As already noted, kickbacks are sometimes difficult to detect because there may be no obvious evidence in the books of the purchasing company. The evidence, if any, will usually be in the records of the supplying company. For that reason companies sometimes include provisions for vendor audits in their contracts with suppliers to monitor key accounts such as entertaining and related expenditure. The incidence of kickbacks and inducements is likely to be higher where a company does not have a clear policy concerning the acceptance of gifts, bribes and inducements.

However, there will often be many indicators of corruption on purchasing files.

BROWN ENVELOPES

For 12 years the managing director of a supplier bribed several directors and executives of a major co-op to ensure that business worth £300,000 a week stayed with his company. Bribes took the form of cash, exotic holidays and prostitutes. To cover the costs the supplier charged the co-op above market rate for its goods which led to the co-op's profits being half the figure expected and to customers paying inflated prices for goods. The fraud was eventually discovered when the co-op began rejecting the supplier's produce on quality grounds.

Warning signs are as for bid fixing above.

Connected companies

Prices or quantities may be manipulated or products substituted by bogus intermediaries. This is most likely to happen where the intermediary is acting for an overseas supplier with whom it is difficult for the purchasing company to have direct contact. Unnecessary or exorbitant charges may be built into the price charged to the purchasing company.

ADD IN THE MIDDLEMAN

A purchasing manager set up a bogus print-buying company, owned by himself and his wife, and routed the group's print buying via the company so that he could add a 100 per cent mark-up to underlying print costs billed by suppliers. He got away with the fraud due to poor budgeting procedures, very little scrutiny of marketing costs by finance or other senior management and no independent review of the suppliers used by the group, the services supplied or the basis of the pricing.

What to look for:

- ownership or status of intermediaries not known
- reason for intermediary arrangements not clear
- vendor complaints not monitored independently

Work done/goods supplied for private purposes

Work done or goods supplied for private purposes is one of the most common purchasing frauds. This involves the fraudster appropriating company assets or using company time for private purposes. The risk of this type of fraud is increased where activities are conducted at remote locations or are not closely supervised, using materials that are readily useable in another trade or for private use.

HOME IMPROVEMENTS

Staff in a maintenance department incorporated into their schedule work on their own homes. They removed the necessary supplies from inventory and falsified their time records (even charging overtime for the private work).

What to look for:

- unusual delivery times or methods
- ambiguous or abbreviated descriptions on invoices

166

- over-ordered or surplus stock lines

- a weak link between invoices and the origination of the order

- poor segregation of duties

Dummy suppliers

Companies may have strong controls over the initial selection of suppliers in relation to major contracts but may monitor the later submission of invoices under the contract less well, when inflated or false invoices may be introduced. Controls may also be weaker in relation to computer installations, office refurbishments, maintenance, design and other consultancy work.

Payments may be made to dummy suppliers for services not provided or amounts posted to accounts of suppliers which the company has in fact stopped using. Dummy sub-accounts or branches may be set up on legitimate suppliers. This makes it more difficult for those reviewing and approving payments to identify unusual suppliers or supplies.

Amounts may be posted to accounts which are 'off budget' (such as recharge accounts) or 'up-front' payments or deposits may be made in respect of bogus contracts. Another fraud in this area is 'teeming and lading' with suppliers. The fraudster changes the payee detail on a cheque, or sets up a bank account in a supplier's name, diverts the cheque to the account and uses later cheques made payable to the supplier to 'settle' the earlier unpaid liability. The following examples illustrate the range of situations in which dummy supplier frauds may take place.

PHOTOCOPIED SUPPLIERS

A criminal gang obtained payment vouchers of an organisation and internal circulation envelopes to enable them to feed fraudulent vouchers into the company's payment system. The fraud involved making payments to overseas bank accounts of bogus suppliers. Some of the supporting documents were photocopied. In other cases payments were made even though none of the necessary supporting documentation was attached and the payment vouchers bore false signatures. Staff making the electronic banking payments did not see it as their responsibility to check the validity of the vouchers.

PHANTOM TRANSPORT COMPANY

A road haulage manager set up a bogus transport company and over eight months invoiced his employer £150,000. He bought luxury cars, foreign holidays and luxurious fittings for his home. He had so many cars he was able to set up a car hire business.

BOGUS CONSULTANCY AND DESIGN SERVICES

The finance director of an information systems company defrauded the company of £1.5 million over a five-year period. For instance, he paid £275,000 for computer consultancy never received. He also paid £348,000 to an interior design company in Florida, falsely claiming that the company had provided services to his employer. In fact the sums were channelled back to him and were used to buy three properties in Florida. He also bought computer hardware and then resold it privately or sometimes gave it away.

What to look for:

- unclear reasons for particular supplies or few details concerning the service provided

- suppliers not generally known to staff, not handled in the normal way, or dealt with exclusively by a director or manager

- suppliers with PO Box addresses, accommodation addresses, residential addresses, the same address as another supplier, as an employee or his next of kin or an employee's former employer

- invoices which are soiled, incomplete, over-abbreviated or altered in some way

- unfolded invoices (that have never been in the mail)

- corporate suppliers with no registered number, using accommodation address or resident offshore

- supplier has incorrect VAT number

- large number of invoices for a particular supplier just beneath approval thresholds

- numerous contras or other adjustments on purchase ledger

- numerous entries in suspense accounts during the year

- confirmation of supplier accounts resisted or unusual conditions suggested

- supplier does not offer usual discounts and special deals

- weak account opening procedures or weak controls over amendments to standing data. Poor control over dormant supplier accounts

- poor controls over paid invoices

- no zero-based budgets or clearly defined budget holders for particular accounts

Misuse of credit notes, rebates and volume discounts

The true cost of purchases may be manipulated through the misuse of credit notes or volume discounts and rebates. For example, credit notes may be used to manipulate profits or to conceal other frauds. Alternatively volume discounts and rebates may be triggered artificially and diverted for the personal benefit of the fraudster.

What to look for:

- abnormal numbers and/or value of credit notes around period ends

- volume discounts/rebates not monitored independently against quantities bought

- stock surpluses (indicating possible over-purchasing) to trigger volume discounts

External purchasing frauds

Bid rigging

Bid rigging is the manipulation of the competitive bidding process by suppliers. Typically, bidders conspire to fix prices and terms for particular contracts. Contracts are then allocated between the suppliers in rotation. There is also the wider problem of cartels operating in a number of industries. As with bid fixing, the effect is that the purchasing company obtains less favourable terms and pays a higher price than it would otherwise have done had a truly competitive process been in operation.

Warning signs are as for bid fixing above.

Advance fee fraud

Advance fee fraud has attracted a good deal of publicity in recent years. Typically, the fraudster takes an up-front fee or deposit and promises to deliver certain goods or services in the future. Once he has pocketed the fee he disappears.

Those most at risk are businessmen who are having difficulty in obtaining a particular product or service, for example access to credit due to weak financial position. The fraudster exploits this vulnerability. Others may be tempted by unusually low prices offered by the fraudster.

CHEAP FERRARIS

A car dealer took £3.5 million in deposits from 1,100 motorists promising that he would obtain Rolls Royces, Ferraris, Aston Martins and Porches at very low prices. He rarely delivered the cars.

LOST: ONE OIL TANKER

A lawyer attempted to sell £14 million of crude oil he did not own. He used fake documents to sell a non-existent consignment of almost £1.2 million barrels of Nigerian crude oil to an oil company through the spot market in Rotterdam. He obtained US$150,000 from a senior official of the company, allegedly for charter fees, and allowed to him to speak to a 'tanker captain' on the telephone, confirming that the consignment was en route to Amsterdam. However, the official became suspicious and tipped off police.

The fraudsters rarely operate from offices, mainly using phones, a photocopier and a fax to access them. Occasionally they ply their trade from home, or utilise the facilities offered by an answering service. Sometimes they can be contacted via a telephone number abroad which actually rings back to a number in the UK.

A particularly prevalent stream of advance fee fraud involves the arranging of bogus credits facilities. Typically, the fraudster promises that on payment of an up-front fee he will either directly fund at a very low rate of interest or more frequently put the prospective borrower in touch with a lender knowing that the funds do not exist and no loan will ever result.

Meetings with prospective borrowers take place, usually in hotels or clubs. The fraudster will explain that the finance will come from off-shore shell banks located in the Far East, Saudi Arabia, the USA, or the British Virgin Islands, all to avoid tax.

The prospective borrower will be told that this route has been tried and tested successfully many times. The advance fee is required to pay for legal expenses and to facilitate the loan. Sometimes the payment is required to demonstrate goodwill and to evidence that the borrower is serious. They will be informed that the 'honest broker's' fee will only be payable after completion.

As part of the loan process the borrower is asked to sign a document called a non-disclosure, non-circumvention agreement or a 'specific performance agreement'. If the borrower fails to comply with conditions stipulated by the lender, usually in a very short time-scale with which it is impossible to comply, then the borrower is deemed to have defaulted and the advance payment is forfeit.

Some borrowers (corporate entities included) have even been persuaded into believing that the non-disclosure element includes reporting the matter to the police. The main reason given for signing these documents is in order to prevent the broker being bypassed in the loan cycle and thereby losing his commission. Lawyers too, have been induced to receive funds from borrowers into their client account which the borrowers erroneously believed to be an escrow account. Those funds have then been disbursed on the instructions of the fraudster and in some cases the lawyers have been successfully sued by the borrowers.

Set out below are some further examples of advance fee fraud.

SELF-LIQUIDATING LOANS AND PRIME BANK GUARANTEES

Prior to payment of the up-front fee, the fraudster indicates approval in principle from the lender but the fraudster indicates that the amount is considered to be too small. It is suggested that an alternative would be to borrow twice the amount required. This is known as 'arbitrage' in the USA or a 'self-liquidating loan'. The excess over the actual amount of loan required is to purchase a prime bank guarantee, or a prime bank instrument or a US Treasury Bond at a discounted rate for a 10-year period. At the conclusion of the term, the interest on trading the bond will repay the loan.

This sort of scenario delivered with panache and confidence and interspersed with what is perceived to be genuine banking terminology is what induces the borrower to part with the fee. The lender will apparently be from the top 100 prime banks. If these words are used then immediate alarm bells should go off. There are only a few banks in the world with the name 'prime' included. The end result is that despite the payment of the advance fee, no loan is forthcoming, with the borrower often being blamed for non-performance.

THE NIGERIAN VERSION

The Nigerian version of advance fee fraud, also known as 419, so named after the section of the Nigerian penal code which deals with such fraud, involves sending letters to victims selected at random, for example from telephone directories, promising vast sums of money in return for the privilege of using the victim's banking details and headed paper. This type of advance fee fraud is very prevalent.

BLOCKED FUNDS

Blocked funds frauds involve the fraudster asking depositors to place funds with a scheme after being shown a bank document called a 'blocked funds letter'. This states that the promoters have a significant amount of collateral with which to raise loans. Details can be forged on genuine bank notepaper and high rates of return are offered to attract depositors. The letter will state that the funds are available 'with full bank authority' and that they are 'clean and of non-criminal origin' or from a 'fresh cut non-criminal source' and are 'blocked for a number of banking days and free of all liens or encumbrances over the period'. No returns are forthcoming.

BLACK MONEY

Black money frauds involve the claimed conversion of blank pieces of paper to US high-denomination dollar bills. The fraudster persuades his victim that he is in possession of thousands of US dollars but, in order to get them out of the country (usually Nigeria), the notes have been treated with a chemical which makes them appear like blank paper. This enables the money to be smuggled out of country because it is not picked up on x-ray machines at airports.

In order to convert the paper back to cash another chemical is required which the victim is informed is very expensive. The fraudster conducts a presentation (using a genuine dollar bill of course) for the benefit of victim He obtains the advance fee from the victim to purchase the larger amount of chemical required and then disappears leaving a trunk full of blank dollar-sized paper.

What to look for:

- abnormally low prices or products or services which seem 'too good to be true'
- non-returnable up-front payments or deposits required
- all dealings through agents
- inability to verify the authenticity of documentation
- all correspondence and documentation is faxed
- complex explanations given for advantageous terms or reasons for undisclosed principal entering into deal
- deal involves complex and unusual financial instruments
- purported principal is overseas and identity cannot be revealed
- the agent is in a hurry to conclude the deal

Short deliveries/goods or services not supplied

Short deliveries and invoicing for goods not supplied is a common problem. Companies at greatest risk are those with:

- weak controls over goods received;
- poor physical security;
- weak account opening procedures; or
- a weak link between the origination of the order, receipt of the goods and approval of the invoice.

MISCELLANEOUS MARKETING

A marketing director approved agency invoices for work which was not done or was in excess of the actual amount due. He took kickbacks from the agency directors. He debited the money to the company's 'miscellaneous' account rather than his own budget, to hide the fraud. The fraud involved four suppliers and went on for two-and-a-half years. The fraud was discovered as a result of concerns raised by a sales promotion manager. The marketing director was responsible for a multimillion pound annual promotions budget.

FICTITIOUS FITTING OUT

Payments were made to a dummy labour supply agency during the development of a supermarket and then forwarded to the supermarket group's project quantity surveyor. The regional quantity surveyor of the developer undertaking the super-market fitting out contract used bank accounts of the labour supply agency, which in fact had never worked on the site, to launder the money back to the project quantity surveyor. The irregularities came to light during an Inland Revenue investigation.

It was clear to the two surveyors that the project was over-budgeted. The developer's surveyor claimed that the supermarket's surveyor had demanded cash back otherwise the supermarket would cease to use the developer. He said he co-operated because the supermarket group was an important client and felt that if he lost their contracts his department would collapse. The labour agency got a share of the money for the use of the bank accounts.

What to look for:

- excessive budgets
- stock shortages
- deliveries at unusual times or at unusual locations
- tampering with measuring equipment

Substandard product fraud

Substandard product frauds can be devastating where the products supplied are for use in sophisticated equipment. Companies most at risk are those that do not have rigorous quality control checks on goods supplied or independent checks on the credentials and capabilities of key suppliers.

Sometimes grandiose claims are made by suppliers about work they have performed for other customers, for example major public companies, overseas governments and members of royal families. It is surprising how often such claims are accepted at face value without any further corroboration.

High risk situations are where suppliers are changed at the last moment, where there are rushed jobs, or where the terms require substantial payment in advance of delivery.

174

FALSE CERTIFICATIONS

The US subsidiary of a major defence supplier was fined US$88 million for supplying military aircraft parts with false certifications for US fighter aircraft.

BOUGHT IN HONG KONG

An electronics engineer was subcontracted by an approved supplier of a major organisation to supply military-grade adjustable voltage regulators for use in submarine torpedoes. In fact he supplied parts which he had obtained from a shop in Hong Kong. He produced false certificates supposedly issued by the company which normally supplied the regulators. He told the approved supplier that he had managed to obtain war stock parts from the USA and from the grounded space shuttle programme.

What to look for:

- suppliers changed at the last moment
- rushed jobs
- contract terms require substantial payments in advance of delivery

Billing for work not performed and overbilling

This type of fraud is similar to short deliveries/goods not supplied above. Susceptible contracts are those where a large number of invoices are submitted, the service is supplied at a remote location or checking performance of individual stages of the contract is difficult.

As with most purchasing frauds a clear link between payment of the invoice and the need for the supply is fundamental.

LITTLE AND OFTEN

Under a contract to service a road fleet of 7,000 vehicles a supplier was not allowed to make a profit on parts supplied. To compensate for this restriction the supplier allegedly added an amount to each invoice. Although the amount added to each invoice was small, the total loss was very considerable.

INFLATED INVOICES

Over four years, a businessman paid hundreds of thousands of pounds in bribes to an employee of a major car manufacturer in return for the award of lucrative artwork contracts. He was responsible for a budget of £2.5 million a year. Another manager in the technical publications department was also involved in the fraud and received £25,000 'hush money', lavish lunches and free flights to France. There was also a middleman involved who negotiated contracts on behalf of the managers. He put out the work to genuine subcontractors but submitted vastly inflated invoices to the car firm out of which the bribes were paid. The company received a tip-off and launched an investigation.

FAMILY CONCERNS

A company had entered into a joint venture with an overseas family-run company to build a large processing plant for a foreign government. The project was in effect run by the overseas joint venture. Each party had invested over £50 million in the project. The company decided to investigate the joint venture because they had concerns about costs and the quality of management information. It turned out that some local managers were in collusion with suppliers to overstate professional fees and other invoices, a contract for pipe construction was awarded without tendering and salaries of locally employed staff were excessive.

What to look for:

- no independent checks on prices or volume discounts
- no competitive tendering
- no zero-based budgeting
- vague terms in contracts and no detailed review of charges such as travel, advertising, consultancy fees, recruitment, maintenance and leasing

Sales

Introduction

There are four main phases in a typical sales cycle:

- receipt of the sales order;

176

- delivery of the goods or services;
- invoicing and recording of the sale; and
- payment by the customer.

In practice there are many more detailed processing steps but it is helpful to keep these four key phases clearly in mind. The most common frauds are illustrated on the following chart.

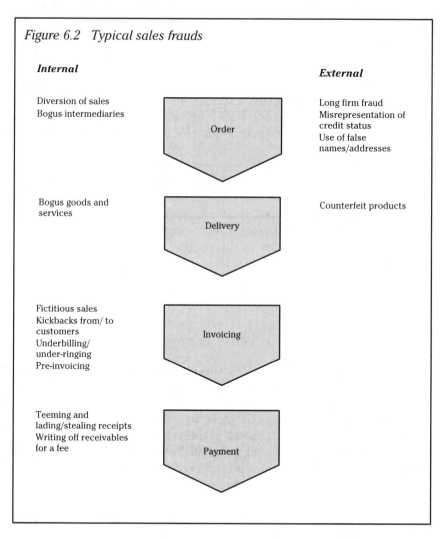

Figure 6.2 Typical sales frauds

Internal

External

Diversion of sales
Bogus intermediaries

Order

Long firm fraud
Misrepresentation of
credit status
Use of false
names/addresses

Bogus goods and
services

Delivery

Counterfeit products

Fictitious sales
Kickbacks from/ to
customers
Underbilling/
under-ringing
Pre-invoicing

Invoicing

Teeming and
lading/stealing receipts
Writing off receivables
for a fee

Payment

In the **order** phase, the main concerns are whether the company receives all the sales orders it should (i.e., they are not diverted) and whether its customers are genuine and do not misrepresent their identity or credit status. Internal frauds include diversion of sales and the use of bogus intermediary companies to manipulate margins and 'cream off' profits. External frauds include the use of false names and addresses by customers, the misrepresentation of credit status and what is known as 'long firm' fraud.

In the **delivery** phase, the main concern is whether the customer receives the product or service which he ordered. The major fraud in this phase of the cycle is the supply of non-existent or substandard goods or services and short deliveries. External frauds include counterfeiting of branded products.

In the **invoicing** phase, the key concern is whether the goods and services are properly invoiced and that the invoices represent actual sales. Internal frauds include fictitious sales, kickbacks to or from customers, underbilling or under-ringing (i.e., of tills) and pre-invoicing.

In the **payment** phase, the main concern is whether cash is collected in respect of all sales and whether cash is deposited and recorded promptly. Internal frauds include 'teeming and lading', sometimes referred to as 'lapping' fraud, and writing off receivables for a fee. There is also a number of frauds which relate more specifically to the cash area itself. I deal with these later in the chapter under cash and payment systems.

Diversion of sales

Diversion of sales usually involves rerouting sales to private companies owned by the fraudster. This may be achieved by the fraudster's misuse of customer mailing lists, the diversion of responses to sales promotions, frustration of existing contracts, by using non-competitive terms or providing poor service. The risk of this type of fraud may be particularly high prior to and following an acquisition or major reorganisation, for example where the vendors remain in the business, where staff have been demoted or where morale is low.

Sales may also be routed through bogus intermediary companies owned by the fraudster or his associates (e.g., brokers or distributors) with the fraudster taking a cut in the form of hidden commissions or unusual pricing structures.

DISGRUNTLED DIRECTOR DIVERTS SALES

The ex-director of a company, which had recently been acquired and divisionalised, and who remained with the group, diverted sales to a rival company owned by him. He ensured his employer's tenders for contracts were non-competitive and that poor service was given on other contracts. He recommended the rival company as an alternative to perform the contracts. Management of the parent company realised something was wrong when several staff left the division and the division was under-performing against budget.

BOGUS BROKER

Over four years the general manager and his deputy conspired to tell tour companies that they could only charter aircraft through a particular aircraft broker. The broker was part of their conspiracy. The general manager and his deputy produced documents with one price for his employer's accounts, less the fake commission, while the broker invoiced customers for a higher amount, diverting the difference to an account with a bank in Zurich. After the fraud was discovered through a tip-off, a package of evidence was received by his employer's solicitors, thought to have been sent by the general manager's former lover. Fortunately, most of the funds were later recovered.

What to look for:

- unexpected loss of customers or a high level of customer complaints (assuming such complaints are monitored independently)
- inconsistent business patterns – for example, sales reduced but spares sales constant (or vice versa)
- no independent appraisal of pricing structures or amounts charged by inter-mediaries. Ownership of supplier companies is not checked

Bogus goods and services

Bogus goods and services frauds are often associated with new ventures involving management or staff without a proven track record. The nature of the customer base is also important. Relevant factors include the vulnerability of the customers and their ability to appraise the product or service.

Frauds involve management or employees manipulating a particular

179

product or service in order to meet profit targets or to siphon off part of the product for personal benefit. This involves the provision of substandard or non-existent products or services to customers. The following examples cover a wide range of business situations: a defence company, a house builder and a ferry company.

DANGEROUS DEFECT

A quality control manager at a defence company uncovered a defect in a missile launcher that could make a missile accidentally fall off a wing. He said that the company ordered him to conceal the defect and eventually dismissed him. He sued his employer and notified the regulatory authorities. Subsequently his employer pleaded guilty to conspiracy to defraud the government and was fined.

HOLIDAY HOMES THAT NEVER GOT OFF THE GROUND

A company allegedly sold thousands of pounds worth of timeshares on properties abroad. It was alleged that no building work was ever undertaken and the scheme would not have obtained planning permission. The pictures in the brochure were of another development.

FERRY SERVICE WITHOUT A FERRY

A company attempted to run a ferry service. A feasibility plan was prepared, a manager, an accountant and a sales manager recruited and a shipbroker asked to find a suitable ferry for charter. Approximately £100,000 was allegedly taken from customers who were led to believe that the ferry service would operate. In fact, the ferry service had no financial backing, no crew, no port and no ship. It was alleged that the customers' deposits were used to defray the operating expenses of the company.

Other examples of bogus product frauds are clocked cars in the motor trade or sale of watered down spirits in public houses or hotels.

What to look for:

* products which are 'too good to be true' – for example, low risk, high return products
* grandiose claims and glossy advertising which cannot be easily corroborated

- services provided at remote locations or at a date far in the future (particularly where up-front payments or deposits are required)
- complex explanations, with exotic reasons for advantageous pricing
- abnormal growth or profitability

Kickbacks to or from customers

Kickbacks to or from customers involve the payment of a kickback of some kind in return for manipulating quantities or prices, or supplying a higher or lower grade of product. The risk of this type of fraud is increased where there is no independent review of prices and/or terms of business for particular customers. Kickbacks may also be paid to employees to write off debts, or issue credit notes or extend credit on payment terms.

LUCRATIVE FRANCHISES

Several senior executives and employees at a subsidiary of a major car manufacturer received kickbacks from motor dealers over several years in the form of cash, expensive jewellery, luxury cars, swimming pools and other gifts in return for the award of lucrative franchises to dealers as well as allocations of certain sought after car models for which demand exceeded supply.

What to look for:

- customers dealt with outside the main system, for example, handled exclusively by a senior member of staff using non-standard documentation
- no pricing information on standing data files or unusual prices, discounts or credit terms
- unusual trends in margins
- alterations on invoices or other documentation

Underbilling and under-ringing

Underbilling involves the suppression of invoices, the understating of quantities despatched or the manipulation of prices or discounts, often in return for some kind of kickback to the employee. Under-ringing is the under-recording of cash sales, for example shop employees not ringing up sales in retail outlets and pocketing the amount not recorded. Payment and credit terminals may be misused, especially where the supervisor's card is left in the machine unattended. For example, bogus refunds may be given to relatives and friends.

What to look for:

- alterations to delivery notes or invoices

- transactions handled exclusively by a senior member of staff using non-standard documentation

- certain customers dealt with by only one member of staff

- no sequential control over invoices

- no independent checks on prices

- weak controls over changes to standing data or the absence of standing data for particular customers

- poor control over 'miscellaneous' sales

- poor control over till rolls

- no reconciliation of stock movements to sales

Teeming and lading/stealing of receipts

Perhaps the best known fraud in the sales area is 'teeming and lading'. This involves the theft of cash or cheque receipts on a sales ledger and the use of later receipts, or receipts from other customers, to 'settle' the outstanding amounts. The fraudster conceals the unpaid amounts for as long as possible until he is able to repay the amount or, more likely, until he disappears.

Teeming and lading frauds are rarely reported in the press. This is because they do not usually involve significant amounts and tend to be committed by more junior staff. However, quite often other frauds may be linked to teeming and lading so this should not give any particular comfort.

Poor segregation of duties, not only between the recording of sales and the handling of cash and cheques but also between these functions and the resolution of customer complaints, increases the risk of teeming and lading significantly.

182

A CREATIVE ACCOUNTANT

A temporary accountant, who was responsible for credit control, stole cheques payable to his employer. He opened two bank accounts in the name of the company. He paid them into the new accounts. The fraud was concealed for a time by bogus journal entries and teeming and lading of sales ledger accounts.

A 'COMPUTER ERROR'

A sales ledger clerk stole a number of cheques. He told the customers to ignore the outstanding items on their statements saying it was a 'computer error'. Eventually he had to make a significant transfer from another account, at which point the fraud was discovered.

ANOTHER CLASSIC CASE

A credit control manager had staff under his supervision who passed cash and other entries to the sales ledger. The manager was responsible for producing the aged debtor analysis. On occasion, when his staff were away or otherwise engaged, he stole cash and other receipts and deposited them in his personal bank account. He updated the relevant accounts himself and manipulated the aged debtor analysis.

What to look for:

- part-paid items on the sales ledger
- large numbers of journals or adjustments on particular accounts, or on bank reconciliations
- unusual fluctuations or inconsistencies on the aged debtor analysis
- alterations to invoices or frequent issue of 'duplicates' on particular accounts
- differences between original and duplicate paying-in slips or incomplete details or alterations
- differences between paying-in slips, cash book details and ledger postings – for example, re the number of items, dates and payee details
- no independent review of customers who do not pay or who delay payment
- no independent despatch of statements or investigation of complaints or queries

Writing off receivables for a fee

Customers may pay kickbacks to staff in a variety of situations. In the collection phase, credit controllers or other staff may be bribed by a customer to write off outstanding debts and to frustrate legal action, for example, by introducing aspects which may make pursuit of an action more difficult. A possible warning sign of this type of fraud is heavy concentration of provisions/write-offs attributable to one employee or division.

Long firm fraud

In long firm fraud the fraudster obtains goods on credit, purporting to be running a bona fide business. Initially orders are small and payments are made promptly. As the supplier's confidence increases so does the size of the orders and further credit is given. After a few months, when the fraudster believes he has obtained the maximum credit he can obtain, he disposes of the goods quickly at discount prices for cash and disappears without trace, leaving the supplier bills unpaid.

Long firm fraud is probably one of the oldest white-collar crimes. The Victorians complained of the fraudulent activities of 'phantom capitalists'. Long firm fraud tends to be carried out on a highly-organised basis by gangs of fraudsters operating a number of linked businesses using false identities. The risk of long firm fraud is greatly increased where customers are situated in remote locations, making face-to-face contact unlikely.

HERE TODAY GONE TOMORROW

A group of fraudsters, using false identities, set up a number of retail businesses, using off-the-shelf companies. Distinctive headed paper was prepared, orders were placed and credit granted. Some of the credit references given to suppliers were from other companies owned by the fraudsters, who gave glowing references of credit worthiness and financial stability. The initial small orders were all paid promptly. Larger orders were then placed and increased credit given. A central warehouse, owned by the fraudsters, but apparently having no connection with them, was used to collect the goods obtained. The items were then sold to cut price stores and market traders at discount prices. After a few months of operation, the fraudsters disappeared without trace, leaving the supplier bills unpaid.

Similar frauds occur in relation to premium rate calls. A number of lines

184

are set up with the telephone company taking a share of the bills, paying income to the fraudster. Fraudsters set up many phones to make calls to the premium rate numbers to generate income. The fraudster then disappears leaving the premium rate bills unpaid and the bills for the telephones used to make the calls also unpaid.

What to look for:

- air of unreality about the principals or their business premises, for example lack of customer orientation
- rapidly increasing turnover for new customers
- no independent checks on the existence or credentials of referees

Misrepresentation of credit status

This type of fraud includes a wide range of practices which involve impersonation or the submission of false or misleading information.

What to look for:

- poor quality documentation
- use of 'accommodation' offices by new customers
- customers who operate through 'front' companies or intermediaries
- incomplete customer details or undue difficulties in completing normal credit references and other checks

Counterfeit products

Counterfeiting of branded goods is a widespread problem. Detailed consideration of this type of fraud is outside the scope of this guide.

Stock frauds

Introduction

I have discussed above a number of frauds which concern the receipt or despatch of goods. The previous chapter dealt with manipulation of stock valuations, quantities and other aspects. Certain frauds relate specifically to the holding of stock or to the distribution channels into and out of stock. The key concern is theft of inventory but there are also issues to do with the theft of returned stock or valuable scrap and the misuse of metering and weighbridge equipment.

Theft of stock

Stock fraud is endemic in certain industries. The frauds are often conducted on a highly organised basis and involve a large number of employees, sometimes acting in collusion with organised criminals. The frauds may remain undetected for many years. Businesses handling valuable and easily movable products (such as electrical goods and motor vehicle spare parts) are especially vulnerable.

For instance, four employees at an electrical goods manufacturer stole spare parts over an eight-year period. The fraud was masterminded by an electrical salesman, assisted by a lorry driver and forklift driver. The salesman's uncle delivered the stolen parts to shops around the country. The spare parts were sold at discount.

Certain frauds occur on the delivery route from the supplier to the company or on the route from the company to the customer. In one case delivery drivers en route from a manufacturing plant of a well-known sweet manufacturer to a distribution warehouse would unload a portion of the load at another warehouse. The delivery driver colluded with the goods-in clerk at the distribution warehouse to sign off the goods received note for the quantity stated on the delivery note whereas the amount actually delivered was less. The delivery driver and the goods-in clerk shared the proceeds of the stolen stock.

In another case employees at a bulk plaster supplier stole plaster and sold it for cash to the local building trade, splitting the proceeds among factory employees as a 'bonus'. The plaster was loaded onto the lorries, weighed and appropriate delivery documentation produced. However, part of the plaster was unloaded at another warehouse used by the conspirators before it reached its destination. The fraud was not detected by the company's customers, who were small to medium-sized building contractors, because most did not have weighbridges and were content to have the plaster tipped into their silos or storage bins. They relied on the delivery note as confirmation of the quantity delivered.

EMPLOYEES PUTTING ON WEIGHT

Employees at a major car manufacturer stole £2 million of spare parts by taping components to their bodies. A union agreement banned body searches. The parts were pooled and then sold to the public in bogus manufacturer's packaging.

What to look for:

- unexplained differences between book and physical stock

- stock turnover in particular locations inconsistent with the general level of turnover

- poor margins or unusual fluctuations

- delivery drivers driving part-loaded vehicles or asking for routes to be amended or asking to do the same routes

- deliveries received or made at unusual times of the day

- no monitoring of stock losses and no regular stock counts

- weak goods received or despatch procedure

- poor control over stock movements at the time of stocktakes

- poor control over unaccepted loads or incorrect loads

- no independent follow-up of customer complaints, for example re substandard products, delays in delivery or short deliveries

Theft of returned stock or valuable scrap

Frauds involving returned stock or valuable scrap are quite common. Rich pickings can be made by the opportunist fraudster.

In one case partly-damaged stock returned by customers to a building material manufacturer was removed by warehouse staff and sold to the public. In another case, an employee at a manufacturing company who was responsible for sending high quality scrap metal to another company for reprocessing colluded with an employee at the processing company to falsify the weights and types of metal sent for reprocessing. The profits from the 'lost' metal were shared between the employees.

Metering and weighbridge frauds

Metering and weighbridge equipment is prone to tampering. Regular checks on such equipment are therefore essential. Frequent break-downs or faults occurring at unusual times should be regarded with suspicion and investigated thoroughly.

BOGUS WEIGHBRIDGE TICKETS

A managing director conspired to defraud a council, in collusion with seven other members of the company, while working on road surfacing contracts worth £2.5 million. The fraud involved bogus weighbridge tickets for road building materials. The company owned its own quarry. The weighbridge operators would generate a false ticket relating to a non-existent load, forge the signature of the driver and send it to the site. Bogus tickets would be incorporated with the real tickets.

Cash and payments

Introduction

As one would expect, the scope for fraud and malpractice in the cash and payments area is huge. The most common types of fraud are:

- misuse of cheques and payment systems;
- manipulation of bank reconciliations and cash books;
- money transfer frauds;
- forged cheques.

In addition to the above, certain frauds in the next chapter relating to dealing may be relevant to treasury departments in larger companies.

Cheque fraud

Cheque frauds involve the use of forged signatures, stolen cheques or cheque-books, misuse of cancelled cheques, unsupported cash advances and the theft of cash or cash equivalents. For example, in one case an employee took three cheques from the back of an unused cheque-book. The employee then forged the signatures on the cheques, making the cheques payable to a connected company. In another case the accounting function of a company's regional office was largely under the control of one person. The individual made unsupported cash advances to himself using old unclaimed credit balances to conceal the debit entries.

DOUBLE DEALER

A bought ledger clerk opened a bank account in a name similar to a supplier used by his employer. The account was opened using a forged driving licence for identification. Two sets of payment documentation were then raised by the employee. The first set, designed to generate the fraudulent cheque, was sent with a large number of other payments for authorisation to a manager. Aware that the accounting system might generate reports highlighting possible duplicate payments, the false payment was for £2,000 more than the amount due to the supplier. A payment requisition form, which the manager had to sign, showing the inflated amount was placed in front of the invoice for the actual amount.

The employee took a calculated risk that the manager would not check each set of documentation to ensure that the amounts were the same. If he had noticed it, the employee would have apologised for making the error. A few days later, a second payment authorisation was raised for the correct amount, using the original documentation. As the supplier was doing significant levels of business with the organisation, the false payment would not appear unusual to anyone in the payment process. The fraudulent cheque was then taken from the mail by the employee once it had been raised and signed. Towards the end of the working day, envelopes containing cheques were left in the office out-tray overnight. The cheque was then presented for payment the next day into the bank account opened for the purpose.

What to look for:

Cheque stock security

- cheque stock kept in desk drawers or filing cabinets

- computer cheques left on printer

- poor voiding procedures for unused or spoilt cheques

- cashier's office in open plan area or in a room without lock or with movable partitions

- no restrictions on access to cashier's area

Cheque processing

- poor segregation of duties between key functions such as ordering and payments

- unnecessary use of cheques when other methods such as direct credit or electronic methods of payment may be used

- payee and amount lines not crossed through

- payee details abbreviated , for example 'IR' for 'Inland Revenue'

- cheques left unattended on desks awaiting signature or despatch

- cheques left in in-trays or out-trays overnight or in unlocked desk drawers or filing cabinets

- cheques sent in internal mail envelopes or specially coloured transmission wallets

Post handling

- cheques sent in semi-transparent envelopes or with indications of contents visible through window, e.g., 'remit to' or 'treasury department'

- envelopes containing cheques left in post basket overnight

- incoming or outgoing post left in bags in vulnerable areas, for example near entrances before staff arrive

Other

- no clear desk policy overnight – cheques or documents including bank account details and signatures left lying around

- poor access control over contractors' staff

- poor security over building, especially during alterations

- weak recruitment screening procedures and/or weak recruitment screening by contractors or agents whose staff have access to your building

- no fraud response plan to capture, evaluate and investigate suspicions of fraud or theft

Electronic payments fraud

Some very large frauds have occurred in this area. Many more have been attempted. The example below involved a payment of £23 million. Another attempted fraud, dressed up as a covert operation to secure the release of British hostages in the Middle East, involved an attempt to divert £40 million to a bank account in the Isle of Man.

Often these frauds are possible because the controls over the release of funds are inappropriate for the amounts involved. For example, at a financial institution processing was carried out by junior personnel and the final release of funds was dependent only on a check that the signatory was authorised to sign. This was insufficient for the amount involved (US$70 million).

ATTEMPT TO DIVERT £23 MILLION

A senior accounts assistant in an oil company conspired to defraud the company of £23 million by seeking to divert an annual lease payment relating to an oil rig to a bank account in Switzerland. The accounts assistant stole the form authorising the transfer of the funds and substituted an international payment application directing the money to the Swiss bank account. An employee at the company's bank queried the payment application when he saw a message written on the top of the application urging the bank to make payment on time.

What to look for:

- payment devices kept outside locked safes

- passwords written on guidance booklets, by screens, etc.

- evidence of payments being made where one or both authorised members of staff have not been involved, even if the payments are legitimate

- payee bank accounts the same as employees' salary bank accounts

- payee names the same as employee names, payee name abbreviated, payee name is the employer's name, etc

- lack of segregation of duties, for example the person making payments also does the bank reconciliation

- manager review of bank reconciliations is not taking place or is only a cursory review

- untidy balance sheet with unnecessary credit balances and provisions

- poor accountability of budget holders allowing incorrect or fraudulent payments to be posted to expense accounts

Manipulation of bank reconciliations and cash books

Bank reconciliations are usually regarded as a strong control. However, such reconciliations must be properly prepared and subject to a thorough independent check from time to time to be effective. Cursory review and approval by management is not sufficient. A number of frauds would have been spotted if reconciliations had been completely reperformed periodically, for example during enforced holiday absence, and the details checked to other ledgers and supporting documentation.

Reconciliations are now frequently prepared using spreadsheet programs. Changing formulae on these spreadsheets is easy. For example, it is quite easy to insert +£29,995 into the totals formula to make the reconciliation appear to balance, the item being a fraudulent payment.

Other concealment devices include:

- rolling matching;
- incorrect description of reconciling items;
- incorrect description of items in cash books; or
- the use of compensating debits and credits in other ledgers to make the bank reconciliation 'work'.

Rolling matching is the incorrect matching of items on reconciliations to facilitate the concealment of fraudulent items. This is most likely to happen when numerous items of a similar amount flow through an account.

What to look for:

- no independent detailed check of bank reconciliations – cursory review only
- excessive numbers of contras and adjustments on reconciliations
- no review of endorsements or alterations on returned cheques

Money transfer fraud

Money transfer frauds involve the misuse of systems by external fraudsters to make fraudulent transfers of funds. Quite often these frauds involve collusion with management and employees. Fraudsters misuse passwords and authorisation codes or forge the documentation authorising transfers. Similar frauds in the financial sector are covered under Other external banking frauds in the next chapter.

What to look for:

- transfers to or from accounts in offshore locations or countries with bank secrecy laws
- transfers to or from individuals who are not regular suppliers
- abbreviated payee names or alterations to the date, amount, payee or other details
- poor control over documents between approval and processing
- processing of significant transactions by junior personnel
- poor security over the room from which transfer instructions are issued or over codes and passwords

Forged cheques

This type of fraud involves the theft of cheques or cheque-books or the manufacture of forged cheques by external fraudsters. The forgeries may be based on cheques, cancelled cheques or returned cheques and other documents containing authorised signatories. Alternatively the documents may be used to obtain cheque-books from the company's bankers. Devices are also used by fraudsters to scan signatures in order to forge cheques or other instructions to banks.

Possible warning signs are as for misuse of cheques and payment systems above.

Other areas

In this section I cover frauds affecting other areas:

- share support schemes;
- misuse of pension funds and other assets;
- company car scheme frauds;
- payroll frauds;

193

- misuse of intercompany and suspense accounts;

- bogus curriculum vitae;

- bogus insurance cover.

Share support schemes

There are many well-known cases of directors using company funds to support the price of the shares in their companies. Off-shore companies and other complex structures are used to conceal the identity of the purchaser. 'Consultancy' or other fees may be paid to counterparties to purchase shares.

The motivation for such schemes is greatest when a company's share price is about to fall, maybe due to the announcement of poor trading results or some other factor such as the imminent departure of a key director/shareholder with shares to sell. Maybe, a senior executive with a large shareholding lives expensively and has borrowed heavily on the shares of the company. Share support schemes may also be used when a company is about to make a significant acquisition, when the market price of the company's shares may be critical.

It is difficult to identify possible warning signs for all the schemes which may be used. The financial position of the company, its trading performance, recent movements in its share prices, stock market conditions generally and any significant proposed transactions, such as a major acquisition, will be important. Evidence of complex structures, including a pattern of purchases by offshore companies or transactions which are shrouded in secrecy, should be regarded with suspicion.

SUB-UNDERWRITING YOUR OWN SHARE ISSUE

Two directors of a company allegedly paid for millions of pounds of shares in their company by laundering company funds through private offshore companies set up for the purpose. One of the directors was a sub-underwriter for an issue of shares and used company funds to meet his obligations as underwriter.

GETTING OUT WHILE THE GOING IS GOOD

The chairman of a quoted company sold a large holding of his company's shares just before an announcement of worse than expected figures, thereby avoiding a loss of approximately £1 million. Shortly afterwards the chairman resigned and trading in the company's shares was suspended. When trading resumed the shares traded at one-third of the original price. The chairman drew up a deed of gift, purporting to give his shares to his girlfriend. In fact he had authorised his bank to sell them after his resignation.

Misuse of pension funds or other assets

Pension funds and other assets may be used to bail out ailing companies. There have been a number of cases where pension fund assets have been stolen or used as security to obtain loans. In other cases assets have been transferred from the employing company to the pension fund at above their market value.

A SINKING SHIP

The chief executive of a construction company which was in financial difficulties allegedly stole a cheque for nearly £1 million and shares in various quoted companies from the group's pension fund.

What to look for:

- access to assets created through legal arrangements – for example, powers of attorney, investment management agreements and trustee companies
- pension fund has different accounting period from employer
- transfers of assets between employing company and the pension fund where the market value cannot be readily ascertained

Company car scheme frauds

Company car scheme frauds usually involve the sale of ex-fleet cars to connected parties at discount prices. External frauds include overbilling for labour on servicing or repairs, in particular where the invoice is passed directly to the employing company (i.e., not inspected by the

195

employee) with the company car. Agency cards may be misused to purchase fuel, spare parts or other items for use on non-company vehicles.

EX-FLEET CARS GOING CHEAP

The manager of a company car scheme stole over 100 vehicles. Many were sold cheaply in secret to senior employees. None of the employees asked where the vehicles came from because they felt they had earned the bargains by hard work.

SECRETARY COLLECTS EX-FLEET CARS

The manager of a company car fleet was suspected of having sold company cars at less than their market value. In the previous 18 months five company cars had been sold to the same secretary.

What to look out for:

- no independent checks on the prices at which, and the parties to whom, company cars are sold
- same purchaser for a range of models
- single source of supply for key services such as repairs

Payroll and pension frauds

Payroll frauds involve the use of dummy employees, unauthorised increases to salaries and bogus commissions, bonuses and overtime payments. The risk of such frauds is particularly high when segregation of duties is poor and where remote locations are poorly supervised.

PHANTOM OF THE FACTORY

A manager at a remote plant, where there was a large number of employees, was responsible for submitting time cards and summary sheets for employees. He input details for a dummy employee over a three-year period.

Where there is poor control in pension administration departments, it can be easy for fraud to be perpetrated. For example, in one case a fraudster identified pensioners without next of kin. When these pensioners died, he suppressed this fact and arranged to pay ongoing pension payments into bank accounts under his control.

What to look for:

- no checks on bonuses, commissions and overtime payments

- employees not on voters' register

- no zero-based budgets

- failure to take employees off payroll when they leave employment. Salary details can be transferred to the fraudster

Misuse of intercompany and suspense accounts

We saw in the previous chapter how intercompany accounts are used in accounts manipulation. Intercompany accounts and suspense accounts can be used to conceal other frauds. Intercompany accounts may not be reconciled regularly or items may be incorrectly described as 'timing differences' when in fact there is a discrepancy, i.e., one set of books is wrong.

Suspense accounts also require careful scrutiny. It is important to review the nature of items passing through suspense accounts during the year (including 'contra' items) even if the account is cleared to zero at the year end. Review of the activity on suspense accounts may reveal unusual patterns of entries.

Sometimes suspense accounts are used when none are needed. This enables fraudsters to shift fraudulent items between various accounts, creating a complex web of entries to cover their tracks.

What to look for:

- intercompany accounts not reconciled and adjustments not posted (all differences treated as 'timing' differences) especially accounts which are not strictly intercompany i.e., with associates or related parties outside the group

- reasons for transactions, particularly with overseas companies, unclear or shrouded in secrecy

- high volume of items passing through suspense accounts, even if apparently cleared at the year end

- large round sum cash movements

197

Bogus curriculum vitae

Many companies do not have effective recruitment screening procedures. Fraudsters may have committed similar frauds in their previous employments. Items on job applications or matters which come up during interview may provide a clue.

JUST THE MAN FOR THE JOB

An individual who had already served a four-year prison sentence for obtaining property by deception obtained a job claiming he had an MBA, fluency in Mandarin, Chinese and Japanese and a glowing reference from a Home Office minister. The CV and the reference were completely bogus.

What to look for:

- references not checked or references being given by friends or ex-workmates rather than management or human resources

- inconsistencies or gaps in employment history not followed up

- grandiose claims

- attempts to mislead, contradictory answers, extreme defensiveness or excessive bravado when questioned about certain matters

Bogus insurance cover

Cases have been reported of bogus insurance policies being offered to companies by insurance intermediaries. These frauds usually involve the forgery of insurance documentation of well-known insurance companies.

NOT WORTH THE PAPER IT'S WRITTEN ON

A company which offered extended insurance guarantees on electrical appliances defrauded a number of major companies of more than £6 million by issuing bogus insurance warranties. The company used photocopying machines to create bogus documents which were passed off as five-year extended insurance guarantees.

What to look for:

- quality of documentation below the standard expected
- unusually low insurance premiums
- intermediary ensures that all contact with the insurer is via him

Conclusion

Table 6.1 summarises the frauds discussed in this chapter. It is not intended to be comprehensive list of all frauds that may occur in manufacturing and services companies. It should be used as an aide-mémoire when undertaking more detailed risk profiling in particular companies. (See page 200.)

Table 6.1 Fraud in manufacturing and services

Purchasing	Sales	Stock	Treasury	Other
• Bid fixing	• Diversion of sales	• Theft of stock	• Cheque fraud	• Share support schemes
• Kickbacks	• Bogus goods	• Theft of stock from distribution channels	• Electronic payments fraud	• Misuse of pension fund assets
• Private supplies	• Kickbacks	• Theft of returned stock	• Manipulation of bank recs	• Company car scheme frauds
• Dummy suppliers	• Teeming and lading	• Theft of valuable scrap	• Money transfer fraud	• Payroll and pension frauds
• Connected companies	• Write-off of debtors for a fee	• Metering and weigh-bridge frauds	• Forged cheques	• Intercompany account frauds
• Bid rigging	• Long firm fraud		• Dealing frauds	• Bogus CVs
• Advance fee fraud	• Misrepresentation of credit status			• Bogus insurance cover
• Short deliveries	• Counterfeit products			
• Substandard product fraud				
• Overbilling				

7

Fraud in the financial sector

Introduction

Companies in the financial sector are susceptible to many of the frauds described in the previous two chapters. These are general types of fraud that may affect virtually any company. But the financial sector is also subject to a large number of more specialised frauds. Some of these are similar to frauds in other sectors but for the most part they are best understood in the context of particular businesses in the financial sector. Some are unique to those businesses.

In this chapter I examine frauds in banking, investment business and insurance.

Banking

Frauds in banks fall into four main areas:

- credit;

- deposit taking;

- dealing;

- other areas.

As in the previous chapter, I look at the key phases in each business process and the points at which the various frauds typically occur.

Credit

Introduction

There are three main aspects to the lending process:

- introduction and appraisal of the borrower;
- taking security and the release of funds;
- payment of interest, repayment of the loan principal and the release of security.

The most common frauds at each stage of the process are illustrated in Figure 7.1. (See page 203.)

At the **introduction and appraisal** stage, the main concerns relate to the identity of the borrower, his financial status, who introduced the borrower and on what terms. Internal frauds include creation of fictitious loans or the granting of loans to connected borrowers, usually disguised by the use of nominee or 'front' companies.

Lending to connected borrowers may also be disguised by what is known as 'deposit transformation': the fraudster places a deposit with a 'friendly' bank, which in turn lends the money, against the security of the deposit, to a nominated beneficiary of the fraudster. Management may also approve loans in which they have an undisclosed interest, for example through joint venture or profit sharing arrangements.

Management may seek to conceal the extent of lending to particular borrowers so that they appear to meet regulatory requirements or disguise the identity of certain borrowers to conceal their credit status. Management and employees may also be bribed by borrowers to obtain credit. External frauds include impersonation and the submission of false information on loan applications.

In the second phase, **taking security and the release of funds**, the key concerns relate to the nature and value of the security, ensuring that there is no release of funds before appropriate security is taken, and whether the loan funds are used by the customer for the purpose for which they were intended. Internal frauds include using the bank's own funds to provide collateral for its lending. External frauds include double pledging of collateral by borrowers, land flips (involving sales between connected parties to boost valuations artificially for collateral purposes), fraudulent valuations, the use of forged or valueless

---

Figure 7.1 Typical credit frauds

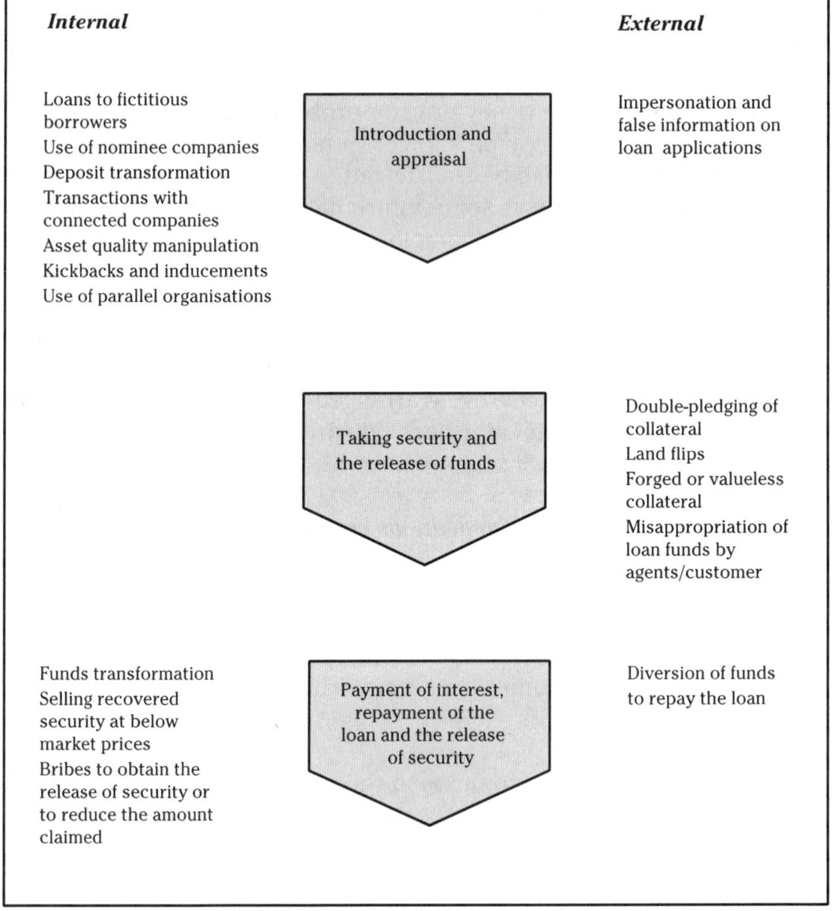

Internal   **External**

Loans to fictitious
borrowers   Introduction and   Impersonation and
Use of nominee companies   appraisal   false information on
Deposit transformation   loan applications
Transactions with
connected companies
Asset quality manipulation
Kickbacks and inducements
Use of parallel organisations

                                                        Double-pledging of
                                 Taking security and   collateral
                                 the release of funds   Land flips
                                                        Forged or valueless
                                                        collateral
                                                        Misappropriation of
                                                        loan funds by
                                                        agents/customer

Funds transformation   Payment of interest,   Diversion of funds
Selling recovered   repayment of the   to repay the loan
security at below   loan and the release
market prices   of security
Bribes to obtain the
release of security or
to reduce the amount
claimed

---

collateral, loan funds used for a different purpose than that indicated on the loan application and misappropriation of loan funds by solicitors and agents.

In the final phase, **payment of interest, repayment of the loan and the release of security**, the main concerns are that payments are made in accordance with the loan agreement and that the payments are in fact made by the borrower. Where a problem arises with the payment of either interest or principal, management may seek to give a false impression of the financial soundness of particular borrowers, to avoid making provisions or to meet regulatory requirements. The fraudster may achieve this by generating false activity on loan accounts, usually by circulating the bank's own money or depositors' funds and 'transforming' the funds into an apparent repayment from the borrower.

Alternatively, management may transfer problem loans to other parts of the group, where they may be subject to less scrutiny by auditors or regulators. Loans may also be transferred to connected parties with an agreement to repurchase at some future date. External frauds include bribes paid to management or employees to obtain the release of the security before the loan is repaid.

Finally, sales of recovered security are often poorly controlled and offer internal fraudsters opportunities to profit personally. In one case, a bank credit officer even arranged loans to co-conspirators to purchase such assets at prices much lower than their market values.

Loans to fictitious borrowers

Loans to fictitious borrowers involve the creation of fictitious loans using false names and addresses and phoney financial information. Other frauds involve individuals or companies with good credit status 'lending' their names to others to obtain loans, in other words acting as 'front men'.

This type of fraud is quite common in the retail banking sector where a large number of false loan applications, each for a relatively small amount, may be involved.

GAMBLING HABIT

Without the customers' knowledge or consent, a branch manager created overdraft facilities on five customers who were entitled to overdrafts but did not use them. He forged 200 cheques drawn on these accounts amounting to US$59 million to fund a serious gambling habit. There was poor monitoring by head office and internal audit of accounts introduced or facilities extended, especially those introduced or handled exclusively by the branch manager. There was also no review of the underlying business relating to significant accounts.

FALSE LOANS USING REAL CUSTOMER NAME

A branch manager defrauded the bank of US$8 million. The fraud involved falsification of customer loan applications using a real customer's name. The fraud was only picked up when the company whose name had been used on fraudulent documents alerted the bank to discrepancies on account records. The fraud was not picked up by head office inspectors who visited the bank each year.

What to look for:

- 'thin' loan files with sketchy, incomplete financial information or photocopied or scrappy documentation

- loans or overdrafts where there is little documentation and management claim the borrower is wealthy and his 'creditworthiness is undoubted'

- borrowers with common names or like-sounding names or a significant number of borrowers introduced by the same source

- borrowers not on the voters' register, missing credit checks or references or discrepancies not followed up

- valuations which seem high, valuers used from outside the usually permitted area or the same valuer used on numerous applications

- commercial customers or significant personal borrowers who are not generally known to staff

- funds released before all the necessary formalities have been completed

- remuneration closely linked to the number and/or value of new loans

- generous extensions or revised terms when the borrower defaults

Use of nominee companies

Other more sophisticated devices are used to conceal fictitious or connected lending. Rather than lend funds in personal names the fraudster may seek to disguise the borrowing through offshore companies or trustee or management arrangements.

Files kept outside the main filing system or documentation kept in the offices of senior officials which apparently does not relate to the institution should be regarded with suspicion. Similarly, evasive replies concerning particular loans or when access to such documentation is requested may provide a clue to such arrangements.

PERSONAL PAPERS

The managing director at a bank made a loan to himself via an offshore company owned by him. The loan file implied that the company was owned by one of the director's contacts rather than the director himself. It suggested that the company was owned by one of his contacts overseas and that the managing director had merely introduced the business. The file indicated that the loan was to meet short-term working capital requirements. However, there was very little information on file about the company, its directors, its activities or financial position. Other documents, which revealed the true nature of the loan, were kept in his office

What to look for:

- 'thin' loan files with sketchy or incomplete financial information

- loans to individuals or companies in remote jurisdictions, outside the area of the bank's or branch's normal operations

- loans to offshore companies with no clear business purpose

- complex structures shrouded in secrecy

- few details on file about the individuals behind particular companies or arrangements

- a strong recommendation from a senior official at the bank but few other details to support the loan

- like-sounding names between borrowers

- sole contact customers (i.e., handled exclusively by one member of staff)

Deposit transformation

A further way in which management may disguise connected lending is to make the loan at one remove by what is sometimes called 'deposit transformation'. This involves the fraudster placing a deposit with another bank which in turn lends money to a nominated beneficiary of the fraudster against the security of the deposit. No record of the pledge or the contingent liability arising in respect of the ultimate loan is made, thereby not only concealing the credit exposure but also retaining the benefit of the deposit to satisfy liquidity reporting requirements.

AN UNUSUAL STRATEGY

An overseas bank with liquidity problems made substantial medium-term deposits with a disreputable bank when the funds were urgently required to meet pressing commitments. It transpired that the deposits had been used by the disreputable bank to secure lending by that bank to a company related to the directors.

What to look for:

- pledges over deposits (disclosed by confirmations which have specifically requested such pledges to be disclosed)

- deposits which are continually rolled over

- long-term deposits placed with other banks when liquidity is tight

- unusual counterparties

- documentation or files held in directors' or senior managers' offices outside the usual filing areas

- evasive replies when access to such documents is requested

- weak controls over the giving and recording of guarantees

Transactions with connected companies

Certain loans may appear to be to third-party borrowers. However, joint venture agreements or profit sharing arrangements, from which a director or senior official of the bank may benefit (on an undisclosed basis), may be linked to the loan. Usually the loan would not have been entered into but for the hidden arrangement.

LETTERS OF RECOMMENDATION

A loan was granted to a well-known business tycoon who diverted an industrial loan for personal use. The credit director and finance director of the bank based their review of the borrower's creditworthiness on letters of recommendation of high ranking officials rather than sound business data and proper security. There was weak ongoing monitoring of the actual use of loan funds. A chief adviser of the country's president gave a letter of reference that was used as a recommendation to obtain the loan. The finance director also claimed that the chairman of the state auditing board had ordered him to continue providing the loan despite irregularities.

207

FALSE FINANCIAL STATEMENTS

Loans amounting to US$236 million were granted to an individual who owned several companies. He diverted funds from loans to 10 of his companies to pay personal expenses and to repay other loans. The banks took financial data supporting the loan applications at face value. The borrower submitted false financial statements, inventory lists and invoices in support of loan applications. There was weak ongoing monitoring of the actual use of funds.

FINANCING PRIVATE BUSINESS INTERESTS

The chairman approved loans amounting to US$1.8 million to finance the private businesses of one of the bank's other directors. The director concerned was also a partner in the law firm which provided significant legal advice to the bank. In his capacity as legal adviser, he represented the bank on loans to his own businesses. In fact the loans were not properly secured and were not repaid. The chairman also received kickbacks from the director in return for the award of other legal work to the director's law firm.

What to look for:

• as for loans to fictitious borrowers and use of nominee companies

• jottings on files which are not consistent with other information on file (for example, names, addresses, telephone numbers of unknown individuals)

• repayments made by persons other than the borrower

Asset quality manipulation

Management may need to conceal the extent of lending to particular borrowers, either to avoid provisions or to meet regulatory requirements. Asset quality manipulation involves various forms of manipulation designed to enhance, artificially, the apparent quality of assets.

LARGE EXPOSURES

The chief executive of a bank agreed with a particular borrower that the finance for a series of large projects overseas should be spread between a number of off-shore companies. The ownership of the companies was carefully disguised so that the true extent of the borrowings to the customer was concealed from the auditors and the regulator. Certain of the projects ran into difficulties. The complex structure enabled advances to be made in respect of apparently new, unconnected ventures to meet loan repayments on the ventures which were in difficulties.

HIDDEN STAKES

A director of a bank approved a loan to an offshore company in order for the company to purchase shares in a public company. A sharp increase in the share price was predicted. A director of the bank and the finance director of the company were joint shareholders of the offshore company. The bank director's shareholdings in the off-shore company were not disclosed to his fellow directors. The anticipated increase in the share price did not occur. Subsequently, the finance director of the public company defaulted on the loan repayments. The director of the bank made a number of repayments on his behalf via another offshore company owned by him so that the loan did not come under scrutiny by his fellow directors or the auditors.

Possible warning signs as for use of nominee companies.

Kickbacks and inducements

Borrowers may offer bribes to management and employees to obtain credit or to manipulate lending criteria. The risk of this type of fraud is increased where the remuneration of loan officers is closely linked to the number or value of new loans entered into. There is also a risk that unwise lending may take place at the end of bonus assessment periods in order to earn commissions.

WHO WANTS TO BE A MILLIONAIRE?

A corporate borrower ran into cash flow problems because it was difficult to sell certain of its assets. At the financial year end, the company's auditors needed proof that it could meet its debts before they could sign the accounts. The branch manager, whose bank was the largest loan provider to the borrower, wrote letters offering 'open-ended' support on bank notepaper, without telling his head office. The letters were not authorised by the bank and its senior management had no idea of the commitment the manager was making on its behalf. Although the manager frequently reported to head office in the USA, he had day-to-day control of the borrower's account. The letters stated that 'the bank is prepared to make available funds to meet any shortfall in cash flow'. The chairman of the borrower paid £1 million to the branch manager for providing the letters.

What to look for:

- excessive amounts of business generated by particular loan officers

- lending criteria overridden regularly by particular loan officers

- sole contact customers

- concentration of lending in particular sectors or through particular sources of introduction

- change in pattern of business towards high risk areas

- strong recommendation by director or lending officer but missing data or documentation on credit file

Use of parallel organisations

'Parallel organisations' are companies under common control of the directors and/or shareholders. Such companies are often used in Asset quality manipulation and funds transformation (see below). However, they may also be used for other purposes, for example, undisclosed sale and repurchase agreements, circular refinancing arrangements and sales at other than market value.

Parallel organisations may also be used to secure the bank's own lending. This is usually achieved by a series of transactions which result in the bank's own funds being transferred into off-shore companies, which are ostensibly third party depositors. The funds deposited in these accounts are then used as cash collateral for the lending.

PRESSING PERSONAL NEEDS

A bank made a short-term loan to an individual overseas to meet 'pressing personal needs'. The loan was secured by a cash deposit from an offshore company. In fact, the individual was a friend of the managing director who had incurred large gambling debts. The offshore company was owned by the managing director and the funds transferred to the deposit account were drawn from other customers' funds held on long-term deposit or under hold-mail arrangements.

PASSING THE PARCEL

A bank purchased loans from a parallel bank (ultimately under common ownership) before its year end in exchange for an unrecorded arrangement whereby the parallel

210

bank would repurchase the loans at face value after its year end. In order to conceal the transaction from the head office auditors, these loans were transferred to a subsidiary which was given unrecorded guarantees to support the loans.

LAUNDRY

The branch manager of a bank dealt personally with certain depositors and their accounts when these would normally have been managed by more junior members of staff. It transpired that the manager was assisting depositors to launder funds through overseas branches of the bank, returning them to the home country represented as deposits by non-residents on which interest was treated as non-taxable.

What to look for:

- unexpected settlement of problem loans shortly before the period end or prior to an audit visit
- unexpected new lending close to the period end
- transfers of loans, especially to companies which are suspected to have some connection with the directors and/or shareholders
- poor controls over the giving and recording of guarantees or similar commitments
- transactions or structures shrouded in secrecy
- changes in the pattern of business with related organisations

Funds transformation

When it is likely that a borrower may default on a loan, management may seek to give a false impression of the financial soundness of the borrowers. This may be to avoid making provisions or to satisfy regulatory requirements. 'Funds transformation' involves concealment of the nature or source of funds. For example, the bank's own funds may be routed, via subsidiaries, branches, associated companies or other companies under common ownership, to 'transform' the funds into an apparent repayment from the borrower. Sometimes the loans involved may be connected with the directors or staff of the bank in some way or set up for some fraudulent purpose.

ROUND THE HOUSES

A bank made a loan to purchase a property development undertaken by the chairman's brother-in-law. The loan was non-performing and there was a shortfall on the security. The bank transferred an amount equal to the shortfall through a branch, a subsidiary and an associated institution under its management and back to the bank as though they were a receipt from the chairman's brother-in-law.

What to look for:

- sources of receipt which are inconsistent with the standing data

- transactions with companies within a group or with its associated companies where the business purpose is unclear

- arrangements involving offshore companies and/or companies under common ownership

- annotations on file which do not appear to relate to the borrower (for example, names, addresses, telephone numbers and other jottings)

- files kept outside the normal filing areas

Selling recovered security at below market prices

Many banks have strong credit procedures and controls relating to the main part of the credit cycle. However, procedures and controls may be much less rigorous in situations where the borrower has defaulted and the bank is in possession of the recovered security. Checks over the prices at which and the parties to whom such assets are sold are sometimes very weak providing the opportunity for officers of the bank to obtain hidden profits or kickbacks.

Bribes to obtain release of security or reduce amount claimed

Just as bribes may be paid to loan officers to obtain credit in the first place, so they may be paid by borrowers to obtain the release of security before the loan principal has been repaid. Bribes may also encourage loan officers to reduce their bank's claims after the loan is in default.

Impersonation

Turning now to external banking frauds, impersonation and the submission of false information on loan applications are significant threats for any bank. Banks most vulnerable to this type of activity are those with inexperienced loan officers or where appraisal of loans is largely a desk top review. Vulnerability to this type of fraud is high during periods of rapid growth when banks may be keen to gain market share.

Another aspect which is crucial at the appraisal stage is assessing who the introducer of the business is and how well he knows the borrower. A bank may think that the introducer, for example a firm of solicitors or accountants, knows the customer well. This might not be the case. The borrower may be a recent acquaintance. The firm may be simply keen to develop a relationship with the customer. It is also important to look at concentrations of business obtained from introducers, in particular loan brokers, and possible connections between the introducer and personnel of the bank.

Examples of false information on loan applications include:

(a) grandiose claims concerning the borrower's business credentials. For example, a borrower, who requested a loan for the purchase and refurbishment of a hotel, claimed to have extensive experience of the hotel industry whereas he had never owned or run a hotel;

(b) false accounts – a borrower falsified a set of audited accounts. The accounts appeared genuine in every way, except the source and application of funds statement did not add up; and

(c) false accounting records or other data relating to the business. For example, directors of an ailing toy manufacturing company used fake computer records of sales to convince banks and finance companies to lend them money.

PIPE AND SLIPPERS

The fraud involved fake identities and switching money from one account to another to create the impression of solid creditworthiness. The fraudster, known as the 'pipe and slippers fraudster' so staggeringly boring was his life, had recently been released from prison and he embarked on a plan to defraud banks of £1 million.

He did not smoke, drink, gamble or own a car, despite obtaining 10 driving licences. He created nine different identities with 11 banks and opened 90 accounts. For each identity he took a driving test to get his licence. This was then used to get accommodation (in which he left the same items: a suit, shoes, a shirt, underwear and herbal teabags) and to open bank accounts. The accounts were serviced with money moved from other accounts so that he could get a good credit rating, with money paid in as if it were a monthly salary.

He would get the maximum loan available which would normally be £15,000 and then he would change that address and use a business centre to deal with the mail. He had a sophisticated card index system, with each identity having its own reference which was divided into different colours for each bank account, so that he could see at a glance how much credit he had on cards and accounts and how much room for further loans. The fraud was found out when a security officer of one of the banks noticed an unusual sequence of account numbers and transactions. He began to investigate and, after speaking to other banks, the fraud was suspected and the case passed to the police.

What to look for:

- grandiose claims not corroborated

- extravagant lifestyle or lavish entertaining of bank officials by the customer

- no on-site appraisal of borrower

- business ventures too good to be true

- inexperienced loan officers

- sole contact customers

- difficulty in obtaining corroboration of the individual's credentials, inconsistent or missing documentation and inconsistencies in personal details (such as voter's register and credit status checks)

False financial information

False financial information may be submitted at the time of application for the loan, during the life of the loan as up-to-date information is requested by the bank, or when the loan goes into default. All manner of information can be falsified including details relating to the nature of the underlying business or contract, its returns, false financial statements, false supporting sales invoices and other vouchers. The following examples illustrate the wide range of deceptions.

SHAM GUARANTEES

The borrower specialised in providing and renting expensive classic cars. It leased directly or bought expensive items from individuals and leased them back. Over six years it expanded from a turnover of £2 million to £38 million. The company was financed by loans from syndicates of merchant banks. The directors deceived the consortium of banks over the true state of the leases on vehicles and equipment to a major lessee. Many of the loans were backed up by sham guarantees. In certain cases advances were made against fixtures and fittings of a borrower which were not allowed to be used as security for a loan. The directors also received bribes for arranging finance for a borrower. The problems were discovered after the company was put into receivership.

FALSE SALES INVOICES

A corporate borrower hired mechanical plant to local authorities and contractors. The firm ran into financial problems, partly due to rapid expansion. The director submitted copies of false invoices for work she claimed her company had done. The bank advanced her 70 per cent of the value of the invoice, on the basis that it would get back the loan with interest when the invoice was eventually paid. The fake invoices involved bills of work in districts not covered by the local authorities and for work on roads which did not exist. The director disguised what was going on quite carefully until the sheer volume of false invoices being put through the system overwhelmed her. The fraud came to light when discrepancies were discovered.

FALSE CVs

A company expanded to become the largest hairdressing chain in Europe. Its rapid growth had been partly based on a rights issue of over £5 million. The primary source of its income was the profit made from franchise salons. The company gave cash advances to franchisees who would use them to secure large bank loans. But as soon as the loans were paid out, all the money was repaid to the company. The lending was based on false CVs of franchisees. The company used the circular lending arrangements, amounting to £11 million, to be treated as income to boost profits.

FALSE DOCUMENTS AND SALES INVOICES

A corporate borrower was in financial difficulties. The directors had hoped that their electrical motor repair business would become the premier repair shop in the UK. The fraud involved the creation of false documents to get loan and overdraft facilities. The borrower creating false invoices to give the impression the company was owed signifi-cant amounts for work done, some of it from major companies.

What to look for:

- scrappy documentation

- inconsistencies within or between documents

- documents apparently from different sources using the same typeface or paper type

- delay in obtaining documents

- missing information, for example VAT numbers on invoices

- evasive replies or lack of knowledge when detail on documents is probed

Double pledging of collateral, land flips and valueless collateral

Many external frauds against banks involve the use of false or misvalued security, for example, the double pledging of collateral, forged or value-less collateral or collateral whose value has been inflated. The latter problem often involves what are known as 'land flips'. These are sales of property between connected parties (usually there is a series of such sales) to boost artificially the valuation of the property for collateral purposes.

Other frauds involve bribes paid to valuers to obtain false valuations. The certificates of other professionals, for example architects' certificates in connection with refurbishment work, are sometimes forged or overstated. The risk of this type of fraud is greatly increased where there are no on-site visits by the bank's staff. For example, in one case if such a visit had been made to the hotel concerned it would have been apparent that although refurbishment work was being undertaken it was of a much lower quality than indicated in the loan application.

FORGED SOLICITOR'S LETTER

The borrower, who was also a practising solicitor, applied for an overdraft facility of £300,000 in connection with a housing development and offered to put his house up as security. The bank then received documentation apparently from a firm of solicitors which appeared to confirm details of the security. However, the solicitor's letter was forged. The house was already subject to a standard security in favour of another building society. When the bank discovered the true position it arranged for the borrower to be sequestrated but found that the borrower had no assets.

Later the same year the borrower had used up all the cash and approached a corporate

216

manager at another well-known bank. Again he offered the same house as security and offered to set aside £275,000 of shares allegedly held on his behalf by a London finance company. He produced a letter apparently from the finance company but again it was forged. The bank was not happy with the documentation and phoned the finance company which confirmed that it held no assets for the borrower. As a result the loan was never advanced. The borrower had conducted a number of developments but had been badly affected by a slump in property prices and soaring interest rates. He was badly placed to finance the completion of his fifth and last development. He believed that there was only a 'temporary blip' in the economy and thought that if he could only complete the development, things would be alright. He committed the fraud in desperation in the belief that all the money would be repaid in a short time.

A DEVELOPMENT IN DOCKLANDS

Seven people connected with a redevelopment in Docklands, including estate agents and solicitors, allegedly arranged for the initial buyers of flats which were being built to resell their properties to various off-shore companies at false market valuations. An overseas bank lent to new buyers on the basis of these valuations assuming that they were open market prices obtained for the properties.

What to look for:

- valuer from outside the area in which the property is situated

- same valuer used in a large number of transactions

- same valuer used by both parties

- series of sales of a particular asset over a short period with values increasing on each sale

- identity of principals difficult to ascertain/use of nominee or 'front' companies

- borrower known to have access to substantial assets (for example, pension fund assets) of a type similar to those pledged

Misappropriation of loan funds by agents/customers

This type of fraud involves the misuse of loan funds by customers, borrowers or their agents.

APPEARANCES CAN BE DECEPTIVE

A number of banks were allegedly defrauded by two individuals who tricked the banks into believing that they were providing short-term loans to fund international trade whereas the cash was going in long-term loans to two bankrupt German companies. The banks were shown bogus bills and letters to convince them that the loans were for international trade.

A BRIDGE TOO FAR

A solicitor obtained over £250,000 from a bank pretending the money was for the use of clients buying property. The solicitor asked the clients to sign blank forms in case bridging loans were required in a hurry. The solicitor had an arrangement with the bank that when bridging loans were required the money would be transferred into his firm's account. However, the money was not used for bridging loans but was instead used to top up his firm's own resources and to fund the solicitor's lifestyle of exotic holidays and lavish entertaining.

Warning signs are as for impersonation/false information on loan applications above.

Diversion of funds to repay loan

Sometimes borrowers decide that they have better use for funds which should be used to repay a loan. The following case is an example of this in a factoring business.

FRAUDULENT FACTORING

The borrower had two companies one of which was a tyre company and the other was a finance company. The bank had granted factoring facilities of £4 million to help the directors to finance their export trade and sales within the UK. The directors failed to tell customers that debts they owed should not be paid to them but should be paid directly to the bank. The money was used as working capital to keep the companies afloat. The directors also submitted bogus invoices to the bank for sales which had never taken place. When the facilities came for renewal there was over £2 million overdue and outstanding to the bank. The companies subsequently went into liquidation.

Deposits

Introduction

The deposit-taking cycle falls into three key phases, as follows:

- verifying the identity of the depositor and establishing the source of funds;

- recording the funds deposited;

- handling the funds in accordance with the customer's instructions.

Typical frauds at each stage of the cycle are illustrated in the following chart.

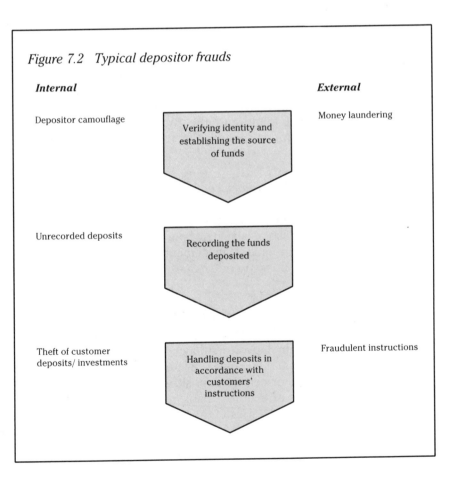

Figure 7.2   Typical depositor frauds

Internal   **External**

Depositor camouflage   Money laundering

Verifying identity and establishing the source of funds

Unrecorded deposits

Recording the funds deposited

Theft of customer deposits/ investments   Fraudulent instructions

Handling deposits in accordance with customers' instructions

Verifying identity of new customers and **establishing the source of the funds** deposited is a key requirement for any bank. The main concern is money laundering. As noted in the Preface, consideration of the legal requirements and the various practical matters which banks should address in relation to money laundering is outside the scope of this guide. In some cases management may collude with depositors to disguise their identity. For example, false names or code names may be used to conceal the identity of customers.

In the next phase, **recording of the funds deposited**, a number of international banking frauds have involved the diversion of deposits to bank accounts controlled by the fraudster (i.e., the deposits are never recorded in the bank's books). Banks most susceptible to this type of fraud are those operating hold-mail arrangements and those taking long-term deposits from overseas customers who are rarely in contact with the bank.

As regards **handling deposits in accordance with the customers' instructions**, the key issues relate to proper segregation of the customers' funds and ensuring that transfers from deposit accounts, or sales of customer investments, are made in accordance with properly authorised instructions. Internal frauds involve the merging of depositor and personal funds and the theft of customer funds or investments. External frauds include the use of fraudulent payment instructions.

Depositors' camouflage

As noted above, management may collude with a depositor to conceal his identity through the use of false names or code names. A large number of such names may be used. Management may also set up accounts themselves using false names or code names to conceal their interest in certain accounts.

Often this will be because the funds which are being deposited are the proceeds of criminal conduct. However, there may be other reasons why the identity of certain depositors may be disguised. For example, a bank may wish to conceal the extent to which its deposit base derives from a particular source or certain depositors may be directors of the bank or their associates or even the bank's own funds used to secure lending to nominated beneficiaries of the directors.

MANAGING DIRECTOR IN DISGUISE

Several accounts at a bank overseas were in fact the managing director and principal shareholder in disguise. Some accounts had like-sounding names. Others were in the names of offshore companies owned by the managing director.

What to look for:

- similar or like-sounding names across various accounts

- offshore company depositors with no clearly defined business or about which there are few details

- depositor files with little information on them, particularly where they are resident in countries associated with drugs trafficking or terrorist activities

Unrecorded deposits

A number of major international banking frauds have involved the diversion of deposits to accounts controlled by the fraudster. Usually the funds are not recorded in the bank's books at all, the deposits being routed through intermediaries or by the bank paying away receipts without recording the receipt or the payment in the accounting records. Often the accounts to which the funds are diverted are located in off-shore locations or countries with bank secrecy laws.

This type of fraud is most likely to occur where bank's depositors are resident overseas and/or where funds are held on long-term deposit or under hold-mail arrangements. As a result the customer may not be in regular contact with the bank and may not receive statements. The risk is increased where the depositors concerned seek to remove their funds from an oppressive home jurisdiction. The depositors may put a higher level of trust in the bank concerned to make the necessary arrangements and take care of the money deposited.

DEPOSITS FUNDED PERSONAL BUSINESS INTERESTS

A director of an overseas bank took deposits from certain overseas customers into code-numbered accounts in a Swiss bank. He had sole contact with most of the customers, who mostly wished to hold their funds on long-term deposit outside their home jurisdiction. The funds were moved from the Swiss bank into other off-shore accounts and used by the director to fund various of his other interests.

What to look for:

- any evidence of deposit taking by any other company of which there are details on the premises, whether part of the regulated group or not

- documentation held in management offices which it is claimed have no connection with the business of the bank

- evasive replies regarding such documents

Theft of customer deposits/investments

Where customers are not in regular contact with a bank or where a high level of discretion is extended to the bank by the customer, the scope for the misuse of customers' funds or investments is increased. The example below is typical of the circumstances in which this type of fraud may occur.

This type of fraud is different to unrecorded deposits above because the customers' funds or assets will have been recorded in the bank's books initially, only later being misused.

GAMBLING WITH CUSTOMERS' MONEY

A branch manager stole £730,000 from a customer's account while the customer was being detained overseas. The manager had been given authority to make investments on the customer's behalf during the customer's absence. However, he spent the money on gambling.

What to look for:

- customers with hold-mail arrangements who only have very occasional contact with the bank

- no independent resolution of customer complaints or review of hold-mail accounts

Fraudulent instructions

Frauds involving false instructions are considered under other external frauds below.

Dealing

Introduction

Dealing fraud is a potential problem in banks of all sizes. Almost every bank and every dealer have their own 'war stories' as to how dealing fraud has been perpetrated. The scale of fraud ranges from the small, perhaps giving rise to no financial loss, to those in which institutions lose millions of pounds.

A simple categorisation of dealing fraud would divide the frauds into two categories:

(a) misappropriation of funds, whereby a dealer takes funds from the institution, either directly or indirectly, for his own purpose; and

(b) false reporting or accounting, whereby a dealer ensures that the financial performance of the area under his control is misreported. This may or may not lead to a loss for the institution but in all cases would involve unauthorised activity. It may also result in a misleading impression being given of the financial soundness of the institution.

Motivation for dealing fraud includes:

(a) direct personal benefit – the dealer siphons off cash for his own use;

(b) job protection – the dealer incurs a loss and, in order to protect his position within the institution, seeks to hide the loss by the use of fraudulent transactions. In many cases the original loss may be due to a simple mistake or an error of judgement;

(c) to increase remuneration – this occurs indirectly by the use of some type of fraudulent transaction to inflate reported profits. In many institutions dealers are remunerated both by means of a base salary and a performance-related bonus. The greater the profits shown in the particular dealer's book, the greater the performance bonus;

(d) protecting the future – this is the reverse of inflating profits, whereby, if a dealer has been particularly successful in one period, rather than recognising all the profit now he secretes an amount away to be released when trading is not so profitable.

In many cases the original motivation for dealing fraud is to protect a current position and not to defraud the institution of cash. Some of the more notable dealing frauds are 'downward spirals' whereby one unauthorised or fraudulent transaction leads to a complex web of transactions, which eventually give rise to a significant loss.

A typical sequence of events involves the dealer incurring, but not reporting, a loss (innocently or otherwise) or reporting a false profit. Having taken this initial step there is a need to generate profit to cover the loss or to realise the profit. In order to do this, the position is increased on the basis that, by taking a bigger position, the ability to make profit is increased. Having taken the bigger position, the market moves against that position such that the original loss becomes greater. The spiral then continues with the need to increase the position even further to be able to recover the loss. The spiral continues further until it becomes very complex, is hard to disguise and is then discovered.

As with lending and depositor frauds above, it is helpful to consider the various types of dealing fraud in the context of a typical dealing cycle. The dealing cycle may be broken down into the following key phases:

- dealer enters into the deal;
- a dealing slip or dealing sheet is completed;
- the deal is entered into the accounting system;
- the deal is matched with the counterparty;
- the deal is settled;
- open positions are valued.

The second and third stages above may be simultaneous in many computerised systems. The matching process may also be computerised.

The most common dealing frauds are illustrated in Figure 7.3. (See page 225.)

When the **dealer enters into the deal**, the key issues are the price at which the deal is struck and the dealer's relationship with the counterparty concerned. Frauds involve the use of false market prices, for example through off-market rings or related party deals. Concentration of business through particular brokers may indicate the existence of broker kickbacks, whereby the dealer receives a payment from a particular broker in return for passing business to the broker.

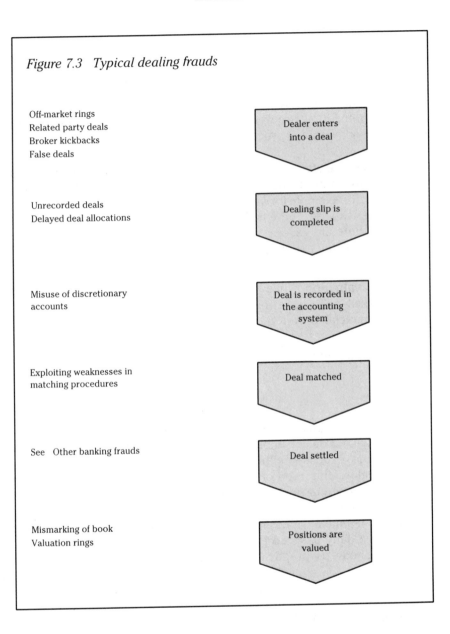

Figure 7.3   Typical dealing frauds

When the **deal slip is completed and entered into the accounting system**, the main concern is that the deal is properly recorded and on a timely basis. Dealers may suppress deals to hide loss-making transactions or delay their input to keep within limits. They may manipulate profits between client accounts and the firm's own portfolio. Dealers may also input fictitious transactions to avoid showing a loss, recognise a profit or disguise a position. Unnecessary suspense accounts should be closed as these are often used by fraudsters to cover their tracks.

On **deal matching**, opportunities for fraud may arise where deal matching procedures are weak or where there are known loopholes in computerised matching procedures.

At the **settlement stage**, a key factor in many dealing frauds is that deals roll up without settlement. Certain contracts do not require immediate settlement, for example forward foreign exchange contracts and certain types of derivatives. There is a higher risk of fraud with instruments of this kind: there are cases of losses of hundreds of millions of pounds being accumulated and concealed.

As regards **valuation**, while many financial investments have deep and liquid markets and market prices are freely available, the newer generation of financial products, particularly derivatives, pose significant valuation challenges. Over-marking a book may lead to bonuses being paid on false profits.

Off-market rings

Off-market rings involve two or more parties dealing at off-market prices. Usually a dealer in one of the institutions concerned obtains a profit at the expense of his employer. However, as shown in the example below, this type of fraud may be difficult to spot unless an institution marks its positions to market each day and performs spot checks on the prices at which deals are transacted, because everyone appears to be making a profit. Most institutions mark their positions to market on a daily basis so this would expose this type of fraud. However, there may be practical problems in doing this in more illiquid markets.

EVERYONE SEEMS TO BE MAKING A PROFIT

A dealer at an institution bought a particular security at 100. He then sold the bond to an investor at 101, when the market price was 103, apparently making a profit of 1. The investor then sold the shares at 103 to another institution which in turn sold them on at a small profit to the first institution. Part of the profit made by the investor was paid as a kickback to the dealer at the first institution.

FALSE MARKET IN BOND WARRANTS

A trader created a false market in bond warrant prices. He bought Swiss franc-dominated put warrants which gave him the right to buy Spanish government bonds. He drove the price of the warrants higher and then sold them back to the bank. He made a profit of £2 million on the deal which was placed in a Swiss bank account. He was going to use the profits to set up his own trading firm. The compliance department picked it up and the funds were returned with interest.

What to look for:

- dealing book not marked to market on a daily basis
- no spot checks on the prices at which deals are transacted
- unusual levels of activity with particular counterparties
- poor supervision in the dealing room

Related party deals

Related party deals are those with counterparties to whom the institution or the dealer is related. Again deals are undertaken at off-market prices with a view to manipulating profits. Sometimes securities are sold to related parties, with an undisclosed commitment to buy back the securities at a later date, perhaps after the year end audit is complete. These frauds often involve esoteric deals or the use of intermediaries, with no clear business purpose.

Sometimes these arrangements involve both related and unrelated parties. For example, in one case involving trading in warrants the price of the warrants was artificially 'ramped' by a complex series of transactions between a number of institutions. In this type of fraud no loss is incurred until 'the music stops' and one of the unrelated parties is left holding virtually worthless stock. Usually this type of fraud succeeds because the unrelated parties in the ring do not fully understand the product.

Warning signs are as for off-market rings above.

Broker kickbacks

A significant volume of transactions in the London markets are dealt through brokers rather than directly between counterparties. Brokers earn a commission on all transactions they arrange. In some cases commissions may be paid to the individual dealer as a form of kickback in order to increase the flow of deals through that broker. Such arrangements are difficult to identify.

What to look for:

- high levels of business with a particular broker
- unusual trends in broker commissions

False deals

Dealers may input fictitious transactions into the system in order to avoid showing a loss, recognise a profit or disguise a position. Clearly the risk of false deals remaining undetected is increased significantly where deal matching procedures are weak.

FALSE HEDGES

The trader exceeded his trading limit by more that US$200 million. He was required to maintain a matched trading book to protect the bank from the risk of loss in the event there was a change in the value of the Mexican peso. He was not supposed to have unprotected positions in pesos exceeding US$2 million. The trader did not actually hedge his positions and had acquired an unauthorised position exceeding US$200 million. When the peso was devalued by about 30 per cent the bank lost about US$70 million. The trader entered fictitious transactions into the bank's computer system to make it falsely appear that he had hedged his position so that it showed he had made a profit. If the bank had not discovered the fraud the trader would have earned a 125 per cent bonus.

What to look for:

- unusual trends in dealers' positions
- very high gross positions compared to net positions
- significant number of unmatched or unconfirmed deals in particular dealing books or with particular counterparties
- a significant number of cancelled deals
- unusually high value of unsettled transactions

Unrecorded deals

There may be a number of reasons why dealers want to delay inputting deals. For example, the dealer may wish to conceal loss-making transactions or hide the fact that he has exceeded certain dealing limits (in many institutions exceeding limits is a dismissable offence).

NO QUESTIONS ASKED

A highly successful foreign exchange dealer, whose remuneration was linked closely to dealing profits earned, took unauthorised overnight positions in forward foreign exchange contracts. He booked the unauthorised deals the following day shortly before booking the deals which reversed the positions. Having made significant profits on one occasion the markets in New York and Tokyo moved against him overnight. He doubled up his positions assuming the market would continue in the same direction. However, the market reversed. The unauthorised activity was not picked up because the back office focused almost exclusively on checking of settlement date details on incoming confirmations ignoring trade date and other details. Also details relating to forward deals were only checked as they reached settlement date. No questions were asked about how the dealer managed to achieve a high level of profits despite a strategy where only very limited overnight positions were permitted.

What to look for:

- high levels of profit by particular dealers in relation to stated dealing strategy
- dealing books trading close to their dealing limits
- unusual trends in dealers' positions
- significant number of unmatched counterparty confirmations

Delayed deal allocation

In institutions which deal for their own account and for clients, dealers may deliberately delay the allocation of deals to clients or the institution, awaiting market movements. An example of this would be buying equities in the morning and then not allocating them to the client or the firm's own portfolio until the position has been sold later in the day such that profitable transactions are passed to an account set up by the dealer with loss-making deals being booked to the client.

This type of fraud can operate in a number of ways with profitable deals being allocated to the institution itself or being targeted at particular clients who then reimburse the dealer for his efforts.

HEADS I WIN, TAILS I WIN

The head of foreign exchange at a bank helped an investor to earn 'profits' of approximately £500,000. Details of transactions were recorded on the dealer's trading sheet in pencil. Then the pencil entries were later overwritten in ink, putting in the known results instead of the speculated figures.

What to look for:

- no time stamping of deal tickets or a review of the time of booking

- alterations to or overwriting of details on deal sheets

- abnormal profits or losses by particular dealers or certain of their clients

Misuse of discretionary accounts

Discretionary dealing accounts, in the hands of experienced dealers, may provide an opportunity for secreting profits, hiding losses or generally manipulating results. While dealers will of course be accountable to the discretionary client, the dealer may use clever accounting devices and exploit timing differences to hide losses or manipulate results for the period he requires.

The risk of this type of fraud is increased where account statements are not despatched by personnel independent of the dealing room. Also in many systems the quality of reporting in relation to client accounts is inferior to the bank's own trading. Poor quality statements can sometimes conceal the nature and extent of a client's exposure. Also, many clients do not check their statements very closely, particularly if they appear to be making profits. As with Unrecorded deals above, it is essential to question abnormal levels of profit achieved by individual dealers in relation to particular client accounts against the agreed dealing strategy.

What to look for:

- unusual trends on particular discretionary accounts

- sole contact clients

- non-standard postings or adjustments to particular accounts
- special arrangements for preparation and issue of statements

Exploiting weaknesses in deal matching procedures

Rigorous deal matching procedures are crucial in any dealing system. All deal details should be agreed with the counterparty as soon as possible. Where such procedures are weak or where there are loopholes in computerised deal matching programs, opportunities for fraud may occur.

It is difficult to identify warning signs for this particular type of fraud. Once programmed, it is likely that staff will place unquestioning reliance on a computer matching process. The problem may therefore go undetected for a considerable period.

A LOOPHOLE IN THE PROGRAM

In a foreign exchange dealing operation the computer would only process transactions where all specified fields matched with the counterparty's details. However, due to a computer programming error the computer did not compare trade date details. Dealers became aware of this loophole. It allowed them to misrepresent their positions by recording them on other than their actual trade dates.

Mismarking the book

One of the more difficult areas in a dealing portfolio is determining market values for reporting purposes at the end of reporting periods. For certain financial instruments quoted prices are available which can be determined and checked with a reasonable amount of accuracy. In other instruments, markets are thinner or pricing arrangements are complex such that there is considerable scope for dealers to over- or undervalue positions in order to achieve their target level of performance.

The tremendous growth in over-the-counter products, particularly derivatives, provides significant scope for misvaluation. Institutions most susceptible to this type of fraud are those where the gap between the experience, knowledge and ability of front office personnel and that of back and middle office personnel, financial control and general management is greatest.

231

In many of the newer products there is no market price. On a large book, a misvaluation by only a few points can have a significant impact on reported profits. Within any institution which has a significant amount of over-the-counter and derivative products, thorough independent review and testing of prices used for profit reporting is an essential financial control.

THE MARKETS DID NOT OBEY ME

An interest rate options dealer at a bank manipulated revaluation rates to hide an unrealised loss of £3 million, because the market had moved against him. Trading in interest rate options had commenced at the bank before back-office procedures were fully in place. In particular there was no facility for the back-office to check the valuation of interest rate options independently.

What to look for:

- no detailed valuation policies and guidelines
- pace of new product launches out of line with systems development
- unusual trends in the value of particular books

Valuation rings

Position values are often checked by comparing revaluation prices to third party sources. In certain cases however the dealer at the institution may have agreed with the third party that in a response to a request for information they should provide non-market prices.

Other banking areas

Introduction

In this section, I examine frauds in other banking areas.

Fictitious borrowers/false information on mortgage applications

During the 1980s building societies and banks were defrauded of considerable sums of money in connection with their mortgage lending activities. In a time of rising prices and significant changes in the financial services industry, building societies and banks sought to gain market share. Higher income multiples were offered and 100 per cent mortgages became more common. Unfortunately lending criteria were often poor, or were poorly applied, and opportunities for the fraudster were consequently considerable. There was also a shortage at that time of staff with the right skills and experience.

Market conditions have changed considerably since that time and most building societies and banks have tightened up their procedures. However, this type of fraud remains a threat and as similar conditions return some of the above problems may occur again.

Frauds involving false or incomplete information are closely linked with the frauds described above. However, the individual making the application may well be the person named on the form but some or all of the other details may be false, for example: false employment details, employment references, tenancy details and references, bogus valuations. Another common fraud involves the fraudster providing false information to obtain the loan. He then makes some payments but soon defaults. The bank or building society then repossess the property. Once they have recovered their funds, the balance is paid to the fraudster. With house prices rising steeply, the fraudster shows a considerable profit for minimal outlay.

Many of the above mortgage frauds also involve collusion with valuers and solicitors and the double pledging of collateral.

Warning signs are as for Loans to fictitious borrowers and Impersonation/false information on loan applications under Credit above.

Leasing

Leasing frauds usually involve leases for non-existent equipment or vehicles. For example, car dealers may submit signed documentation to leasing companies from customers who have in fact changed their mind and decided to pay the car dealer cash: the dealer therefore gets paid twice for the same car. Similarly leasing companies have 'double dipped' into bank finance of their lease portfolios by writing fictitious leases on the same underlying asset.

Other frauds have involved equipment manufacturers forging the signatures of customers entering into leases with leading finance houses for non-existent computer equipment or lessees giving false acceptance certificates and using the finance for some other purpose.

CARS 'SOLD' TWICE

A car dealer sold cars on hire purchase. The customer would sign the relevant documentation which was sent to the hire purchase company for approval. However, often the customer would decide not to proceed with the hire purchase agreement and paid cash instead. The dealer accepted the cash and requested the customer to forward the documentation back to him rather than return it to the hire purchase company. The hire purchase company would pay the dealer for the car and he would commence making the repayments in place of the customer. This was repeated many times. Eventually the repayments fell behind and the hire purchase company contacted the original customer at which point the fraud was discovered.

DOUBLE LEASING

Leases for millions of pounds of computer equipment were used to obtain money twice from financial institutions on the same assets. The fraudsters leased out valuable computer equipment to a number of companies and then illegally used the leasing documents as collateral to raise money from more than one lender at a time to save their debt-ridden company. The fraud came to light after the borrower had gone into liquidation.

INTANGIBLE ASSETS

The managing director and finance director of a computer equipment company forged signatures of county council customers and entered into leases with leading finance houses for non-existent computer equipment. The company was well-respected and sold Unisys and IBM equipment and had a thriving computer maintenance operation. The directors bought Jaguars and Porsches and acquired a company-owned farm. When the company ran into financial difficulties bogus leases were written bearing the forged signatures of the county council customers.

LEASING REGISTRATION NUMBERS

A car dealer used unused registration numbers for new cars to obtain cash from hire purchase companies. He then sold the same car with a real registration number to a genuine customer, thereby getting paid twice.

What to look for:

- no physical inspection of the leased asset
- abnormal levels of business via particular agents
- inconsistencies in lease documentation

Omitted contingencies

Omitted contingency frauds involve the giving of unrecorded guarantees or other commitments. There is no immediate movement of funds making these frauds easier to conceal. Quite often such undisclosed guarantees and commitments are connected with other transactions, such as the transfer of a problem loan to another part of the group or an associate. The risk of this type of fraud is increased where there are weak controls over the giving and recording of guarantees and other commitments.

FALSE GUARANTEES

The vice-president of the London branch of an overseas bank conspired with a business consultant to defraud the bank by issuing guarantees to certain investors without the bank's knowledge. He claimed that he was acting on behalf of the bank.

SIDE DEAL

The chairman and principal shareholder of a bank, who also owned and was a director of a bank overseas, gave a guarantee in the name of the bank to a customer of the overseas bank. The management of the bank were unaware that the guarantee had been given.

What to look for:

- evidence of guarantee fees or telex messages to counterparties with whom the bank does not normally deal
- documentation kept in management offices to which access is restricted

Passing through

Passing through involves paying away receipts without recording the

235

receipt or the repayment in the accounting records, usually to enable benefits to be paid direct to directors or employees.

TAKING A CUT

Certain Swiss banks paid commissions to another bank for the introduction of substantial client funds for discretionary management. The directors who had arranged the introduction believed that they personally rather than the bank should benefit from the commissions and, with management collusion, the commissions were paid away on receipt to personal accounts of the directors. Neither receipts, or payments through the correspondent accounts were recorded.

What to look for:

- large number of contra items on nostro reconciliations
- sole customer contacts

Rolling matching

As explained in the previous chapter, rolling matching is the incorrect matching of items on reconciliations to facilitate the concealment of fraudulent items. Rolling matching is most likely to happen when numerous items of a similar amount flow through an account. The reconciliation may appear to work. However, full reperformance of the reconciliation will reveal that the reconciling items are not those shown but other items which appear to have been matched.

The risk of this type of fraud is increased where there is no periodic reperformance of reconciliations. Cursory review of reconciliations by management is insufficient. Excessive numbers of contras and journals may be a warning sign.

Diverted postings

Diverted postings may be used in virtually any area of a bank. For example, a bank may enter into transactions so that a customer is able to obtain some benefit, often illegally, such as export credits, grants or a tax benefit. In return the customer may agree for his account to be used in an irregular manner by the bank. For example, loans may be concealed by debiting them to the account of such a customer and providing the customer with documentation to 'hold him harmless' for the loan.

What to look for:

- unusual terms or activity on particular accounts
- any evidence that a bank is actively involved in helping persons in other jurisdictions to break local laws

Misuse of volume accounts

Where large numbers of transactions flow through a particular account, this may enable the fraudster to conceal fraudulent transactions more easily. For example, the fraudster may charge relatively small amounts regularly to interest expense accounts, crediting the equivalent amount to his own or his nominee's account. It may be difficult to detect this type of fraud because exact amounts may be charged so that the correlation between interest expense and deposit liabilities is maintained. Similar types of manipulation may happen in other areas of a bank's operations.

The risk of this type of fraud is increased where there is no independent review of personal or interest rates charged or credited on particular accounts.

PRO RATA FRAUD

The management of a bank charged amounts each month to interest expense crediting the equivalent amount to their own current accounts. To avoid detection, exact amounts, calculated by reference to the total deposit liabilities on a day-to-day basis, were charged so that the correlation between interest expense and deposit liabilities was maintained.

What to look for:

- terms of business which are unusual
- journals and adjustments posted to volume accounts which are not adequately explained

Cross firing (or cheque kiting)

Cross firing involves the accumulation of balances on bank accounts based on uncollected cheques drawn on similar accounts at other banks. The fraudster takes advantage of the timing delays inherent in the banking system to increase, artificially, his reserves or reduce his cost of funding. Often a multiplicity of accounts is used.

What to look for:

- many deposits of similar and/or round sum amounts

- a high proportion of transactions regularly with another bank

- deposits soon withdrawn

- flow through account does not seem to have a business reason

- accounts with low average balance but a high volume of transactions

Cheque fraud

I discussed cheque fraud in the previous chapter in relation to manufacturing and service companies. It may be worth looking at organised cheque fraud from the banks' point of view and reviewing a few more examples. Cheque fraud includes impersonation, giving false details, altering payee details, forging signatures and manufacturing copies of company cheques. Sometimes the photocopied cheques are so good that only forensic tests distinguish them from the real thing.

COLOUR COPIERS

Four individuals made near perfect copies of stolen blank cheques on a stolen laser photocopier. They paid the bogus cheques into bank accounts under false names before withdrawing money from cash points. During a period of six months they printed £100,000 worth of cheques in a lock-up garage, cashed nearly half and stole a further £60,000 in a series of thefts and burglaries. The photocopies were so accurate that only forensic tests distinguished them from the real thing.

219 FALSE BANK ACCOUNTS

Two individuals used false names to open 219 accounts across the country. They gave addresses taken from voters' registers and asked for cheque books and cheque guarantee cards to be sent to them. They then had the mail redirected by the Post Office on the pretext of moving house. The individuals used five accommodation addresses which ended up at a collection point in Slough. The individuals used a mobile office, with a filofax and a card index system to keep track of their transactions. A Post Office clerk recognised an address used by the individuals and alerted investigators because she knew the people who really lived there. The police then undertook surveillance operations.

What to look for:

- alterations to cheques
- illegible signatures
- inconsistencies in printing
- customers resident outside the normal trading area of the branch or bank
- undue haste to open accounts
- unusual behaviour of the applicant
- inconsistencies arising from credit status and other checks

Electronic payments fraud

Some of the largest frauds, or attempted frauds, have involved the misuse of money transfer systems. The fraudster may attempt to transfer funds, securities or other assets. Many of the attempts are only discovered by chance rather than any particular strength in the banks' preventive controls.

CODE NUMBERS SCRAMBLED

The employee who worked in the computer systems department at a bank's headquarters stole customer data, including code numbers by which transactions were conducted from clients' computers. A collaborating computer engineer sent to the bank from a temporary personnel firm decoded the scramble on the code numbers.

However, there was also a variable code number which changes with each transaction. The fraudsters were able to break through the security barrier by acquiring data on recent transactions, which may be displayed on clients' computer screens, and deciphered the alteration pattern. Using a PC, the group transmitted a large amount from a customer account. The next day they transferred a similar amount from three bank branches to an account at another bank. An attempt to withdraw the funds all at once raised suspicions at the second branch.

PASSWORD ABUSE

A clerk hacked into an electronic cash transfer system and attempted to send 70 million Swiss francs to a bank account in Zurich. He used a colleague's computer password to authorise the money transfer to the bank, where an account had been opened the day before in the name of one of the fraudsters.

Although he was only 23, he had an aptitude for computers and had helped set up a system at the bank. The system gave him power to make large transfers. He used his own secret password and another stolen from a colleague to make the transfer.

He was caught because he did not know that the limit on cash transfers was US$30 million (£19 million). He also got the VAT amount on the advice wrong. When the money arrived at the bank in Zurich the alarm was raised before it could be sent to a bogus account. The clerk said that he had been recruited by a gang of international fraudsters and could not back out because of the 'fear factor'. He was promised £4 million for his part in the fraud. When the bank's computer logs were checked, it was discovered that the clerk had made three previous abortive attempts at the fraud.

FORGED CUSTOMER LETTERS OF AUTHORITY

The fraud involved forging a letter of authority from a customer of one bank and requesting money to be transferred to an account of another. The fraudsters would ring target companies on the pretence of buying a product and suggest payment through CHAPS. Armed with the firm's account details, they would forge corporate letterheads and directors' signatures and instruct the companies' banks to make payments to accounts held by stooges willing to be used in return for a cut of the proceeds.

The fraudsters then removed the money from these stooge accounts before the alarm was raised. A total of 131 attempts were made of which 33 were successful, netting just under £2 million. If all attempts had been successful the amount netted would have been £7 million. To make sure the pattern of a major coordinated fraud was not recognised the fraudsters deliberately spread their efforts around the country.

The fraud was picked up by following a trail of false documents which were all signed with a misspelling of the word 'sincerely' in 'yours sincerely'. The spelling mistake led 20 different police forces to recognise that a major coordinated crime had taken place. Certain members of the gang were arrested attempting to deliver a forged letter of authority to a branch of a well-known bank.

What to look for:

- control over final release of funds insufficient for the amounts involved – for example, checking only that the signatory is authorised to sign

- transfers to or from accounts in offshore locations or countries with bank secrecy laws

- transfers to or from individuals who are not regular customers

- abbreviated payee names or instructions and alterations to the date, amount, payee or other details

- poor control of documents between approval and processing

- processing of significant transactions by junior personnel

- poor security over the room where transfers are made or over codes and passwords

Investment business

Introduction

In this section I look at some of the more common frauds in investment business. A number of the frauds are similar to frauds discussed elsewhere in this book. For example, the frauds involving bogus investments are similar to the frauds involving bogus goods or services discussed under sales in Chapter 6. All of these frauds involve the sale of products which are 'too good to be true', marketed in a convincing way to a vulnerable customer base. They usually involve a complex web of deceit including false accounting records and bogus documentation. The businesses are often seemingly very successful, having achieved extraordinary growth.

Selling clients investments without authority overlaps with certain of the depositor frauds discussed earlier in this chapter. Dealing room fraud has been discussed in a banking context. Most of these frauds are equally prevalent in investment business. Share ramping was discussed in the previous chapter. These frauds may be perpetrated by anyone who has access to inside information: officers of the company, dealers in the companies' shares, merchant bankers and other advisers.

241

Bogus investments

Bogus product frauds have been particularly prevalent in the financial sector in recent years. These frauds are similar in nature to the bogus product frauds discussed in the previous chapter. Typically, private investors invest savings in seemingly low risk, high return products. The products are attractively 'packaged' and the fraudster makes sure all the 'right' documentation is in place. The funds are either invested in highly speculative investments on which the fraudster hopes to make secret profits, or are diverted for personal use.

Sometimes investors are induced to invest in bogus shares of a speculative nature or offering some inducement. For example, in one case people were deceived into believing that investing in a particular company's shares would exempt them from the poll tax. In another case it was claimed that the company was developing a miracle way of detecting salmonella and listeria bacteria.

ALL THAT GLITTERS IS NOT A GILT

The directors of an investment management firm defrauded thousands of small investors. The firm promised the investor that the money would be invested in gilt-edged securities. When the firm collapsed there should have been more than £115 million invested in gilts whereas there was just £1.9 million. The investors' money had been invested in various highly speculative schemes resulting in losses of over £40 million. The money was also used to fund a lavish lifestyle and to buy properties, yachts, jets and luxury cars. The small investors, mainly elderly people, were taken in by glossy brochures and advertising, believed that their money was secure in gilt-edged stock. The company was run from plush offices. The firm offered portfolios which it claimed attracted capital gains tax rather than income tax and guaranteed a minimum monthly return. The firm paid returns of capital expected by clients from new money invested by other clients.

AN ANAGRAM FOR OFFSHORE

The director of an investment management company told clients that he was investing their money in offshore trusts, promising returns varying between 21 and 100 per cent a year. He actually spent the money on a system of horse-race betting. His impeccable social connections and personal charm led investors to trust him. Investors inquiring about their money were told it was 'offshore' – a mixture, according to the fraudster of 'off' and an anagram of 'horse'. The individual was at the same time employed as a public relations officer in a firm of accountants on £24,000 a year. No one at the firm or his company became suspicious about the fact that he lived in a £500,000 house, had three children at private schools and held lavish parties. He spoke a great deal about his private means and an annuity he had.

THREE ROLLS ROYCES, A BOAT AND A GAMBLING HOBBY

The director of a small investment consultancy persuaded more than 100 people to invest £1.75 million purportedly in fixed-term guaranteed-income bonds paying 14-18 per cent interest. In fact, the funds were not invested at all, save in his own bank account. He paid investors the interest and capital they were due from new funds received from other investors. The investors were mainly elderly people who had invested their life savings or redundant people investing redundancy pay-offs. The individual used the money to fund an extravagant lifestyle. He had three Rolls Royces (and had a fourth on order at the time of his arrest) and a boat. He also gambled heavily.

The warning signs are similar to the aspects highlighted in connection with bogus product frauds in the previous chapter.

What to look for:

- products 'too good to be true' – for example, low risk high return products

- glossy advertising and high pressure sales techniques targeted at a vulnerable and inexperienced client base (for example, the elderly, unemployed or inexperienced investors)

- explanation of transaction is complex or investments are in companies based on one-off ventures or promoting some 'miracle' product

- abnormal levels of growth in profitability or margins achieved

- documentation held in the offices of senior officers of the company which it is claimed have no connection with the business

- complex accounting arrangements, over use of intermediaries, companies in offshore locations or other factors which make it difficult to trace the movement of funds or investments

243

Trading without authorisation

There have been a number of reported cases of individuals attempting to carry on investment business without authorisation from the appropriate regulator. While it will be clear whether or not authorisation has been obtained, it may be less clear whether further authorisation is required for new business areas.

Perhaps more common, although often unreported, are businesses which submit false or misleading information to the regulator. Examples include misdescription of assets or omission of liabilities to inflate the net worth of the company so as to continue to meet capital adequacy requirements.

What to look for:

- new business developments where detailed advice has not been sought concerning the regulatory implications
- tight liquidity position
- unusual trends
- transactions with suspected related parties

Selling or lending client investments without authority

This type of fraud includes selling shares or other securities on behalf of clients without their authority, or surrendering client endowment policies and single premium bonds and investment bonds without their consent. Alternatively, client securities could be used as collateral to secure the liabilities of the fraudster, perhaps represented as having been 'stock lent' by the client.

INVESTMENT ADVISER CASHES IN CLIENT POLICIES

An investment adviser sold clients' endowment policies, single premium bonds and investment bonds. His clients were mainly retired people of modest means. He forged clients' signatures and surrendered policies without their consent in an attempt to recoup stock market losses amounting to £1.6 million.

What to look for:

- abnormal level of client sales or policy surrenders given stated investment strategy or unexpected departures from agreed investment strategy
- evidence of significant personal dealing
- missing documentation or authority letters or unusual aspects on client files

Share ramping

I discussed share ramping and other similar schemes in Chapter 6 (see other frauds) and in the section on dealing frauds earlier in this chapter. Share ramping involves financial advisers, company executives or others buying substantial amounts of a company's shares at inflated prices to give a false impression of their value. Similar frauds may occur via e-mail and on Internet news groups tipping 'penny' or other low value or obscure shares.

THE PANAMANIAN BUBBLE

The managing director of a financial services company, who acted as financial adviser to a number of small quoted companies, used a Panamanian company to buy on credit four million of the seven million shares available in a particular company at inflated prices, thus giving a false impression of their value.

What to look for:

- abnormal increases in the prices of shares of companies for which the company acts as adviser or sponsor
- loans or transactions, the commercial purpose of which is unclear
- complex structures/transactions with offshore or 'front' companies

Front running

Dealers may make profits on their own account by personally entering into deals ahead of transactions to be made by the fund they manage. This type of fraud may be difficult to detect unless detailed analysis of transactions is undertaken. Clearly the absence of strict rules on and monitoring of own account dealings increases the risk of this type of fraud.

Churning

Churning involves the excessive buying and selling of securities for the main purpose of generating commission. This usually occurs where a broker is acting in a discretionary capacity or as investment manager for a particular client.

What to look for:

- unusually high levels of activity on particular clients or high commission levels for particular clients or brokers
- apparent departures from agreed investment strategy
- client rarely in contact with the broker – for example, abroad for long periods

Bogus documents/stolen share certificates

Most investment businesses take good care of share certificates, bearer documents and other valuable assets in their custody. However, frauds in this area are surprisingly common.

STOLEN SHARE CERTIFICATES

Three individuals defrauded banks, stockbrokers and financial institutions of £12.5 million by inducing them to accept share certificates which had been stolen from a major securities house. They tried to sell them through other brokers and to raise loans using the stolen share as security.

What to look for:

- weaknesses in physical security procedures
- overdue reconciliations of custody records to securities held on the premises or to other depositaries
- significant number of items on reconciliations which cannot be explained
- insufficient resources or inexperienced staff allocated to safe custody activities

Fraudulent instructions

Fraudulent instructions may include forged signatures on share transfer forms, forged power of attorney, bogus fax messages or unauthorised use of codes and passwords to transfer securities electronically.

The risk of this type of fraud is increased where significant transactions are undertaken without contacting the customer directly or where there is poor security over codes and passwords.

FORGED POWER OF ATTORNEY

Two individuals allegedly plotted to obtain shares from a bank. The bank held the shares on behalf of one of the individual's great aunt. He had flown to his great aunt's villa abroad and obtained a specimen signature. A letter was then allegedly forged saying that he had power of attorney for her. The letter was used in an attempt to obtain the shares.

What to look for:

- instructions out of line with clients' usual activities

- abnormal haste to complete the transaction

- unusual aspects in documentation, for example small differences in letterheads, paper used, typescript, handwriting or postmarks

Insurance

Introduction

As with investment business, a number of the insurance frauds discussed in this section are similar to frauds discussed elsewhere in this book. For example, persuading customers to cancel policies against their interests, forged surrender of policies or claims and misappropriation of funds invested are similar to certain of the banking and investment business frauds discussed above. Some of the frauds involving false insurance claims are similar in certain respects to the external purchasing frauds discussed in Chapter 6. However, as before, it is useful to look at these frauds in the context of insurance business to understand the nature of the threat.

Bogus policies

These frauds include producing bogus insurance products, such as capital investment bonds, bogus cover notes and insurance policies and the manipulation of risk classes by agents.

NON-EXISTENT INSURANCE COMPANY

Four individuals collected premiums on commercial liability policies, performance bonds and financial guarantees for building contractors. They issued policies through an insurance agent in which one of them was an officer, in the name of a non-existent insurance company apparently incorporated in Anguilla. They provided potential policy holders and agents with false financial statements which showed that the insurance company had substantial assets to meet claims.

Persuading customers to cancel policies against their interests

This type of fraud enables insurance companies or their agents to generate commissions fraudulently by persuading customers to cancel existing policies against their interests and take out new ones.

TOO GOOD TO BE TRUE

An insurance agent induced policyholders to take out new policies, giving them misleading information about interest rates and dividends. However, instead of terminating the old policies he took out loans on them, only later terminating the old policies and rolling them over into new ones.

What to look for:

- abnormal level of early policy surrenders
- unusual trends in commission levels

Forged surrender of policies/claims

Forged surrender of policies often occur where customers' policies have become dormant. The agent forges surrender documentation and pockets the surrender proceeds himself.

FORGED SIGNATURES

A life insurance agent identified policyholders who had ceased to pay premiums. He then forged the policyholders' signatures on policy surrender documents and sent them to head office requesting that the cheques be sent back to him for delivery. He forged endorsements and banked the cheques.

Misappropriation of funds

Misappropriation of funds can occur in a large number of situations: for example, diverting funds handed over by investors for investment in policies, or insurance company employees submitting fictitious claims relating to non-existent dependants of eligible policyholders.

DEFRAUDING INVESTORS

A life insurance salesman defrauded 400 investors of their life savings. The salesman accepted funds for investment in policies. He arranged for a monthly income to be paid to the investors, misappropriating the larger part of the funds invested. The insurance company did not admit legal responsibility but paid substantial compensation to the victims of the fraud.

What to look for:

- unusual trends in commissions earned by particular salesmen

- no independent spot checking of information on claim forms

- customer complaints/general correspondence not monitored independently

False statements/failure to disclose relevant information

False statements and failure to disclose relevant information covers a very wide range of matters, such as age, state of health, previous convictions, financial details and other insurances held. Most insurance companies are alert to the risks in this area.

Bogus policyholders

Bogus policy holder frauds usually involve impersonation and/or submission of false information.

MEN OF STRAW

An individual who ran his own accountancy practice allegedly defrauded insurance companies of £1.9 million in respect of pension schemes set up for bogus companies. He set up an advisory insurance company to help clients in his accountancy practice. In the course of his accountancy business his clients gave him details of themselves and their families. It was alleged that he later used these details when putting forward forged documents to insurance companies. It was also alleged that he set up bogus companies and attributed to them bogus employees. He then took out pension schemes for these bogus businesses. In return he received large sums of money by way of insurance commission.

What to look for:

- common or like-sounding names between various policyholders
- no spot checks on information on application forms
- unusual trends in payment of premiums
- incomplete or scrappy documentation accompanying applications

Staged deaths/accidents/thefts/arson frauds

This type of fraud is a major threat to all insurance companies. Cases include false claims on life policies, bogus accident claims, arson or otherwise destroying the insured assets, and false claims by insurance company employees based on customer policies.

Certain insurance companies now rely on databases which enable multiple claims for the same loss, claimants' financial commitments, records of County Court judgments and anomalies in names and addresses to be detected.

Warning signs will depend on the particular circumstances. These frauds are often only uncovered by detailed appraisal of claims to ascertain all the facts relating to the claim.

Inflated/false/composite claims

Inflated, false and composite claims can also occur in a wide range of situations. Most insurance companies are alert to the risks in this area and make use of sophisticated databases and cross-checks to identify fraudulent claims.

The dividing line between an optimistic assessment of loss (especially business interruption) and fraud is a grey area. For example, in business interruption claims it may so happen that the period in which the event of the claim occurred would have been the best period ever. In some instances the claimant may make false representations, for example regarding orders received.

Conclusion

This chapter has given an overview of the main types of fraud encountered in the financial sector. They are summarised in Table 7.1 below.

Table 7.1 Fraud in the financial sector

Credit	Deposits	Dealing	Other banking	Investment business	Insurance
• Fictitious borrowers	• Depositor camouflage	• Off-market dealing rings	• Mortgage fraud	• Bogus investments	• Bogus policies
• Nominee companies	• Unrecorded deposits	• Related party deals	• Leasing fraud	• Trading without	• Fraudulent policy
• Deposit	• Money laundering	• Broker kickbacks	• Omitted contingencies	authorisation	cancellation
transformation	• Theft of customer	• False deals	• Passing through	• Unauthorised selling or	• Forged surrender of
• Connected companies	deposits	• Unrecorded deals	frauds	lending of client	policies
• Asset quality	• Theft of customer	• Delayed deal allocation	• Rolling matching	investments	• Misappropriation of
manipulation	investments	• Misuse of discretionary	• Diverted postings	• Share ramping	funds
• Kickbacks	• Fraudulent	accounts	• Misuse of volume	• Front running	• False statements to
• Parallel companies	instructions	• Exploiting loopholes in	accounts	• Churning	gain insurance
• Funds transformation		matching systems	• Cross firing	• Bogus documents or	• Bogus policyholders
• Impersonation		• Mismarking positions	• Electronic payments	share certificates	• Staged deaths,
• False financial		• Valuation rings	frauds	• Fraudulent instructions	accidents, thefts,
information					arsons
• Double pledging and					• Inflated and false
land flips					claims
• Diversion of funds to					
repay loan					

8

Managing fraud in the future

Introduction

This chapter discusses practical ways to manage fraud risk, focusing on the people skills that will be fundamental to managing fraud in the future.

Listed companies in the UK of course need to take account of the Combined Code on corporate governance and the related Turnbull guidance on internal control. Guides are available on how to implement these requirements, including Implementing Turnbull: A Boardroom Briefing published by the Institute of Chartered Accountants in England and Wales, and Internal Control: A Practical Guide published by KPMG. I do not propose to cover the general risk management and internal control guidance set out in these publications. The emphasis in this chapter is on specific measures that will make a significant difference to the management of fraud risk.

Linking risk to value

The starting point is to demonstrate to the board and senior management team the added value of improved fraud risk management. If a company has recently suffered a fraud incident then for a short period of time the business case may be clear to all concerned. A few months later the need may be less clear as other matters move up the corporate agenda.

It is helpful to explain how fraud impacts the value chain. For example, in a typical retail business, the core business processes relate to brand and image delivery, product or service delivery and customer service delivery. These processes are illustrated in Figure 8.1 (See page 255.)

Using the concept of the 'shadow profile' introduced in the opening chapter, business risks (honest) in each area can be compared with the fraud risks (dishonest).

For example, high staff turnover may be driven by poor motivational skills of management, an unattractive working environment or pay levels out of line with market rates. On the other hand, staff may be leaving because they do not like working in a corrupt business unit or department. The costs of recruiting and training can be calculated. The wider impact on brand image can be assessed as ex-employees spread the word and talk to the press about how the business is run.

In the supplier selection and sourcing area, what might appear to be loss of value through an inefficient purchasing processes and poor buying may in fact be due to kickbacks and corruption. Suppliers may be overcharging the business because they have favourable contracts negotiated by buyers who are receiving kickbacks. These frauds may also affect other areas such as buying of advertising and promotion services and visual merchandising. Cutting inefficiencies in purchasing may cut costs by 10–20 per cent. Cutting out corrupt purchasing practices often saves a similar percentage.

Similarly in the stock management and distribution areas, what might appear to be a logistical problem in getting the right stock in the right place at the right time may actually be more to do with 'leakage' of stock due to staff theft or collusion between delivery and goods in staff. Cutting stock leakage by half can yield savings of millions of pounds in many retail chains.

For each identified area of saving, in the value chain it is helpful to estimate the savings that may be achieved. If that is difficult in certain areas, then it is usually possible to estimate the likely scale of the problem based on industry surveys and information obtained from fraud specialists.

Figure 8.1 Examples of fraud in a retail value chain

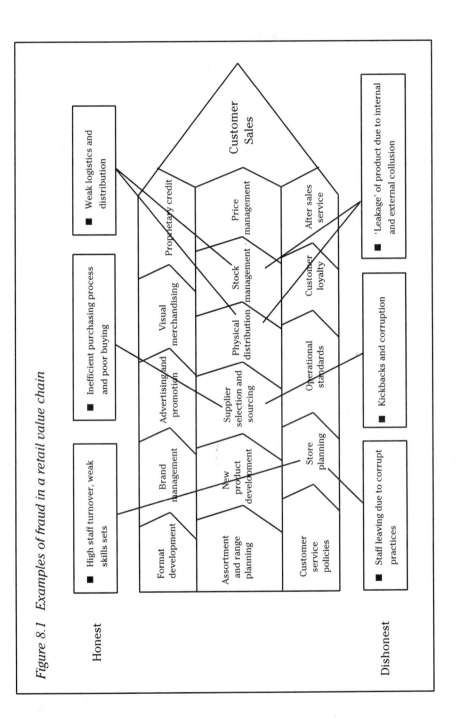

Fraud fundamentals

Certain initiatives are crucial to the fight against fraud. The five fundamental elements are: clear values and ethics, effective personnel policies, fraud awareness at all levels of the organisation, strong fraud reporting and response plans, and the development of good interviewing and probing skills among directors and managers. These measures need to be brought together in a coherent anti-fraud strategy.

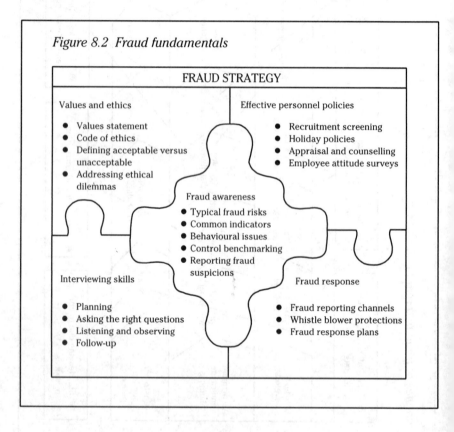

Figure 8.2 Fraud fundamentals

FRAUD STRATEGY

Values and ethics

- Values statement
- Code of ethics
- Defining acceptable versus unacceptable
- Addressing ethical dilemmas

Effective personnel policies

- Recruitment screening
- Holiday policies
- Appraisal and counselling
- Employee attitude surveys

Fraud awareness

- Typical fraud risks
- Common indicators
- Behavioural issues
- Control benchmarking
- Reporting fraud suspicions

Interviewing skills

- Planning
- Asking the right questions
- Listening and observing
- Follow-up

Fraud response

- Fraud reporting channels
- Whistle blower protections
- Fraud response plans

Fraud strategy

Initially, the fraud strategy can be a straightforward document, adopted by the board. Typically it should contain:

- the company's stance on fraud and other breaches of the ethical code;

- what will be done and by whom in the case that frauds or other breaches are suspected;
- the key initiatives which the company proposes;
- who will lead these initiatives;
- clear deadlines and measures for monitoring the effectiveness of implementation.

Values and ethics

Fraud and integrity issues are often given short shrift in the development of values charters and codes of ethics. It is seen by management as a negative aspect in a document extolling positive corporate principles such as teamwork, trust and respect. This makes it more difficult to give appropriate status to the company's position on ethical issues.

Organisations which successfully promote high standards of ethical conduct have a lower incidence of fraud and find out about fraud incidents earlier.

The starting point is a clear statement or charter setting out the company's core values. This should be communicated through team briefings and other forms of corporate communications such as posters and the company's Intranet.

The company's detailed position on ethical issues will usually be set out in a code of ethics. The fraud message is one of several important issues which the code should address. The code should encourage ethical conduct and set out assurance mechanisms to monitor and enforce the application of the principles.

Defining what is unacceptable behaviour is important in reducing the grey areas which fraudsters often exploit to justify their actions to themselves and fellow employees. For example, a company which supplies services to governments will wish to set out a policy on bribery and corruption of public officials. A principle, perhaps including an example, which clarifies the distinction between a facilitating payment (usually acceptable) and a bribe is helpful.

There are many methods of bringing the issue of what is acceptable to

257

the forefront. Some illustrations of ethical dilemmas to clarify what is expected of employees in a set of realistic situations can be very helpful. This can be expanded on during fraud awareness training programmes.

The fundamental message is that staff at all levels in the company are bound to work under a set of rules which everyone should accept. Those who break the rules, including those who commit fraud, are working against corporate goals and to the detriment of shareholder value.

Common implementation issues are as follows:

(a) the code does not reflect the company's culture and management style. This often happens where a model code or another company's code has been copied with little thought or adaption. The code needs to use language and terms that staff will relate to;

(b) the group has several different ethical codes in various divisions, business units and countries. This usually happens where the group has grown by a series of acquisitions;

(c) the code does not give examples regarding what is acceptable or unacceptable;

(d) the code is not presented in an effective way. Many codes of ethics are dry, typed documents with no helpful examples or constructive guidance. Issuing the code as a well-presented booklet using the company's logo and colours with a foreword by the chief executive can transform how the code and the messages it contains are perceived and embraced;

(e) there is no forum for bringing out and dealing with ethical dilemmas faced by staff. A regular forum in each business unit to talk about ethical issues can be very valuable. There should also be clear reporting channels for those who wish to raise specific concerns about unethical practices.

Effective personnel policies

I discussed in Chapter 3 how people issues can contribute to fraud risk. Many of these aspects relate to personnel policies.

Recruitment screening

Recruitment screening is a weak area in many companies. Often checks on prospective employees and their CVs are not performed independently of the person recruiting or at all. Two of the cases I discussed in Chapter 3 showed how procedures were overridden by senior management because they thought they knew the individual well.

In a significant proportion of fraud cases one finds that there was some lie or inconsistency on the fraudster's application to join the company or during interview. Aspects to check include:

(a) verifying identity to passport;

(b) checking qualifications where possible against to up-to-date registers of members or other publicly available databases;

(c) checking the names of educational establishments attended (for example, University of Sussex versus Sussex University) and whether the person actually went there;

(d) probing gaps in career history and reasons for leaving jobs;

(e) obtaining telephone as well as written references. Find out contact telephone numbers independently rather than relying on the candidate. Assess who is giving the reference and their position in the particular organisation;

(f) beware of name dropping on CVs; question work done for well-known companies or clients.

Holiday policies and work patterns

A simple but very effective anti-fraud measure is to require all staff to take at least two weeks continuous holiday at some point during the year and monitor that this actually happens. For staff in sensitive positions, it is worth ensuring that all matters are handled independently during their absence. A significant number of frauds come to light during such periods of absence. Most frauds are hard to keep going, you need to be there.

Workaholics and staff working unusual hours, for example working weekends but not working regular hours during the week, should be monitored. It does not necessarily mean there is a fraud problem, but remember that unusual work patterns are a feature in many fraud cases.

Appraisal and counselling

Appraisal and counselling sessions should be used to identify situations where there is low morale or unusual management styles. The factors underlying these situations may need to be probed with care and those doing the appraising need to be trained to ask questions about these more difficult matters.

Employee attitude surveys

Employee attitude surveys can be valuable in identifying some of the people and cultural issues discussed in Chapter 3. For example, percep-tions of the commercial culture may come out in such surveys. This depends, of course, on the right questions being asked and appropriate conclusions being drawn.

The limitations of surveys need to be understood. For instance, a sur-vey might identify the cultural confusion discussed in Chapter 3 ('empowered' versus 'command and control' cultures). The sub-culture issues highlighted in the opening chapter, where staff were saying that 'the culture drives people to make the best profit possible . . . certain things force individuals not to act with integrity', will usually require more advanced interviewing skills to uncover.

Fraud reporting and response

Fraud reporting

As noted in Chapter 2, staff in a department where fraud has occurred often knew or suspected that fraud or malpractice was taking place. However, it is often not clear to whom those suspicions should be reported or the protections for the person reporting the suspicions.

Even if risk management and control in a company is strong, it is important to capture suspicions of fraud which employees may have, otherwise the company is missing out on a very important source of front-line intelligence. Once the suspicions have been reported it is then equally important that there are appropriate plans to follow-up and, if necessary, investigate the suspicions.

Clear reporting channels should be included in the ethical code and widely publicised through other media such as noticeboards and the company's Intranet. The company may wish to supplement these channels with external anonymous hotlines. There are of course pros and cons in introducing such hotlines.

Table 8.1 Some pros and cons of anonymous hotlines	
Pros	Cons
Deterrent effect	Can generate malicious information
Cut through internal bureaucracy	May be viewed by employees as 'grassing up line'
Can also be used to deal with health and safety, environmental and harassment issues	Requires resource to respond to allegations
Highlight problems early	May encourage staff to avoid using normal internal fraud reporting channels
Many organisations have found it effective Relatively cheap to set up Can be outsourced	

Many of the potential problems can in fact be addressed by careful planning and implementation. In practice, many of those who report via anonymous hotlines are ready to give their name and details.

Fraud response plan

There should also be a fraud response plan which sets out clearly the actions that will be taken and who will take them when fraud occurs. The plan should cover such issues as:

- actions to mitigate further loss

- criteria for evaluating suspicions, covering credibility and motives of the whistle blower and the quality of available evidence

- capture and protection of evidence, including IT-based records

- consideration of further fraud problems

- process for setting up an appropriate investigation and the personnel, both internal and external, who should potentially be involved

- publicity issues

- giving appropriate rights to the suspect and ensuring the company complies with its disciplinary procedures and with employment law

- insurance issues

- police liaison

- ensuring that appropriate lessons are learned across the group as a whole

Fraud awareness programme

The fraud awareness programme is the vehicle to launch many of the above initiatives. The core of the programme should be based around an initial profiling of the key fraud risks facing the business. This profiling needs to be as specific as possible not only to the company but also to a particular business unit.

For example, an initial profile of risks impacting the hospital operations of a private health care provider may be as set out in Figure 8.3.

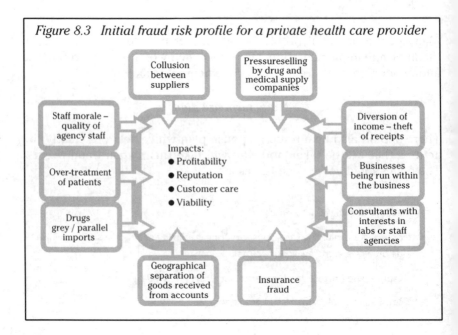

Figure 8.3 Initial fraud risk profile for a private health care provider

An initial profile of fraud risks in an oil company might include the following:

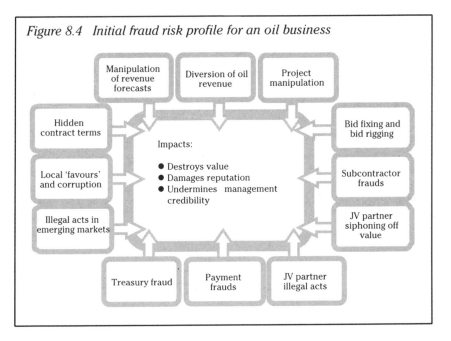

Figure 8.4   Initial fraud risk profile for an oil business

Preliminary consideration can be given to prioritising fraud risks, assessing amounts at risk, likelihood and impact. Each of these risks can be explored with the group, discussing exactly how they might occur in the business.

The session needs to bring out some of the typical indicators of fraud and unusual behavioural aspects.

The session can quite quickly lead to the team challenging how good current controls to manage the risks are. This encourages constructive debate on control improvements. A quick benchmarking exercise may be valuable to assess how well the company currently addresses fraud issues: (See Figure 8.5 on page 264.)

Addressing these questions in a constructive format provides a good basis on which to progress to more detailed fraud risk profiling.

The session can also introduce the ethical code, fraud policy, fraud reporting and response arrangements.

		Score 0 - 10
Figure 8.5 Example of quick team benchmarking exercise		
1	What is the quality of our anti-fraud strategy?	☐
2	Is responsibility for managing fraud risk well defined?	☐
3	How clear are reporting channels for reporting suspicions of fraud?	☐
4	Are there clear protections for those reporting fraud?	☐
5	How effective is our fraud awareness programme?	☐
6	How effective are our recruitment screening procedures at stopping a fraudster joining the company?	☐
7	How developed is the understanding of fraud risks facing our company?	☐
8	How has the organisation matched these fraud risks to controls to see how well they are managed?	☐
9	How effectively does our company learn from fraud incidents?	☐
10	How aware of fraud indicators are head office and regional personnel during reviews of numbers or other management information?	☐
	Total	☐

Interviewing skills

Asking the right questions is a key management skill. In today's fraud arena the ability to think laterally and probe effectively are fundamental. Training in effective interviewing and monitoring should be linked to the fraud awareness programme discussed above, as a follow-on module.

Development of interviewing skills is not commonly part of management training. The interviewing skills required are not those needed for fraud investigation, which requires more specialised techniques, nor the more generic interviewing skills used in recruitment. The need is for management to be able to ask questions in a constructive yet sufficiently challenging way as they review various aspects of the business to pick up on early indicators of fraud. This training is needed at board, senior management, business unit management and at supervisor levels.

This skill is best developed using interview simulations based on realistic scenarios. A few pointers to the basic skills required are discussed below.

There are four main aspects to good interviewing:

- planning;
- questioning;
- listening and observing; and
- follow-up.

Planning

Planning is rarely given the time it deserves. Most organisations operate under pressures of time and resources. But even 15 minutes of concentrated planning can make a huge difference to the effectiveness of an interview. Without, planning a number of things can go wrong.

The interviewee may not be clear what the actual purpose of the interview is. This needs to be clearly indicated at the outset of any interview. You cannot do this if you are unsure yourself what you want to achieve. Poor planning will be evident to the person you are questioning. If that should occur, control may be quickly wrested from you and the interviewee will be in a position to set the agenda.

Understanding the role of persons being seen is important. It is pointless asking questions of someone who cannot possibly know the answers. At best this wastes time, at worst the answers may be guesswork designed to avoid loss of face. Invariably that will mean that misleading or inaccurate information is acquired.

Failure to provide background information prior to the interview, lack of information generally or discrepancies between statistics and general staff or public perceptions may themselves all be issues worthy of questioning during the interview.

Questioning

Many meetings can be nothing more than 'fireside chats' which explore areas that both parties feel comfortable with. Most of us are naturally reluctant to ask difficult questions. We feel embarrassed at seeing someone else struggling or not having an answer. Done well however with questions put in context, someone without a ready answer is more likely to see there is a constructive reason for the question.

Open and closed questions each have their role. Closed questions requiring a 'yes', 'no' or other one word answer are effective ways to fact find. Open questions which require the person being questioned to expand on their answer can be used to paint the wider picture. Remember however that these questions also allow the potential for you to be side-tracked so be aware of the need to remain in control and on course.

Who, what, when, where, why and how questions, when used effectively, can quickly help you set the scene. Who did this? When was it done? Where was it done? Why? And so on.

Reflection is another technique that you can use during interviews to obtain more information, at the same time giving you the chance to formulate further questions or obtain some breathing space. Suppose for example someone says, 'the project was completed ahead of schedule' but you do not have a copy of the schedule and it has not been referred to before. By repeating the word 'schedule?' as a question, it quickly turns the response into a further question.

Avoid over-planning and the appearance of scripted questions. Tenaciously sticking to a script can lead you to ask questions for which you have already had an answer. As well as being embarrassing, it can annoy the interviewee who may feel you have not been listening. Plot a matrix of issues you want to cover and chart a course in advance. Try and find the right words, the right question for the moment. Do not work with pre-set lists of questions. You will not come across as on top of your brief.

Using an interview matrix will help you stay on course, and where necessary put in course corrections. Typically, this will be a one-page grid prepared at the planning stage with key topics or prompt words noted on it. A provisional route is plotted. It is easy for someone to side-track you if you are unprepared. A good interviewer needs to plan for and decide how to deal with diversions. If the side-track is going somewhere useful then consider going there. If it is not, then get back on track. Sometimes, people may do this in an attempt to take you into territory where they feel more comfortable or where they think you will be uncomfortable. If this happens, try and evaluate why.

Having avoided being side-tracked, there may be areas that you wish to return to. One technique you can use is to tell the person you are interviewing that you will return to the subject later. Signal what you intend to do perhaps by saying 'I want to ask a few more questions about that matter, but I would like to return to it later on'. Make a note and remember to return to the point in due course. When you do, make life easier for the person you are interviewing by re-establishing the context; 'Earlier on when you were talking about the project, you mentioned the schedule, what schedule are you referring to?'. This is much more effective than asking out of the blue, 'Tell me about the schedule?'.

Coordination is also key. 'Wildfire' questioning is unprofessional and may divert a colleague from pursuing a productive line of questions. Decide beforehand who will ask what and when. Agree the timing of hand-overs between questioners. It is much better to put a pen down as a sign than to look panic stricken when you have nothing else to ask. Good coordination provides support, bad coordination undermines the questioners' credibility.

Listening and observing

In trying to ask the right questions, do not discount how interviewees answer questions. People often give answers which are emotionally charged. Lots of body language may indicate that they feel strongly about something. Hesitation, sighs, eye movement, sharp intakes of breath and posture may all indicate that this is a subject that is close to the interviewee's heart. Many questioners fail to capitalise on this 'added value' information. They fail to pursue what could be described as a 'come on – ask me' response. It may be that simply remarking on the body language, 'It seems like that is a difficult subject' or 'That seems to bother you', may well produce further information.

The choice of words used to answer questions is also important – the throw-away remark about management style or a joke about the culture – 'It's like Colditz here' – should be pursued. Ask what is meant by these remarks and you may get an answer.

My experience is that these remarks are used to flag up concerns or opinions about important cultural and organisational issues. Failing to ask may be letting down the person you are questioning. They may have decided that you have credibility, that they trust you. They may have decided that you are the person or committee they want to share their concerns with.

When you planned your session, hopefully, you acquired lots of background information. Organisation charts or diagrams illustrating processes or procedures can be a key tool to take with you. The old cliché

267

Table 8.2 Basics of good interviewing

Planning	Questioning
What is your aim?	Use open or closed questions as appropriate
What do you want to have achieved at the end?	Who? When? Where? Why? How?
How will you ensure you stay on course?	Avoid sticking rigidly to a script. Be flexible
Do you need supporting evidence or information in advance?	Do not repeat questions if you have already had the answer
Do research to ensure you will be seen as credible	With two asking questions – coordinate
	Use reflection to turn answers into further questions
	Establish the context when referring to earlier answers
Listening and observing	*Follow-up*
What is the body language saying – posture, hesitation, etc.?	Are further interviews or meetings required?
Listen for emotive language – what underpins this?	Do you need to see other people?
Avoid negativity in your questions	Will an unresolved issue stay on the agenda?
Use diagrams or notes to clarify questions or answers	Consider verifying answers by confirming actual practice
Use the answers to develop lines of further questions	
Do not be intimidated – challenge answers and pursue points	

that a picture paints a thousand words is true in this situation. Use charts and diagrams to assist your understanding. Get the person you are interviewing to annotate diagrams or draw their own. You may well discover issues and impacts of which you were unaware. Diagrams can assist you in re-establishing context or when you want to re-visit a subject. Of course diagrams and drawings also provide an excellent visual reminder afterwards.

Follow-up

You have conducted a well-planned interview; you have asked the right questions; the person or persons you saw drew lots of diagrams and you have achieved most of the aims you set for the meeting. What next?

Follow-up is key. Do you need to see anyone else? Are further interviews required with this or other persons? Will unresolved issues remain on the agenda? Do you need evidence to back up what you have been told?

Table 8.2 summarises the main points in the above guidance.

Fraud risk profiling

The fraud awareness programmes discussed above will have laid the foundation for more detailed profiling of risks. The need for and importance of such profiling will now be more clearly understood. This will enable the company to see in more detail the specific fraud risks it faces and provide a basis on which it can challenge the quality of existing controls. Many approaches to risk identification and control analysis are too complicated. I favour a straightforward approach, maintaining clarity at all times and keeping the 'big picture' in view.

Profiling the detailed fraud risks in the organisation typically involves five main phases, as shown in Figure 8.6. (See page 270.)

The initial profile developed during the awareness programme can be expanded. For example, in many industries there is plenty of public domain information about frauds which have affected companies in that industry internationally.

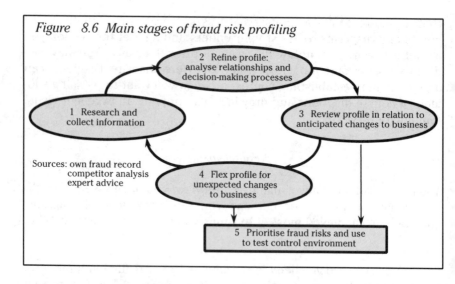

Figure 8.6 Main stages of fraud risk profiling

1 Research and collect information

2 Refine profile: analyse relationships and decision-making processes

3 Review profile in relation to anticipated changes to business

Sources: own fraud record
competitor analysis
expert advice

4 Flex profile for unexpected changes to business

5 Prioritise fraud risks and use to test control environment

Industry forums and groupings can be valuable. These may be coordinated to a degree through the industry associations, for example the Association of British Insurers in the case of the insurance industry, or maybe informal meetings between, for example, heads of internal audit in a particular industry. Some insurance companies are now prepared to fund fraud risk profiling and fraud awareness programmes and offer lower premiums in response to the implementation of measures to cut fraud risk.

Expert input is of course valuable from experienced fraud investigation and risk management specialists who have seen similar problems in other companies.

The aim is to develop a more detailed profile for each main business unit. For example, the fraud risk profile of a manufacturing company may develop in the sales area along the lines shown in Figure 8.7. This will provide a clear map of the typical risks which might affect the company.

In practice of course responsibility for particular risks will sit at many different levels within the organisation. For example, the risk of salesmen generating false sales invoices to reach their sales and bonus targets might be highlighted by any one of the following: a sales supervisor, sales director, sales account clerk, stock controller, divisional

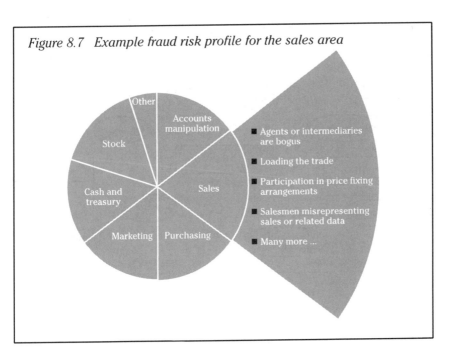

Figure 8.7   Example fraud risk profile for the sales area

accountant, divisional finance director, divisional managing director or head office review team.

Given the range of people and disciplines which may be needed to highlight a particular fraud, this emphasises the importance of a multi-disciplinary approach to assessing fraud risk and running fraud risk workshops.

Mapping the key risks is the first important step but it is then necessary to assess:

- what internal and external relationships could impact the business;
- how key decisions are made during these relationships and by whom;
- how the decision-making process could be manipulated through fraud.

Analysing these relationships in more detail helps to explore particular risks which may arise in dealing with customers, agents, intermediaries, with business partners, regulators and suppliers. For example, in the

Figure 8.8 Mapping key relationships and decisions

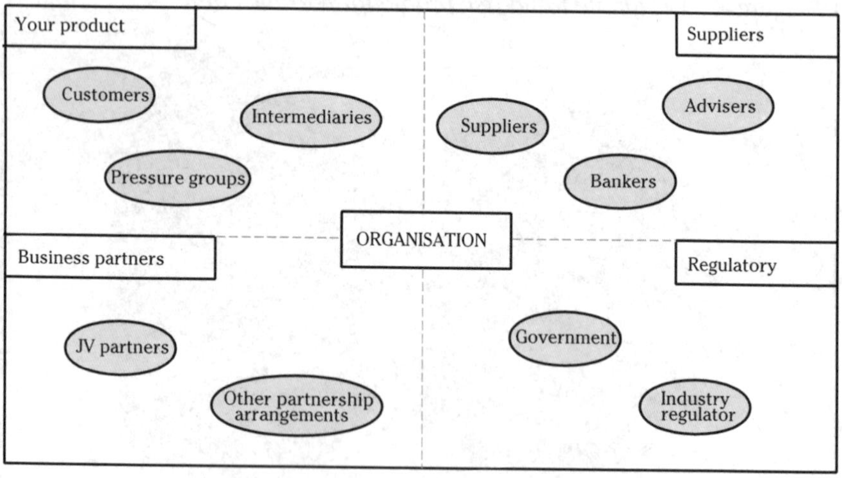

sales area the following decisions will be made in dealing with customers:

- pricing of products;

- discounting arrangements;

- delivery arrangements;

- free supply of products for promotions;

- subsidies given in relation to production and marketing of the product;

- terms of credit;

- sale or return clauses (usually preventing selling on of the product);

- exclusivity rights;

- loan of hardware to best present the product; and

- guarantee of supply.

Associated with each of these decisions are fraud risks. For example in relation to pricing of the product and discounting arrangements the following risks might open up.

Table 8.3 Mapping fraud risks to key decisions	
Key decisions	*Fraud risk*
Pricing of product	• Salesperson receives induce-ments to give unauthorised price reductions
	• Salesperson agrees with customer higher prices in the short-term (so as to meet bonus targets) but for significant unauthorised future price reductions or discounts
Discounting arrangements	• Data regarding sales manipulated so as to claim falsely volume discounts
	• Unauthorised discounts given
	• Discounts for early payment given by manipulation of payment data

The profile then needs to be reviewed in the light of anticipated changes in the business, for example:

- implementation of new IT systems;
- acquisition or disposal of parts of the business;
- changes in reporting structures or responsibilities;
- corporate restructuring;
- changes in regulatory or competition frameworks;
- significant redundancy programme.

Business changes may introduce new fraud risks, they may also impact prioritisation of fraud risks.

Prioritisation should be based on:

- amount at risk;

273

- likelihood;
- impact on image.

Each of these aspects will need to be considered carefully.

The final stage is to match prioritised risks to existing controls. The clearest way of mapping this is to chart the identified risks along the main stages of the relevant business process (for example, the sales process) to see more clearly exactly where the fraud risks cut in. As illustrated in the following chart, there may be under- or over-control.

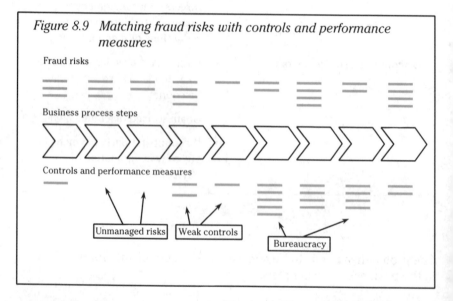

Figure 8.9   Matching fraud risks with controls and performance measures

Management then needs to take a decision whether to mitigate the risk by introducing further controls or to accept the risk. Certain fraud risks are insurable.

Conclusion

In the opening chapter, I highlighted some lessons from yesterday's financial disasters: overwhelming pressure, the trend of escalation and the 'disaster waiting to happen'. Stopping frauds in their early stages depends on management and staff at all levels being alert to fraud risk and to the warning signs. This alertness can be developed by well-structured fraud awareness programmes and risk profiling sessions. Awareness needs to be refreshed at least annually. Fraud risk profiles need to keep pace with changes in the business and in personnel. If people have suspicions, clear reporting channels should capture their concerns. Increased alertness and improved interview and review techniques will help directors and managers to ask the right questions.

So, will the nightmare scenario with which I began the book be your company in 2005: a £100 million 'black hole' opening up in the group's results?

Could other frauds outlined in this book hit your company? Is fraud already draining value from your business? Are you unwittingly creating the conditions in which fraud will thrive? When is the right time to start addressing these questions?

For companies that want to create, and keep, value, the answer is not 2005, next year or next month. The time for action is now.

Index

Entries are in word-by-word aphabetical order.
References are to page number.

accounts, manipulation of   16, 129,
      156–157
   accruals, under/over recording
      142–143
   advance billing   134–136
   assets, pledging   149–150
   bad debt, manipulation of   137
   capitalisation of costs   144
   cash   149
      teeming and lading   150
   cash flow, misuse of   151
   claims   154
   cost manipulation   149
   credit status, misrepresentation
      137
   discounts/undisclosed benefits
      136
   factors influencing   130
   false consulting contracts   143–144
   false sales   131
   fictitious contracts   151–152
   hidden contract terms   140
   joint ventures with connected
      parties   153
   key risks   130
   misrecording   140–142
   overdraft, unauthorised   150
   payments, delaying or advancing
      144–145
   profit smoothing   138
   purchases, manipulation of   139
   reports, inconsistent   155
   rigged forecasts   133–134

accounts, manipulation of – *cont.*
   stock
      manipulation of value of
         146–147
      misvaluation of   145–146
      quality, false   148
      quantity, entering false data on
         147–148
      write-downs   146
   suspended items   152–153
   transfer pricing   154
   transfers other than at market
      value   152
   work-in-progress, fixing of   141
accruals
   under/over recording   142–143
advance billing   134–136
assets
   pledging   149–150
   quality manipulation   208–209
auditors
   several firms of   31
autocratic management style   24–25
awareness programme   262–264

bad debt
   manipulation of   137
banking, see **financial sector**
beating the system   20
behavioural characteristics   22
   boaster   22
   deceiver   22–23
   loner   23

behavioural characteristics – *cont.*
manipulation   22
self-sacrifice   26
shut door policy   26
unusual   25–26
boredom   21
bribes
release of security, to obtain
212
budget   5
percentage of sales, problems
with   13
business culture   11, 15, 17, 41
business ethics
no code of   29
business relationships
prior   47–48
business strategy   42–45
poorly defined   31

capitalisation of costs   144
case studies
accounts manipulation   16
cutting material costs   42–43
double whammy   59
electronic banking   9–12
make or break   40
management structure   59–61
matrix management   66–68
purchasing fraud   12, 66
strategic drift   44
cash flow
misuse of   151
cash and payment frauds, *see*
manufacturing and services
causes of fraud
change and discontinuity   39–40
delayering   37
downsizing   37
empowerment   36–37
fraud arena   35 *et seq.*
globalisation   35–36
management style   39
matrix management   37–38, 41
outsourcing   38–39
pressure   9–10
technological change   36
cheque fraud   238–239
claims   154
common indicators
risk factors and   23
communications   75
fraud and ethics policies   76–77

communications – *cont.*
learning from other businesses
76
poor organisational learning   76
company car scheme   195–196
compensation tied to performance
28
complex structures   30
computer fraud   97
access, increase in   99
active content and Trojans
119–120
advantages of technology   98
data, theft of   122–123
disaffected employees, attacks
from   99
division of work, difficulty in   99
e-mail   120–121
extent of   100–101
external abuse, likely increase in
97
hacking   114–118
input-related   102–106
Internet, on   109–114
IT security   124–127
bulletin boards   127
digital signatures   127
penetration testing   127
software   126
output-related   108–109
outsourcing   100
pornography   120–121
problems brought with
technology   98
program or system related
106–108
software theft   121–122
tracking   101–102
viruses, worms and hoaxes
118–120
connected companies
transactions with   207–208
consulting contracts   143–144
contingencies
omission of   235
contracts
fictitious   151–152
hidden terms   140
control
commitment to   29
weaknesses   10, 18
cost manipulation   149
credit   202–204

credit – *cont.*
status, misrepresentation 137
cross firing 237–238
culture and ethics 53
cultural confusion 54
cultural pressures 55–56
empowered cultures 83
entities not assimilated 57
ethical dilemmas 58
need-to-know culture 56
poor ethical code 57
curriculum vitae
bogus qualifications and
references 198

data
theft of 123–124
dealing, *see* **financial sector**
deposit transformation 206–207
deposits, *see* **financial sector**
direct controls 88–94
contract types 90
problems with 91
purchasing spend, analysing 89
purchasing staff, skill of 90–91
suppliers used
knowledge of 89–90
nature of 90
undermining 91–93
disaster waiting to happen 3–4, 13,
17
discounts/undisclosed benefits 136
discretionary accounts 230
diverted postings 236–237
double pledging 216–217
dysfunctional board 62

electronic banking 9–12
electronic mail, *see* **computer fraud**
electronic payments 239–241
elements leading to fraud, *see* **causes
of fraud**
employees, *see* **people**
equipment corruption 93–94
escalation 3, 10, 13, 16–17
ethics
culture and, *see* **culture and ethics**
fraud and ethics policies, *see* **fraud
and ethics**
values and 257–258
expensive lifestyles 26–27

false contracts 143–144

false deals 228
false sales 131
fictitious borrowers 232
fictitious contracts 151–152
financial data
false 214–216
financial disasters
learning from yesterday's 2–3
financial sector 252
banking 201
asset quality manipulation
208–209
bribes to obtain release of
security 212
connected companies,
transactions with 207–208
credit 202–204
deposit transformation
206–207
double pledging 216–217
electronic 9–12
financial data, false 214–216
funds, diversion of 218
funds transformation 211–212
impersonation 212–214
kickbacks and inducements
209–210
loan funds, misappropriation of
217–218
loans to fictitious borrowers
204–205
nominees companies 205–206
parallel organisations 210–211
recovered security, selling of
212
cheque fraud 238–239
cross firing 237–238
dealing 223–232
broker kickbacks 227–228
delayed allocation 229–230
discretionary accounts 230
false deals 228
matching procedures, abuse of
231
mismarking the book 231
off market rings 226–227
related party deals 227
unrecorded 229
valuation rings 232
deposits 219
camouflage of 220–221
fraudulent instructions 222
theft of 222

financial sector – *cont.*
  deposits – *cont.*
    unrecorded 221–222
  diverted postings 236–237
  electronic payments 239–241
  fictitious borrowers 232
  insurance fraud 247
    bogus policies 248
    bogus policyholders 250
    false or inflated claims 251
    false statements 249
    forged claims 248–249
    forged surrender of policies 248
    misappropriation of funds 249
    staged events 250
  investment business 241
    bogus 242–244
    bogus documents 246
    churning 246
    fraudulent instructions 247
    front running 245
    lending client investments
      without authority 244
    selling client investments without
      authority 244
    share ramping 245
    stolen documents and
      certificates 246
    theft of 222
    trading without authorisation
      244
  leasing 233
  letters of authority, forged 240
  mortgage applications 232–233
  omitted contingencies 235
  passing through 235
  rolling matching 236
  volume accounts, misuse of
    237
fraud
  causes of, *see* **causes of fraud**
  defining 1–2
  ethics and 76–77
  reasons for 18 *et seq.*
  response procedures 11, 15–16,
    94–95
    effective 15
    lack of 15
  risk of 4–6
  strategy 11
  summary of risks of 96
fraud risk profiling 269–275
  awareness programmes 269

fraud risk profiling – *cont.*
  industry forums 270
  mapping risk 271–274
  see also **risk management**
funds
  diversion of 218
  loan, misappropriation of 217–218
  transformation of 211–212

greed 21
growth and systems development
  mismatch between 32

holiday
  untaken 27

illegal acts 26
impersonation 212–214
inducements, *see* **kickbacks**
insurance cover, bogus 198–199
insurance frauds, *see* **financial sector**
inter company accounts
  misuse of 197
interviewing skills 264
  listening and observing 267–269
  planning 265
  questioning 265–267
investment business, see **financial
  sector**
IT, *see* **computer fraud**

joint ventures
  connected parties, with 153

key risks 130
kickbacks and inducements 20,
  209–210, 227–228

letters of authority
  forged 240
liquidity problems 32
low morale 27

management structure 11, 58
  chairman, role of 63
  chief executive, role of 63
  complex company structures 70
  dysfunctional board 62–63
  finance, status of 69–70
  matrix management 63–66
  role definition 68–69
managing fraud
  awareness programme 262–264

managing fraud – *cont.*
  fundamentals   256
  interviewing skills   264
    listening and observing   267–269
    planning   265
    questioning   265–267
  linking risk to value   253–255
  personnel policies   258–260
  reporting and response   260–262
  risk management, *see* **risk management**
  strategy   256
  values and ethics   257–258
manufacturing and services   159, 200
  cash and payment frauds   188
    bank reconciliation, manipulation of   192
    cash book, manipulation of   192
    cheque fraud   188–190
    electronic payments fraud   191–192
    forged cheques   193
    money transfer fraud   193
  purchasing fraud   159–162
    advance fee fraud   170–173
    bid fixing   162, 169
    bribes, receipt of   163, 164
    connected companies   165–166
    dummy suppliers   167–169
    external   169
    home improvements   166
    information brokers, role of   163–164
    internal   162–169
    kickbacks and inducements   165
    overbilling   175–176
    selection and ordering   162
    services supplied for private purposes   166
    short deliveries   173–174
    substandard product fraud   174–175
    work done for private purposes   166
    work not performed, billing for   175
  sales frauds   176–178
    bogus goods and services   179–181
    counterfeit products   185
    creative accounting   183

manufacturing and services *cont.*
  sales frauds – *cont.*
    credit status, misrepresentation of   185
    diversion of   178–179
    kickbacks to or from customers   181
    long firm fraud   184–185
    stealing of receipts   182
    teeming and lading   182
    underbilling and under-ringing   181–182
    writing off of receivables   184
  stock frauds   185
    metering frauds   188
    returned stock   187
    theft of stock   186–187
    valuable scrap   187
    weighbridge frauds   188
material costs
  cutting   43
misrecording   140–142
morale
  low   27
mortgage applications   232–233

nepotism   48–49
nominee companies   205–206

off market rings   226–227
overdraft, unauthorised   150

parallel organisations   210–211
payments, delaying or advancing   144–145
payroll fraud   196–197
pension funds, misuse of   195, 196–197
people
  career moves   50
  disaffected, attacks from   99
  factors   11, 45–46
  high staff turnover   53
  holiday, untaken   53
  lifestyles   53
  low risk alertness   50–52
  management style   53
  morale issues   52–53
  nepotism   48–49
  prior business relationships   47–48
  recruitment screening   46–47
  skills gap   49–50

people – *cont.*
staff turnover   27–28
unquestioning obedience of   30

performance
compensation tied to   28
measures   86–88
weaknesses in   11, 14
personal pressure   20
personnel policies   258–260
personality and status
mismatch between   25
poor quality staff   27
pressure
performance   19
personal   20
points   2–3, 9–10, 12, 16
problem areas   10
profits
excess   31–32
smoothing   138
purchases
manipulation   139
spending on, analysing   89
staff, skill of   90–91
purchasing fraud, *see* **manufacturing and services**

recovered security
selling of   212
recruitment screening   46–47
remote locations poor supervision of   30–31
reports inconsistent   155
reputation poor   32
results at any cost   28
revenge   21
reward structures   18, 70–75
bonuses   71–73
earn-outs   74
market rates, disparities with   74–75
rigged forecasts   133–134
risk management
anti-fraud strategy   77–79
assessment, lack of   15, 17, 42

risk management – *cont.*
credit area control objectives   82
detailed risk assessment, objectives of   81
direct controls   88–94
fraud risk assessment   79
impact and prioritisation   85
key performance indicators   86–88
likelihood   85–86
risk identification   85
sales area control objectives   81–82
traditional approaches to   84–85

sales fraud, *see* **manufacturing and services**
services, *see* **manufacturing and services**
share support schemes   194–195
skills gap   49–50
staff, *see* **people**
stock
frauds, *see* **manufacturing and services**
manipulation of value of   146–147
misvaluation of   145–146
quality, false   148
quantity, entering false data on   147–148
write-downs   146
strategic drift   44
strategic risk assessment   80–81
suppliers
knowledge of   89–90
nature of   90
suspense accounts, misuse of   197
suspended items   152–153

transfer other than at market value   152
transfer pricing   154

valuation rings   232
value, creating and keeping   1

work-in-progress, fixing of   141

282